GRAVE MATTERS

෴

A JOURNEY THROUGH
THE MODERN FUNERAL INDUSTRY
TO A NATURAL WAY OF BURIAL

Mark Harris

SCRIBNER

New York London Toronto Sydney

SCRIBNER

A Division of Simon & Schuster, Inc.
1230 Avenue of the Americas
New York, NY 10020

First Scribner trade paperback edition December 2008

SCRIBNER and design are registered trademarks of The Gale Group, Inc., used
under license by Simon & Schuster, Inc., the publisher of this work.

For information about special discounts for bulk purchases,
please contact Simon & Schuster Special Sales:
1-800-456-6798 or business@simonandschuster.com

DESIGNED BY ERICH HOBBING

Text set in Bembo

Manufactured in the United States of America

1 3 5 7 9 10 8 6 4 2

Library of Congress Control Number: 2006050622

ISBN-13: 978-0-7432-7768-6
ISBN-10: 0-7432-7768-6
ISBN-13: 978-1-4165-6404-1 (pbk)
ISBN-10: 1-4165-6404-7 (pbk)

The author gratefully acknowledges permission from the following source
to reprint material in its control: Oxford University Press, Inc., for an excerpt from
"Round River: A Parable" by Aldo Leopold, from Round River: From the
Journals of Aldo Leopold, edited by Luna B. Leopold, copyright ©1972.

In memory of those whose passings are told in these pages:

Catherine Booth

Ted King

Evelyn McKenna

Ruth Mullen-Saulinas

Chris Nichols

Sharyn Nicholson

Leonard Nutter

Alison Sanders

John Slowe

In the sweat of thy face shalt thou eat bread, till thou return unto the ground; for out of it wast thou taken: for dust thou art, and unto dust shalt thou return.

GENESIS 3:19

Dust unto dust is a desiccated version of the Round River concept. . . . A rock decays and forms soil. In the soil grows an oak, which bears an acorn, which feeds a squirrel, which feeds an Indian, who ultimately lays him down to his last sleep in the great tomb of man—to grow another oak.

ALDO LEOPOLD,
author and naturalist

[After] the moment of death . . . we should get the hell out of the way, with our bodies decently planted in the earth to nourish other forms of life—weeds, flowers, shrubs, trees, which support other forms of life, which support the ongoing human pageant—the lives of our children. That seems good enough to me.

EDWARD ABBEY,
author and environmentalist,
who was buried in his sleeping bag
under a pile of rocks in the Arizona
desert in March 1989

Contents

GRAVE MATTERS

Preface

On a blustery late afternoon near the end of May, I joined a band of hikers that trekked a mowed path snaking through the grounds of the Greensprings Natural Cemetery Preserve. Our rough trail took in a large swath of this hundred-acre burial site in the heart of New York's Finger Lakes region, leading us into wetland and meadows, and, as we ventured off trail, into a large, wooded tract that borders the four thousand-acre Arnot Forest. It was there, under a canopy of maples, ash, and beech that we came upon fragile-looking wild geraniums and tiny, seven-pointed starflowers, saw the delicate purple gaywing rising resolutely from the forest floor.

Emerging from the woods on our return to the keeper's cottage, red-winged blackbirds gliding in the distance, we climbed the meadow hillside that constitutes Greensprings's main burial ground, each grave site staked with a fluttering red flag. No body had yet been buried at the time of our visit; Greensprings's dedication was planned for the following day. But walking the cemetery grounds that afternoon, experiencing up close this thriving ecosystem of the Southern Tier, I couldn't help but believe that many people will seek their final rest here. One doesn't need to be an outdoors enthusiast to feel the powerful pull of the Greensprings promise: a return to bucolic, bountiful countryside in as simple and natural a way as possible. Per cemetery policy, no vaults or embalming will be allowed. Caskets must be basic and made from readily biodegradable materials. Fieldstones may mark the grave site, but native trees and shrubs are welcome as well. The idea is to allow the body to rejoin the elements, to use what remains of a life to regenerate new life, to return dust to dust.

It's a concept hugely at odds with modern burial—and it's catching on. Greensprings is one of some dozen woodland burial grounds that

1

have sprung up in this country since a family physician named Billy Campbell opened South Carolina's Ramsey Creek Preserve to burial in the fall of 1998. A score of others are in the planning stages.

Natural cemeteries like Greensprings are literally regreening the deathscape in America. But as I discovered when I journeyed into the growing, green burial underground that's beginning to surface in this country, it's just one of many strategies we're embracing in search of more meaningful, more fitting, and, ultimately, more natural alternatives to the generic send-off proffered by the local funeral home. And if my research and travels of the last two years are any indication, it's doing nothing less than rewriting—and, in the process, re-righting—the American Way of Death.

I turned up a host of alternatives in my search. I found families who had their loved ones' ashes added to fireworks that blasted out colorful displays, still others who had ashes pressed into diamonds that looked like the real thing. Given an interest in environmental issues, I was most attracted to—and thus chose to focus on—what has become known as natural burial. Like "organic" or "green" or any of the variants on eco-friendly, "natural" defies easy definition. In this new burial movement, a few characteristics stand out. For one, natural burials tend to consume significantly fewer resources than standard funerals, going light on the goods and services that fill out the General Price List the local mortician is required to hand anyone who knocks at his door. Caskets, when used at all, are of plain, wood make; embalming is almost always avoided. As a consequence, these funeral costs tally into the hundreds and low—not many—thousands of dollars. Families generally also take a more active role in the conduct of the funeral.

In the end, these families choose natural burial because it achieves the very end our modern funeral industry labors to prevent at literally all costs: to allow, and even invite, the decay of one's physical body—its tissue and bone, its cache of organic components—and return what remains to the very elements it sprang from, as directly and simply as possible. In their last, final act, the deceased in this book have taken care in death to give back to the earth some very small measure of the vast resources they drew from it in life and, in the process, perpetuate the cycles of nature, of growth and decay, of death and rebirth, that sustain all of us. For Sharyn Nicholson, one Virginia native I write about, that meant being buried on a wooded hillside in view of her mountain cabin, wrapped in nothing but a shroud. Avid angler Leonard Nutter found his final rest in an aquatic environment, his ashes scattered over the Pacific waters he trolled off the coast of Southern California.

Such natural return is, of course, little more than a return to long tradition. Much of what constitutes natural burial, as I show throughout this book, was once standard practice in this country, the default, not the exception. Practiced well into the twentieth century in some places, this truly traditional send-off was a largely simple affair, light on the pocketbook, conserving by nature and, no doubt, as meaningful to the assembled mourners then as the more elaborate and well-orchestrated funeral is to some of us today—and, very likely, even more so.

Families in this book are reviving those not-so-aged traditions—be it laying out and "waking" a loved one at home, or hiring a local carpenter to build a coffin of plain pine boards—as well as one ancient rite of disposition that predates civilization itself: cremation, an option expected to be our most popular way to go by mid-century. At the same time, they're giving old custom a decidedly modern twist. The woodland burial grounds springing up in this country, for example, may descend from the pastoral, "rural" cemeteries that flourished in the early to late 1800s, but they also show the strong conservationist focus of the Baby Boomer environmentalist who first inspired them. In these leafy environs, the dead more than rest in blissful, green repose: their burials help preserve significant, threatened land from the bulldozer and, in some cases, work to restore it to ecological health. Other options offer entirely novel, natural retirement. When Carrie Slowe added her husband's cremated remains to the concrete slurry of a "reef ball" that hardened and was later sunk into the Atlantic Ocean, she not only returned her mate to the waters that held such firm purchase on his affection, she created habitat for new life under the sea.

Not surprisingly, some of the families looking outside the mainstream at the time of death are the very ones who inhabit its margins in life. In my forays into the new deathscape I turned up vegetarians, massage therapists, Waldorf school teachers, as well as one amateur organic gardener who wore dreadlocks and idolized Bob Marley. It's a mistake, though, to categorize all, or even most, adherents of this form of alt.burial as habitués of Whole Foods Markets or hybrid-drive motorists. In my experience, the majority largely comprise what for lack of better description I'd simply call "regular" folk. In addition to those above, my research put me in touch with a hospital nurse, a court stenographer, an elementary school teacher, and an employee at a sporting goods factory who stamps the company logo onto golf balls. There was also a retired meatpacker in Iowa who attends Sunday Mass, and one engineer now buried in a natural cemetery who even expressed a dislike for "environmentalists" and admitted to being less than fond of nature hikes. The families in this book span Gen X to the Greatest Generation, include Republicans as well as Democrats (and Greens), and literally inhabit Middle America and other parts of the compass. As I've seen it on the ground, natural burial is a big tent, not fringe, phenomenon.

What unites this disparate group is the welcome promise of natural burial: simplicity, low cost, and return to the elements, be they on land or sea. Or, as one gentleman who buried his wife in a plain, pine casket put it to me one frosty January afternoon: "It just strikes me as the most logical thing to do."

I've included a broad range of burial options under the rubric of "natural." Clearly, some are more natural than others. Shrouded burial in a woodland cemetery that's devoted to restoration of the land is likely the more conserving and less polluting choice than cremation, with its consumption of natural gas and electricity and release of mercury and other potentially hazardous emissions into the atmosphere. (Though how green any burial turns out to be depends on the given burial. Air-freighting a body to a distant woodland ground for shrouded interment—as has happened—say, must surely negate much of its positive impact on the planet.) Nonetheless, I've arranged the progression of chapters from generally less to more green, with cremation and the options for memorializing with one's ashes at the front, the book ending with burial on one's own rural land or in a natural cemetery.

A word about cremation. Incinerating a body produces an environmental impact of some degree (though just how much depends on any number of factors, including whose figures you believe). Cremation makes it into this book because, its ecological footprint notwithstanding, the average cremation consumes fewer resources and emits less pollution than the outfitting and conduct of the typical, modern funeral. The resulting ashes may—and in these pages do—then return to the natural environment out of which, as the Genesis verse that graces this book's epigraph puts it, we are taken.

An enterprising investigative reporter or doctoral student will some day document the many detrimental environmental consequences that result from the production of the standard funeral. In the meantime, I've attempted to present a scenario of potential and likely effects based on the limited published research to date. Yet while the known evidence may read a bit thin here, I hope it's sufficient to make the point that goes to the heart of the matter of modern memorialization: that the once simple and natural act of laying our dead to rest has been transmogrified into a large-scale industrial operation that, like any other manufacturing process, requires the inputs of vast amounts of energy and raw materials and leaves a trail of environmental damage in its wake.

All the individuals in this book are real (though, in certain cases, I have changed names and identifying characteristics)—with a few exceptions. Myra, Jim, and Jenny Johnson, as well as the funeral director Tom Fielding, are composite characters based on information I gleaned from various printed materials and from the many conversations I had with family members and with funeral personnel I interviewed for background purposes. The narrative that comprises their interactions in chapter one and parts of chapter two did not take place. However, all the events that transpire there—from the Johnsons' arrangement conference to their daughter's embalming in Fielding's prep room and subsequent interment—are nonetheless real to life. The Johnsons' engagement with Fielding in his parlor is typical of what an average family experiences when they sit down with a funeral director on his home turf. The prices he quotes them for goods and services are pulled directly from current price lists I gained from existing funeral homes. As for Jenny's embalming, it's what's known in the trade as a "normal case," and derives from my interviews with funeral directors and from articles, videos, and textbooks assigned to students of mortuary science.

I have also created pseudonyms for the funeral goods—caskets and vaults, mostly—mentioned in the first two chapters. I thought it neither fair nor particularly useful to single out, say, a particular casket for scrutiny when it's not significantly different than the similar model of a competing manufacturer. A vault may fill with water because no vault is impervious to the elements forever, not because it's Brand X.

The funeral industry, surely, won't welcome this bald assessment of its services, but my intent is not to bash the dismal trade. (Whatever criticism it deserves Jessica Mitford already leveled, deftly and with devastating wit.) My goal is to simply offer a picture of the kind of funeral a bereaved family can expect to be presented with when it walks through the parlor doors of Any Funeral Home U.S.A. and, then, show how the effects may play out on their loved ones and on the environment.

My interest, in the end, lies less in the modern funeral, however it's delivered, than in the burgeoning, natural alternatives that are springing up to supplement and, I believe, ultimately change it.

Show me the manner in which a nation cares for its dead, and I will measure with mathematical exactness the tender mercies of its people, their respect for the laws of the land and their loyalty to high ideals.

Attributed to William Gladstone,
British prime minister (1808–1898)

ᏳᎹᏋᎥᎧ

CHAPTER ONE:

The Embalming of Jenny Johnson

At nine o'clock on a brisk October morning, less than twelve hours after they'd left the Brakertown Memorial Hospital, Jim and Myra Johnson arrive at the Fielding Funeral Home to make arrangements for the burial of their eighteen-year-old daughter, their only child, Jenny.

Tom Fielding greets them at the door. The funeral director in the three-piece suit and polished wingtips is the one who'd taken Jim's first call the previous night, telling him that Jenny had suffered a heart attack in her college dorm room; he'd been the one to meet them at the hospital after Jenny had died, had told them he'd handle all the necessary arrangements. Ushering the couple into the parlor's hushed receiving room—harp music sounding in the background, votive candles burning on a pair of side tables—Fielding doesn't try to console or comfort his new clients. After nearly twenty years in the business, Fielding believes that whatever solace a funeral director can offer bereaved families comes less from grief counseling than from the ritual of the well-run funeral service—something for which he has developed a reputation in this small city. So after motioning the Johnsons onto a couch and taking a seat himself on the other side of the coffee table, Fielding comes gently but quickly to the point. "I'm very sorry for your loss," he begins. "Let me assure you we'll do everything we can to help you plan a service that honors the life of your daughter. Have you given any thought to the kind of arrangements you'd like to make?"

After a pause, Jim speaks up. On the way over this morning, he tells Fielding in a halting voice, he and Myra agreed they wanted to give Jenny the kind of funeral that's traditional in their Catholic family. A viewing. Service at St. Matthew's. Burial in Holy Savior. Her family owns a number of plots at the cemetery, Myra adds, and her parents have offered them one, next to Myra's grandmother.

Fielding jots the Johnsons' directions onto a legal pad in his lap. He then pulls out a gray sheet and lays it on the coffee table, turning it to face them. Known in the trade as the General Price List (GPL), the double-sided sheet itemizes all the goods and services the Fielding Home offers, along with their prices. Two package deals at the top of the page would certainly meet their needs, Fielding says: a traditional funeral service with evening viewing ($3,595) or a traditional funeral service with one-hour viewing prior to service ($3,295).

The packages bundle most everything they'd need for either type of funeral, except for the casket, vault, cemetery fees, and other miscellaneous charges. If they'd rather, however, the Johnsons can pick the services they want individually, choosing from the nearly three dozen separate items that follow. To whatever they choose, however, Fielding will add a base fee of $1,395 for his handling of arrangements. And because the Johnsons have requested a viewing, they'll also have to agree to embalming ($825).

Like most of his clients, the Johnsons don't think to question Fielding's request to embalm, even though the GPL states that embalming isn't required by law.

If they'd asked why he insists on it nonetheless, Fielding would have replied with an explanation he mostly cribbed from industry talking points. "Embalming replaces body fluids with a chemical solution that retards natural decomposition and enhances the appearance of your daughter," he'd say. "Without it, she might not be presentable to your family and friends for a viewing that's still a couple of days away." Had the Johnsons known enough to ask Fielding if he'd instead hold Jenny in a refrigeration unit until the viewing, which also would have slowed her decay (and at a fraction of the cost of embalming), Fielding would have said he doesn't offer refrigeration because it won't make Jenny look "nearly as good as she could be" in the casket.

Still, federal law prevents Fielding from embalming Jenny for a fee without first gaining her guardians' express permission. (The Federal Trade Commission had imposed the rule in 1984 after families had complained that some funeral directors, without asking, had embalmed bodies that clearly didn't need it. Among those were remains headed directly to the crematorium, as well as those of orthodox Jews, whose faith opposes the practice.) When Fielding makes his request, he keeps it short and to the point: "Your wish for a viewing includes embalming," he tells the Johnsons. "That okay?" Jim hesitates, perhaps for the first time considering what embalming may mean for his daughter, before slowly nodding his head. Fielding will later translate that nonverbal agreement into writing when the Johnsons sign the contract he'll draw up at the end of this meeting.

A couple of related items are bulleted beneath the embalming section. Fielding checks those he'll require for Jenny—hair styling, which he'll turn over to a beautician ($90); and dressing and "casketing" the remains ($50). Fielding himself can outfit Jenny from the wardrobe of professional funeral wear he keeps in stock, in this case a white burial gown whose backside has been cut out for easy dressing ($135). He'd also touch her up with cosmetics specially formulated for application to bodies infused with embalming dye. But when he asks Myra if she'd prefer that Jenny be dressed in her own clothing—a prom or bridesmaid gown, maybe—and that her own makeup be used, Myra says yes, she'll bring them in.

The options for viewing, Fielding continues, vary with place (church or funeral home), time (day, night), number of days, and actual length. After considering all the variations, the Johnsons decide to hold a viewing in the funeral home, with visiting hours from five to seven the night before the funeral ($410). On Fielding's recommendation, they agree to have their priest lead a praying of the Rosary and end the viewing with a prayer (for which a $100 gratuity will be needed). The Johnsons can bring in a disk of music to be piped over the sound system; if they'd prefer live organ music, Fielding says he'll provide a soloist ($100). The Johnsons tell Fielding they'll drop off a disk of light classic music, one Jenny used to play to help her fall asleep at night.

The actual funeral service will be held the following morning at St. Matthew's ($610, Fielding's charge for coordinating arrangements with the church and preparing for a funeral there, roughly the same price for holding the funeral in his own parlor). Fielding often works with St. Matthew's and tells the Johnsons the church charges a fixed fee of $200 for the hour-long funeral Mass and the services of the priest, altar servers, and organist. Fielding then asks if Jim and Myra can provide him with the names of four to eight pallbearers to carry Jenny's casket in and out of the church, and to the grave site, which they do. (Had they not, Fielding would have hired his own, $50 per pallbearer.)

St. Matthew's is a five-minute drive from Fielding's, the cemetery another ten minutes from there. He'll use a gray Cadillac hearse to transport Jenny to both places ($215). If the Johnsons think they'd rather not drive on the day of the funeral, Fielding can provide them with a six-door Cadillac limousine ($195); other close relatives can follow directly behind in the company's fleet of four-person Lincoln sedans ($85 per vehicle). An escort car, if they want one, will precede the cortege, carrying Fielding and the priest to the cemetery ($60).

The Johnsons are obligated, however, to lease Fielding's "flower van" ($95). Jenny's likely to receive many floral arrangements for the viewing, and he'll need a separate vehicle to forward them to the church and cemetery afterward. A police escort will probably be needed, too ($150). The only other transportation cost, Fielding adds, is his charge for picking up Jenny at the hospital and bringing her back to his funeral home ($205).

The average funeral in America runs to $10,000, accounting for one of the single most expensive purchases a family will make in its lifetime. At this point the Johnsons are already over the $4,000 mark, and that's before the casket cost and cemetery fees are added in. Fielding isn't privy to the Johnson's financial situation. (For older clients, he'd get a better idea of that when he asks them how many copies of the death certificate they'll need. A higher number generally indicates greater wealth, as financial institutions usually demand death certificates to disperse funds.) But if the mounting price tag worries them, the Johnsons aren't showing it. Staring silently down at the itemized list, they look too consumed in their own grief to closely follow Fielding or question the need for—and price of—certain services. Like most of his clients, the Johnsons are new to the business of funeral making, and at this late date they lack the knowledge, energy, and time to figure out what's best for their daughter and their pocketbook. Cost may not even figure into the

Johnsons' plans. In Fielding's experience, young parents tend to want to pamper their children right up to the end—as a sign of love, out of a sense of guilt—regardless of what they can afford.

Fielding now turns to the calendar. "Today is Saturday," he begins. "We could have a funeral as soon as Tuesday, with a viewing Monday night, as long as the church and priest are available." That would give him an opportunity to submit an obituary for tomorrow's paper, giving the community enough advance notice and any distant family time to fly in. Holy Savior Cemetery would have the forty-eight-hour lead time it needs to prepare a grave site, saving the Johnsons the additional weekend overtime fee ($60 per half hour).

Holy Savior is a Colonial-era cemetery by the river that's overspread with mature trees. On weekends, it's filled with joggers and walkers seeking a quiet refuge from the town's bustle. It's a beautiful spot, and, in terms of funereal real estate, fairly exclusive. The Johnsons don't know it, but Myra's parents saved the couple nearly $900 when they gifted them a plot for Jenny. The parents' generosity doesn't cover the burial costs, however. Pulling out a sheet labeled "Holy Savior Interment Fees List," Fielding shows Myra and Jim that they'll still have to pay $900 for a backhoe to scoop out—or "open"—Jenny's grave, and then "close" it following the service. The cemetery also charges an additional $130 to install a concrete "foundation" at the head of the grave to support the marker or monument the family will eventually place there. There's an additional onetime fee of $150 for the ongoing maintenance—mowing, mostly—of the plot.

Fielding anticipates the graveside ceremony will last about twenty minutes. He'll coordinate everything in advance with the cemetery ($350), and provide a tent over the site and thirty chairs for family. The actual grave markers the Johnsons will need to purchase on their own. Fielding recommends that they contact local manufacturers listed in the telephone book. Depending on what they want, they can expect to pay anywhere from several hundred dollars for a modest flat marker to several thousands for a granite or marble headstone.

Fielding now comes to the most delicate part of the arrangement conference: the casket selection. It's often at this point that the reality of death hits a family hardest; it's also when the family's confronted with one of the most expensive items in the entire funeral. Fielding lays the groundwork before proceeding. "I'd like to take you now into our casket selection room," he says. "We offer nearly two dozen models, in both wood and metal. They range in price from $500 to $10,000. So, if you'll please follow me." Fielding then rises and hands the Johnsons a casket price list before leading them out.

The selection room lies at the bottom of a long, broad flight of steps. It's an open, low-ceilinged space, with soft light from recessed lamps illuminating an array of open caskets that fan the perimeter of the room; a smaller sample circles a pillar in the room's center. At the sight of the plush caskets, Myra and Jim both falter. From long experience, Fielding knows these parents are picturing their daughter in one of these caskets, realizing they'll be choosing her final resting place. It's a sobering moment, and Fielding continues into the room alone, leaving the family to join him when they're ready.

When eventually they do, Fielding directs them to a trio of coffins he says represents the basic options. Aside from the obvious differences in styles, he explains, caskets vary according to the material from which they're fashioned. Wood caskets offer the natural warmth and beauty of fine furniture, though they will decay over time. Metal is more resilient and resists the elements. Of the latter, bronze and copper tend to be more expensive because they're semiprecious metals that are virtually indestructible; in fact, Fielding says, archaeologists have retrieved ancient artifacts from copper coffins in near pristine condition. Stainless steel is less durable, but it's cheaper and won't rust. Signs on the caskets indicate the metals' "gauge," a lower gauge indicating a thicker metal.

"If protection of a loved one against water and soil is important," Fielding begins, "a sealed casket might be best." These sealer models, which come in metal only and boost the price of a casket by hundreds of dollars, are outfitted with rubber gaskets that help keep out the elements when the casket's closed. (Federal law prohibits Fielding's from contending that gasketed caskets keep a body from decomposition, which they don't.) Other differences in quality and cost have to do with construction—curved corners are more desirable than sharp, metal hardware is superior to plastic—and such interior features as the fineness of the stitching, color selection, and plushness.

When he finishes his practiced spiel, Fielding slowly ushers the Johnsons past an arc of burnished coffins, moving from least to most expensive. The gray, cloth-covered Rustic ($500). Steel Cortege ($1,595). Stainless-steel Branson ($4,450). Mahogany Congress ($8,200). Solid bronze Eternity Gold ($10,000). For outdoor enthusiasts, Fielding points out, there's a chestnut-colored steel casket with camouflage interior and an image of a deer embroidered into the inside head panel ($7,300). Mourners can write messages with Magic Marker all over the body and interior lid of another casket ($4,500). A few models feature interior "memory drawers." In one of these Fielding has arranged an ensemble that features a Bible and a set of baseball trading cards before the small, framed picture of a handsome, smiling boy on a pitcher's mound.

What's best really depends on personal preference and how one feels about the value of protecting a loved one, Fielding offers. "I'll leave you now and let you peruse as much as you'd like. If you have any questions, I'll be just outside the door."

The Johnsons wander the room in a fog. Eventually, they stop at the Damask Rose ($4,500), a bronze casket with a plush, pink-tinted interior. Myra would later tell Jim she was attracted by its feminine quality, the images of roses stitched into the lid and skirt, the colored fabric, the soft pillow and blanket that reminded her of Jenny's bedroom. The price was high, but, they felt, worth the protection bronze afforded. (Had they known, they could have gone online and, tapping into the score of Internet brokers, ordered the very same casket for overnight delivery for twenty-five percent less. By law Fielding would have been required to accept it, and without charging a handling fee.)

Back upstairs, Fielding and the Johnsons come to the final selections. One concerns the "outer burial container," a requirement of Holy Savior (though not of any local, state, or federal law). "This is a box the casket's buried in," Fielding explains, laying out a set of miniature models. "It's lowered into the ground, the casket is set inside, and a heavy lid is placed on top." Originally designed to deter grave robbers, this "coffin case," as it was once called, is mandated by most cemeteries to keep the ground from caving in around the grave site when the casket degrades. That's not an issue with an impermeable bronze casket like the Damask Rose, Fielding admits. But even more than the coffin itself, a quality case does afford "the best" protection from the elements.

Holy Savior permits two kinds of burial containers. The most inexpensive is a basic grave liner, a bottomless box made from lightweight concrete ($665). It will hold the soil's weight but allows the intrusion of water and the elements. A vault, on the other hand, envelopes the entire casket in a fiberglass or stainless-steel inner liner that's further encased in reinforced concrete; its thousand-pound lid is joined to the body with a tongue and groove joint, sealing top to base. Vaults are more expensive than grave liners, costing as much as $10,000, Fielding explains, but "if protection is important, it's the better choice." He offers a number of them in a range of prices. After reviewing the models and reading the description from Fielding's handouts, the Johnsons choose the mid-priced Clematis, a near three-thousand-pound, steel-lined concrete vault whose exterior is finished in pink and sports a single bloom on its lid ($2,100).

Family and friends will be sending flowers to honor your daughter, Fielding says, moving on. He'll arrange them around the casket when they arrive. If Jim and Myra want to provide a "floral tribute" of their own as well, they can do that through him. Working with a local florist, he's able to offer a variety of fitting arrangements, which are pictured in a small catalog he pulls out to show them. Considering the theme and colors of the casket interior, the Johnsons choose the "casket spray" ($350) from Fielding's Traditional Rose Collection, an arrangement of fifty pink roses to be placed on Jenny's casket during the viewing and funeral. If they'd like, Fielding says, the Johnsons' friends can order flowers directly from him as well.

Only a few details remain. With Fielding's guidance, the Johnsons decide to purchase a register book for the service ($40) and a packet of prayer cards, the Twenty-third Psalm on one side, Jenny's obituary on the other ($30). At this point, Fielding asks the Johnsons for Jenny's personal information—age, social security number, names of surviving relatives—for the death certificate he'll file with the county and for the obituary to run in tomorrow's paper. The Johnsons ask for six copies of the death certificate to be sent to them ($6 each).

When he's done, Fielding reviews the arrangements with the Johnsons. He then transfers their selections onto an itemized contract and tallies the costs right there at his desk. The total cost of the embalming, funeral, and burial of Jenny Johnson comes to $12,376.

After seeing the Johnsons out, Fielding returns to his desk and calls the regional casket company rep to order the Damask Rose, for delivery Monday morning. Arrangements have already been finalized for the viewing that evening of an elderly "case," whose embalmed and prepped remains now repose in the air-conditioned slumber room across from his office. With a few free hours ahead of him, Fielding decides to start Jenny's embalming.

A body can decompose rapidly after death. Its cells, proteins, and tissues begin to break down almost immediately, and pathogenic bacteria in the gut that are normally held in check during life maraud throughout a fresh corpse in as little as four hours. The sooner an embalmer gets to work the fewer the difficulties he'll face in preserving a body for viewing.

The embalming, or prep, room sits in the basement of the Fielding Funeral Home, a Victorian-era abode that Fielding's grandfather retrofitted in the 1940s to process the dead. It's a small, compact space whose only access is a broad, metal door that's equipped with a keypad lock. State law requires that any embalming room be "secure" against public "entrance," to protect the privacy of the dead. Access to Fielding's basement is limited and restricted, but he installed a keypad lock on the door nonetheless to keep out those few curious clients who invariably wander down from the parlor upstairs.

To most outsiders, the odor of an embalming room is distinct and powerful, an acrid smell reminiscent of high school dissection labs. When Fielding punches in his code and opens the door, he barely detects it. His adaptation to the pungent chemical, a phenomenon common to embalmers, allows him to work here without experiencing the typical burning throat and runny, itchy eyes. But not without some cost to his health. The Occupational Safety and Health Administration (OSHA) deems formaldehyde a potential occupational carcinogen, and decreased sensitivity to it increases the likelihood that embalmers unknowingly overexpose themselves to the toxic gas, boosting their odds of contracting brain, colon, kidney, and other cancers for which the trade shows elevated rates.

A faint light ebbs into the prep room from a lone, ground-level window at the far wall. The window's clear panes were long ago replaced with small, opaque blocks, for privacy's sake (and per state law). Feeling along the edge of the doorjamb, Fielding finds and then flicks a light switch, flooding the room in a brilliant, white light.

In an effort to further legitimize its profession in the eyes of the public, the funeral industry sometimes refers to embalmers as "derma"—or skin—"surgeons." And with its gleaming white tiled floor and walls, well-stocked glass cabinets, porcelain sinks, and metal trays laden with syringes, scalpels, clamps, and other instruments of the medical establishment, Fielding's workspace closely resembles a hospital operating room. But for the quiet. Years ago Fielding lined these walls and ceiling with soundproofing tiles, so none of the noise attending his work—the clicking of the embalming machine, the vacuuming aspirator, a dropped scalpel—would disturb the tranquillity of the funeral quarters upstairs. The tiles also block any outdoor noise from penetrating the embalming room. When the door's closed and locked behind him, Fielding can't hear the hum of traffic or even voices in the conference room directly overhead. Besides the din from the embalming procedure, the only sound here comes from circulating fans and the radio he sometimes tunes to talk shows or a classical music station.

Before getting down to work, Fielding checks the room to make sure it's stocked with the supplies he'll need for Jenny—bottles of embalming and cavity fluid, sealing compound, Superglue, hypodermic needles, forceps, scalpels, lengths of clean hose. The door he props open to accommodate a mortuary cot, and then turns on a pair of fans, one drawing in fresh air, the other venting the caustic vapors of the formaldehyde, menthol, phenol, and other chemicals he'll be handling in this tight, enclosed space.

Fielding expects the embalming of Jenny to last under two hours. Unlike some of his colleagues who boast of twenty-minute embalmings or of those that go light on preservative, he isn't one to cut corners. In his experience, shortcuts in time, procedure, or material weren't worth the risk of having a casketed case blurp, bloat, expel gas, or even leak during a public viewing. Those disasters obviously upset the family, and at minimum compel the embalmer to return the body to the prep room and start from ground zero.

Jenny has been cooling in his basement refrigeration unit since he retrieved her from the hospital late last night. The fridge's constant thirty-eight degrees will slow her decomposition and keep bacteria in check. Still, on the off chance that the trim, young athlete may unwittingly harbor some yet transmittable disease—tuberculosis or AIDS, perhaps, whose pathogens can, for a time, survive the death of its host—Fielding sheds his jacket and tie and dons the protective uniform of the trade: a full-length, waterproof bodysuit, a pair of Tyvek shoe covers, a surgical cap, and latex gloves. Over his mouth and nose he ties a gauze mask, and pulls a clear plastic splash guard over his face.

Covered from head to foot, Fielding wheels Jenny from the fridge into the embalming room, parking the mortuary cot next to the porcelain embalming table, and locks the door. Grabbing the edge of the plastic bag she's zipped into, he pulls the teen onto the table, taking care not to bump the body, which could raise bruises he'd have to cover over later on.

Fielding then draws down the brass zipper and works the bag off the body. Clad in a green hospital gown and pair of shorts, Jenny shows little sign of trauma. No blood, wounds, or bruises. No broken bones. Just a few needle sticks he'll eventually close up with Superglue. Thankfully, the county coroner had signed off on an autopsy, since Jenny had been under a doctor's care for the congenital heart condition that had triggered her heart attack. Even a routine autopsy—in which the skull and chest are opened, rib cage removed, and organs (including the brain) pulled out, dissected, and, with the exception of the brain, stuffed back into the abdomen, which is then stitched up—complicates the embalmer's labors. Some cases are so thoroughly mutilated on the autopsy table that an embalmer is compelled to reconstruct lost features with his toolbox of waxes, webbing, plaster of paris, glues and the like, and otherwise artfully cosmeticize a body to a viewable state.

Taking up a pair of scissors, Fielding snips off the hospital gown covering Jenny, and carefully tugs off her clothing—shorts, underwear, socks, tennis shoes—which he'll launder and return to her parents. The gold chain and pendant around her neck he unclasps and sets aside, tapes in place the high school class ring on her finger to prevent it from slipping off during the embalming.

Though somewhat ashen from her time in Fielding's refrigeration unit, Jenny shows little outward sign of decomposition or contamination, no visible distention or swelling. Fielding nonetheless spritzes her from top to toe with a strong disinfectant and then scrubs her with germicidal soap.

The topical spray won't reach any pathogenic bacteria inside Jenny, which could still leak out when Fielding manipulates her on the embalming table. So before bending and flexing her limbs stiffening with rigor mortis, Fielding takes a pair of packing forceps and pushes wads of cotton soaked in phenol into Jenny's anus and vagina. He follows the wet cotton with tufts of dry, fully packing each organ. (Instead of cotton, Fielding could have used any of the "A/V closure" devices for sale in the trade catalogs—A for anus, V for vagina—threaded plastic plugs that screw snugly into their targeted cavities.) He likewise stuffs dry cotton deep into both ears.

Before her death, Jenny had pulled her blond hair into a tight ponytail, now disheveled. Fielding will later wash her hair, and have his beautician on call style and dress it. At this point, though, with the teen freshly bathed and her skin more supple than it would be when infused with embalming fluid, he lathers Jenny's face with cream and shaves it. Like many embalmers, Fielding shaves all his clients—men, women, and children—as a matter of course. Makeup's easier to apply to a smooth, hairless face, and it won't show the powder he'll dust onto Jenny's features before her casketing. He moves the blade in long, slow strokes, taking care not to abrade skin. Any cuts he makes now won't heal.

As do most of his fellow funeral directors, Fielding insists on embalming any case on view because it delays the body's inevitable decay. But preservation is only part of his goal; presentation's just as vital to a successful viewing. For Fielding doesn't merely want Jenny to hold up in the casket; he wants her to look both lifelike and at peace. In the end, the modern embalmer is just as much artist as dermasurgeon. With his arsenal of chemicals, tools, and techniques, he's an illusionist who literally changes the face of death, transforming the ashen, lifeless corpses in his care into lifelike bodies at rest.

The funeral trade has christened the embalmer's creation a "memory picture," a pleasing illusion of a loved one who has simply slipped off to sleep, and insists it's necessary. A family must view the deceased's remains, its argument goes, to accept the fact that a death has occurred and to begin the necessary grieving and subsequent healing process. And the more pleasant and true-to-life the "picture" the easier it is to acknowledge the death and, perhaps, let go.

The artistry involved in arranging that snapshot consumes most of the embalmer's labor. And much of it happens here, with what's known as "setting the features."

The embalming chemicals Fielding will shortly inject into Jenny arteries will firm her soft tissues to a rigid and unalterable state. Now's his best chance to set her into final form. Standing at the head of the table, Fielding raises her head onto a rubber block where a pillow will eventually be placed, and sets the elbows and shoulder blades onto elevated rests. (He could have achieved the same ends with less effort and more precision with "arm positioners," prefab metal forms into which arms are locked.)

Fielding's broken up most of Jenny's rigor mortis, but he continues to manipulate the limbs, and begins to massage the muscle stiffness out of regions that are most visible at a viewing—the forehead, cheeks, eyelids, and hands. When he feels the hands relax, he cups them around a ball of dry cotton and joins them at her lap, right over left. A final twist of her head, fifteen degrees to the right, ensures that mourners will see her face—not just its profile—when they approach the casket. The angle also keeps Jenny from looking like she's staring fixedly at the ceiling, an unappealing position dubbed "stargazing."

A small-busted woman like Jenny poses fewer presentation challenges for Fielding than a larger one. If she'd been endowed with "pendulous" breasts, as one mortuary text puts it, Fielding might have felt compelled to bind them together in the center of her chest in an effort to grace her with "a more natural appearance" (and also permit her arms to be brought in closer to her sides, preserving casket space). For the rebusting, he'd have joined the breasts with a foot-long piece of duct tape. Some of his colleagues follow a more traditional technique that involves running a half-curved needle threaded with suture into each breast at a point just off the nipples and pulling the suture taut, to bind the breasts. An injection of embalming fluid would have then firmed the breasts into place, after which Fielding could have safely stripped off the tape (or, in the case of those fellow embalmers, pulled out the sutures).

More than most features, the appearance of Jenny's eyes and mouth will determine just how natural Jenny looks to her friends and family. Fielding's goal here is to establish what's known in the business as a "pleasant" demeanor. Achieving it proves to be one of the trickier parts of the embalmer's job.

To set the eyes, Fielding can at least rely on two modern inventions of the trade: a tub of "stay cream" cement and a pair of eyecaps. The eyecaps, which are pressed from plastic, are lens-shaped domes covered with raised spurs. After squirting disinfectant onto Jenny's eyeballs and swabbing them dry with cotton, Fielding dips two of the caps into the stay cream and positions each one onto an eyeball. With a needlelike hook he first pulls Jenny's upper eyelids two-thirds of the way down and then raises the lower lids to meet them at an imaginary "line of closure" the industry believes best creates the "illusion of sleep." Fielding then tamps on the lids, sticking them to the spurred caps. When the stay cream dries it will permanently cement the lids to the caps and, on the underside, the caps to the eyeballs. (Some of his colleagues skip the stay cream and simply run a line of Superglue along the lid rim, a strategy Fielding believes unnecessarily risks getting glue into the lashes).

The mouth requires more preparation since rigor mortis has locked it shut. Taking the lower jawbone in hand, Fielding works it up and down until it finally slacks and gapes open. Fielding squirts disinfectant into the opening, killing off bacteria that could darken a ring of skin around the lips and stuffs cotton into the throat.

Fielding has a choice of methods to close Jenny's mouth. (The rigor mortis that locked it would have retreated on its own within twenty-four hours, again gaping it open.) One is to sew the jaws shut from inside the mouth. This bit of internal stitching, dubbed "muscular suture," entails passing a needle threaded with suture through muscular tissue at the base of the inside lower gum, pushing up into a nostril via the inner gum line, punching through the septum into the opposing nostril, and then coming back down into the mouth by way of the gums. The embalmer then pulls the suture taut, closing the jaws, and ties off.

For Jenny, Fielding takes a more common and easier approach. His tool is a spring-activated "needle injector," a cross between a syringe and a workshop staple gun that shoots barb-tipped wires. Its target is the upper and lower jawbones. Pulling back Jenny's upper lip first, Fielding places the tip of the injector at a point of strong bone above the canines, and pushes the trigger. With an audible crunch, a barb drives into bone, securing its five-inch length of wire; a second barb he shoots into a similar spot on the lower jaw. Fielding then pushes Jenny's tongue behind her teeth and twists the wires together, drawing her jaws shut. (Before the advent of the needle injector, embalmers achieved the same ends with a method known as "tack and thread," which required hammering into the jawbones long carpet tacks connected to strong cord.)

It's now up to Fielding to restore a peaceful appearance to Jenny's frowning, sunken mouth. Again, he works to achieve that "pleasant look." Many embalmers simply pack and seal the mouth, stuffing cheeks with cotton and gluing the lips shut. But Fielding's experience has shown that cotton tends to wick moisture from the cheeks, discoloring the mouth. It also sops up "purge," the abdominal or respiratory discharge that sometimes blurps into the mouth (or out the nose), which then has to be mopped out and repacked. Fielding chose instead to use a nonabsorbent mastic filling. Pulling open Jenny's cheeks, he squirts a wad of mastic into both hollows with a fat syringe (though some embalmers find it more convenient to inject into the cheeks via the nostrils). Switching nozzles, he then pushes a narrow ribbon of mastic into the upper and lower gums to fill out the lip line. Compound oozes out of the mouth, which he scrapes off with a spatula.

Filled with mortuary putty, Jenny's mouth is easy to form. Fielding pushes the lips into a gentle upward curve. To ensure the lips stay closed during the embalming, he smears them with "seal cream." He'll glue them permanently shut later. He remembers the needle sticks, and over each prick squeezes a drop of Superglue.

The preembalming, which lasts less than half an hour, is complete. If she'd been dressed in pajamas and had more color in her cheeks, Jenny might look like the college freshman who rolled out of bed yesterday morning and prepared for class. But Fielding knows she wouldn't stay that way for long. Jenny is actively decomposing from the inside out, and it was his job to at least temporarily slow that inevitability long enough so she could be put on view two days from now.

The actual preservation he approaches in two stages. The first, known as arterial injection, involves draining the blood from Jenny's circulatory system and replacing it with liquid preservative. The fluid's main ingredient is formaldehyde, a potent, soluble gas that kills bacteria and fortifies tissues against decomposition; it also contains, among other agents, the solvent methanol, phenol (a preservative), and a pinkish dye formulated to stain body tissue to a lifelike tint.

From the cabinet Fielding pulls four sixteen-ounce bottles of a formaldehyde—"formalin"—cocktail and pours them into the three-gallon clear tank atop a Portiboy embalming machine. The tank fills with water, cutting the solution, and mixes it for injection into Jenny's artery.

Fielding's preferred injection site is the carotid artery, which lies just below the surface of the skin, along the right side of the neck near the collarbone. On Jenny, he draws a sharp scalpel here, opening a two-inch-long gash that exposes a grayish mass of fat and tissue. Switching scalpel for blunt hook, Fielding probes within the mass until he locates the cream-colored artery; he pulls the vessel to the surface and, slipping a thin file beneath the vessel, secures it. Returning to the cut, he likewise raises and secures the neighboring bluish jugular vein.

An artery and vein now protrude from Jenny's neck. With scalpel in hand, Fielding saws an opening into the tough, rubbery artery and guides the head of a metal tube into it, pointing the head toward the heart. A hose affixed to the tube's free end runs to the Portiboy, whose pressure and flow rate Fielding adjusts for a body that looks to be one hundred twenty-five pounds or so. He then trips the machine to life. With a loud, regular clicking sound, the Portiboy begins to pump pink embalming fluid through the tube into Jenny's artery.

With the machine's relentless force behind it, formalin pushes blood from arteries into veins. Fielding is careful not to dial up the pressure. Excessive pressure can bloat a body within a matter of minutes, making it look fifty pounds heavier. The blood is now building up. To release it, Fielding slices a hole into the raised jugular and into it inserts the shaft of the drain tube, pushing south until the tip banks against the upper chamber of the heart. Brackish blood streams from the tube and spills into the gutter that rims the embalming table. From there it flows into a porcelain basin at the head of the table called a "slop" sink and gurgles down the drain on its way to the city sewer system.

With the Portiboy ticking away, arterial fluid being pumped in, blood being forced out, Fielding begins to vigorously massage Jenny's arms and legs to encourage the flow. A couple of times he stops the massage to attend to blood clots that block up the veins. Some embalmers push down on the chest to dislodge them; Fielding pumps a priming lever on the end of the drain tube. When he does, a few clots plop into the slop sink, looking something like currant jelly. These clots are small. Bigger clots, which resemble, and are called, chicken fat, he sometimes needs to smash by hand to keep them from clogging the drain.

After twenty minutes, three-quarters of a gallon of blood are drained from Jenny, and the dark color in the hose begins to brighten, one sign embalming fluid is filling the girl's circulatory system. A pink, lifelike tinge has returned to Jenny's ashen skin as colored dye trickles into underlying tissue. When Fielding pinches Jenny's now plump fingertips and earlobes, the skin rebounds as it would in life. Fielding shuts down the Portiboy, removes both drain nozzles from vein and artery, and ties off the vessels with surgical thread. He stuffs the knot into the incision, follows it with cotton, and squirts a powdery sealing compound over both. Taking a curved needle threaded with suture, Fielding then closes the wound with a baseball stitch.

In the thumbnail definition of embalming he recited for Jenny's parents, the arterial component he's just completed is all he referenced. What he didn't tell the family, and what he still has to accomplish, is the other vital half of the embalming procedure: the cavity injection.

Arterial embalming preserves Jenny's tissue and skin by creating an unwelcome environment for bacteria. It leaves largely untouched, however, the many billions of bacteria that reside—and thrive—within and around her visceral organs. In the early days of embalming, practitioners eliminated those decay-causing microorganisms by cutting open and "eviscerating" the corpse, pulling out abdominal organs and flushing the cavity (and then, depending on the historical period, repacking them with everything from spices to grain alcohol). The invasive activity, popularly known as "ripping the corpse," remained standard embalming procedure for virtually thousands of years. With the rise of modern embalming in mid- to late-nineteenth-century America, however, the nascent industry devised a more sanitary and, in a sign of the times, efficient strategy for disinfecting the abdominal cavity. Instead of opening and cleaning out the abdomen, embalmers learned to siphon out its contaminants through a single, small hole in the abdomen. The tool they designed specially for the purpose is a long, hollow needle called a trocar.

The slender trocar Fielding holds above Jenny is typical of the variety. It's a narrow, two-foot-long metal tube that runs to a sharp, arrowlike point, with slits to the fore of the shaft. An opening at the other end connects to clear, plastic tubing that hooks to an aspirator, a device on a slop sink's faucet that creates the suction a trocar needs to vacuum up—or "aspirate"—abdominal contents through its slitted shaft and carry them into the sink.

The trocar can be fitted with fresh tips, but Fielding hones the point of his with a small whetstone prior to each embalming. The business end of the trocar has to be sharp enough to pierce the tough abdominal wall and reach the organs. The embalmer's ideal point of entry is a soft spot of flesh two inches to the left and north of the navel. With a practiced probe of fingers, Fielding fixes that spot on Jenny and places the silver tip of the trocar there. And then, grasping firmly, he drives it into her stomach.

Jenny shifts on the table as the trocar enters, and moves in motion as Fielding proceeds to impel the shaft in and around her abdomen. To the outsider, Fielding's thrusting—or "belly punching," as early viewers of the practice described it—appears blind and random. But there's method behind it. Each thrust works to puncture a separate organ—first Jenny's heart, lungs, and stomach, and then colon, intestines, liver, and bladder. With an audible sucking sound, the trocar vacuums up the visceral matter it liberates with each puncture: congested blood, accumulated fluid and gases, fecal matter, urine, the semidigested hamburger and fries Jenny ate for her final dinner, and masses of bacteria. Fielding then sweeps the trocar over and around the perforated organs, sucking up additional cavity content.

As he does, darkened mass passes through the clear hose and splashes into the slop sink. After a couple of minutes, it stops. Fielding then clicks off the aspirator and withdraws the soiled trocar from Jenny's abdomen. (If brain matter had begun leaking from Jenny's nose—a sign of advanced cranial decomposition—Fielding would have inserted a small "infant" trocar or a curved metal hose called a nasal aspirator into her nostril and, pushing up into the cranium, sucked out brain tissue and built-up gases before shutting down. He'd have then injected fluid into the aspirated cranium, and then plugged the nose with cotton to keep fluid from leaking out.)

To preserve and further disinfect the area he's just cleared, Fielding moves to flood it with formaldehyde and phenol. Unlike arterial fluid, the liquid cavity compound is used undiluted; it's so astringent that within seconds of popping the cap off a sixteen-ounce bottle, even Fielding's desensitized eyes water and his nose burns. Through his tears he attaches a fresh length of hose to the bottle, connects the other end of the hose to the trocar, and holds the bottle aloft. Again Fielding drives the trocar into Jenny's stomach, thrusting more slowly now in order to evenly and fully distribute the fluid gravitating from bottle to trocar. After two bottles are drained, he stops. (If Fielding had been working on a male and seen that arterial solution had not reached the genitalia, he would have then inserted the trocar separately into the shaft of the penis and scrotum.)

A pool of cavity fluid bubbles up onto Jenny's stomach as Fielding withdraws the trocar. He flushes it away with cold water. Into the opening he's created he packs fresh cotton, which will allow the escape of any "reaction gases" that form when the embalming fluid mixes with cavity contents.

It's nearly one o'clock. Almost ninety minutes have passed since Fielding first slipped on his plastic gloves and snipped off Jenny's hospital gown. Her embalming is now complete. With a hose that has been running for most of the procedure, Fielding washes Jenny once more, scrubbing off dried blood and shampooing and conditioning her hair. Her body he pats dry with a soft towel, and rubs massage cream into her face and hands to keep them from drying out.

A portable dressing table sits along the far wall of the room. Fielding wheels it over to the prep table and slides Jenny onto it, grasping her by the leg and neck. Formalin has replaced the blood that once coursed through her body, so she weighs about the same as she did prior to embalming. He takes a moment to swab the inside of her nostrils with Nair, to loosen unsightly nasal hairs from their follicles. A white sheet is then draped over her clean body, Fielding positioning the sheet off the nose so the cloth's weight won't flatten the most visible feature on her face.

Fielding could now dress and casket Jenny if he had to. But he prefers to let his cases "firm" when time allows. So he parks Jenny in a corner— she'll hold for a good week now with little change, without the need for refrigeration—cleans the room, and after discarding his protective gear, clicks off the light and shuts the door.

Early Monday morning, the day of Jenny's viewing, Fielding returns to review his work, as he has every day since her embalming. Pulling the sheet off her this morning, he sees that the colored embalming fluid has fully perfused the girl's body, which now glows with a natural-looking hue and is firm to the touch. Except for Jenny's abdomen, which is visibly distended, a textbook sign there's an active pocket of bacteria somewhere in the gut. If he lets it go, the bacteria will continue to proliferate, potentially forcing Jenny to purge. Fielding decides to reaspirate. Transferring Jenny to the embalming table, he pulls out the cotton plug in her abdomen and slips in the trocar. This time the metal tube vacuums up bacteria, gas, and old cavity fluid; afterward, he saturates the area with fresh cavity fluid and stops up the open bore in her stomach for good with a threaded, plastic cone called a trocar button.

Despite the cream he applied, Fielding sees that Jenny's lips have wrinkled in the interim. They're a highly visible focal point, so he elects to "hypo" them back into shape. With a small-gauge needle, he injects a mastic of "tissue builder" into four points along the outer edges of the top and bottom lips. He's careful to inject slowly, working to plump but not bloat the lips. (The few times he's overfilled lips, Fielding has had to cut them open with a scalpel, scrape out excess builder and then glue the lips back together.)

For the last time, Fielding washes and dries Jenny, applies more massage cream to her face and hands, and returns her to the dressing table. The Nair he worked into the nostrils has loosened her nasal hair, which he now wipes out with a cotton ball attached to the end of a pair of forceps. Fielding's not one to use a lot of makeup, and fortunately in this case doesn't have to. Myra has dropped off the daughter's makeup kit, a recent picture of Jenny at the senior prom, a rosary, and her white prom gown. He stipples onto her smooth, shaved face the kit's pinker hues, to raise a blush he believes will complement the rose colors of the casket and her gown; he follows the makeup with light rouge. White baby powder is then dusted on top of that, so the face won't reflect light shining from the lamps she'll be sitting under in the reposing room. Using the prom picture as a guide, Fielding proceeds to darken the eyebrows with pencil and, after mixing a bit of cosmetic oil with her lipstick in the palm of his hand, paints the lips with a fine brush.

Only the face and hands will be visible in the casket. As in life, their color must match—and Jenny's, Fielding plainly sees, do not. Returning to the makeup kit, he brushes more pink onto the backside of the girl's hands, applies the rouge and powder; he then clips, buffs, and cleans beneath her fingernails. The cuticles themselves now look somewhat washed out in contrast to the rest of the hands, so Fielding paints the nails with a light pink polish. And stops. He'll wait until Jenny's lying in state upstairs to make final touch-ups, so he can see just how she looks under viewing room lights.

The prom gown Myra dropped off, he's happy to see, is long-sleeved, saving him the effort of having to cosmeticize her arms for color and to cover over those needle sticks from the hospital. Its neckline swings low, though, exposing the incision he made just above her collarbone when raising blood vessels for the arterial embalming. No worry. He'll cover it with a scarf later on.

Jenny's gown is loose and billowy. But he can't easily slip it onto a body whose arms and hands are locked in place. He'll have to cut the backside out of the gown and work it onto Jenny's frame. Before he does this, Fielding pulls a pair of watertight plastic pants onto the teen and dusts the insides with a deodorizing mold killer. The cotton he packed into Jenny's vagina and anus during the preembalming is usually sufficient to keep smelly discharge from leaking out and spoiling both her clothes and the casket bed for the next two days, but the plastic pants are cheap insurance.

Fielding slips a pair of panties over the pants. A bra and socks follow. On top of the panties he lays a cotton cloth, smoothing Jenny's lap so the dress won't emphasize the contour of her crotch. The gown he now cuts and fits to the girl, places a pink scarf around her neck. Myra had accompanied the dress with a pair of stiff shoes, but they'll only fit her feet if Fielding slits them down the back, which he doesn't do, preferring to place them as is at the far end of the casket. Finally, Fielding returns the gold chain to Jenny's neck and removes the tape that had secured her ring during the embalming.

As Fielding fine-tunes his handiwork, the beautician arrives. They confer on the styling of Jenny's hair, which Fielding asks her to match to the picture he hands over. The beautician sets to work and, after cleaning the embalming table and returning materials to their proper place, Fielding heads upstairs.

Half an hour later he returns, accompanied by an assistant, who helps wheel the Damask Rose casket into the prep room and position it next to the dressing table. The assistant opens the lid, and each man takes one end of the stiffened teen and lifts her off the table and into the casket. After closing the casket, both men roll it out of the room and up a ramp that leads to the receiving room.

When the casket is in place, Fielding opens it and primps the embalmed, dressed, cosmeticized, and coiffed eighteen-year-old for viewing. The pillow below Jenny's head, he sees, is overstuffed, elevating her head at an awkward angle. Fielding cuts a third of the padding from the backside and sets the reshaped pillow beneath her head, now more comfortably positioned.

Jenny's head is already turned fifteen degrees to the right, the side facing mourners. Fielding wants more of her head to show so that her face can be seen clearly as her casket is approached. Using the Damask Rose's cranking mechanism, he raises the mattress bed until Jenny's right shoulder is level with the casket's rim, and then tilts her entire body ever so slightly to the right. He now tucks loose clothing in and around the body, readjusts the scarf, and entwines a rosary in her fingers. Jenny's color is perfect under the lights. With a clean brush, he dusts off makeup that colors a bit of hairline, and combs stray strands of hair back from her face.

Looking down at Jenny, Fielding is satisfied. Under his careful hand, the young girl now looks at rest. In her gentle repose is the "memory picture" he wants her family to leave with, the lasting illusion of a beautiful girl who has slipped quietly, peacefully off to sleep. None of them, of course, will ever know the effort it took to achieve that look.

Resource Guide: *The Embalming of Jenny Johnson*

What:
Embalming is a three-stage process of preserving a corpse for viewing: setting the deceased's "features" as they will appear in the casket, draining the body of blood and replacing it with a formaldehyde-based preservative, and then inserting a sharp-pointed "trocar" into the abdomen in order to puncture the body's inner organs, vacuum up the released bacteria and surrounding visceral fluids, afterward flooding the "cleared" area with more preservative.

The Laws:

No federal law requires that a body be embalmed. States rarely require it, and then sometimes only when a body is being transported within or across state lines or when the deceased died of a contagious disease.

In the latter case, embalming is sometimes mandated despite the lack of definitive evidence to show that the procedure does, in fact, protect the public from disease a cadaver may harbor. The few studies that examine the public health benefit to embalming show decidedly mixed results, one indicating, for example, that tuberculosis bacilli may remain active in an embalmed corpse. In reviewing the evidence, a 2004 report by the British Institute of Embalmers states that "the disinfectant properties of embalming fluids are unclear." Embalming may, in fact, increase the risk of spreading, not containing, disease, as another British report on communicable diseases suggests, stating: "Opening cadavers infected with tuberculosis is dangerous." Recognizing the potential health hazards, the state of Hawaii prohibits the embalming of a body infected with any of half a dozen communicable diseases, including smallpox and yellow fever.

About half of all states require that a body be preserved if not buried or cremated within a few days of death, but permit methods of preservation other than embalming. Those may include refrigeration or the use of dry ice (or even frozen ice packs that are regularly changed).

That said, a funeral home is under no legal obligation to handle funeral arrangements for an unembalmed body, and may refuse to do so unless the burial/cremation occurs within a short period following the death and no viewing take place.

How:

Funeral homes that own refrigeration units may agree to refrigerate a body and offer an abbreviated public and/or private viewing. They're more likely to agree if the remains present no major trauma.

The funeral director may try to insist on "preparing" an unembalmed, refrigerated body for viewing, which may involve washing, "disinfecting," and dressing the body as well as "normal cosmetic restoration." The latter could include somewhat invasive procedures, such as gluing lips and eyelids closed and the use of eyecaps, among others. Make sure you and the funeral director agree on what exactly he or she will do to "prepare" the body in his or her care.

Cost:

Expect to pay $200 to $400 for such preparation (in lieu of embalming). Prices for refrigeration vary widely, anywhere from $50 a day to many hundreds of dollars, depending on the willingness of the funeral home to work with unembalmed remains. You'll pay a lot less and afford your dead a multiday wake by holding a funeral in your own home—see chapter six for details.

What You Need to Know:

For a death that occurs in a hospital, Lisa Carlson, author of *Caring for the Dead* (1998, Upper Access Books), advises families opposed to embalming to ask the staff if they may spend time with the deceased there. The funeral director may even allow families a brief "visit" with their deceased in the funeral home, for a nominal charge (sometimes listed on its price sheet under "private family viewing").

For a death that occurs at home, such as under hospice care, don't rush out to call the funeral director. This is time you may spend with the deceased in the private, quiet setting of your home.

To find funeral directors/providers who understand and are willing to provide families with green burial services (including embalming-free viewings), see the state-by-state list maintained by the Green Burial Council (www.greenburialcouncil.org, click on "Providers").

Embalming restores a lifelike appearance to the deceased. Refrigeration does not, which may only matter if you expect the dead to resemble the living.

[T]oday a large group of chemical products are made available to perform the [embalming] process. These products are used as arterial fluids, cavity fluids, co-injection fluids, non-arterial preservatives (powders, gels, cauterants, aerosols and creams), supplement products (solvents, sealants, adhesives), cosmetic products, cleaning compounds (cleansers, soaps, antiseptics, disinfectants, deodorizers) and other miscellaneous products (tissue builders, feature builders, etc.). For this study, about 600 different products were identified.

National Funeral Directors Association,
Funeral Home Wastestream Audit Report (1995)

༄

CHAPTER TWO:

After the Burial

When Tom Fielding returns to Holy Savior Cemetery after driving the priest back to St. Matthew's, the grounds crew is just lowering Jenny's casket into her grave. Yesterday afternoon these same men had scooped out four tons of dirt from this rectangle of ground with a backhoe, dumping the soil into a trailer bed now parked out of sight at the rear of the property. Later they had sunk the concrete base of Jenny's three-thousand-plus-pound burial vault into the freshly excavated hole with a mechanized stanchion, and then laid artificial "grass sets" around and down into the grave itself, covering any evidence of dirt with a brilliant green.

The priest had committed Jenny Johnson's body to the earth earlier this morning, sprinkling a ceremonial handful of sand onto the casket, but it's that vault, not the ground itself, the cemetery crew is lowering Jenny into. Like most cemeteries, Holy Savior insists that a vault be used to keep the ground from sinking into the grave when the casket eventually collapses and creates a depression that mars the uniformity of the grounds and makes mowing difficult. For families, the vault's value is decidedly more personal: the structure erects yet another barrier between their loved one and the natural elements that surround her.

Vault manufacturers invest heavily in that stand against nature, every year pouring more than one and a half million total tons of reinforced concrete in their vault boxes and another fourteen thousand tons of steel into the lining. The vault Jim and Myra Johnson purchased for their daughter is typical of the type. Made from a ton of high-strength reinforced concrete, the Clematis is a knee-high bunker that's lined with a waterproof polymer and, over that, a sheet of stainless steel. A gasket of rubber formulated for use in septic tanks and storm sewers rims the lip of the vault's base. When the twelve-hundred-pound lid is set on the gasket, it forms a tight seal that one manufacturer dubs "the last line of defense against mother nature."

The cemetery crew handles the final stages of interment, but Holy Savior requires funeral directors to oversee the sealing of the vault. Fielding comes to stand near the vault lid, which rests on a stand, with rails running to the grave. A pair of cemetery workers then tackles the main work of the closing: pushing the lid down the rail to a position directly over the vault, cranking the device that undergirds the vault until the base meets the lid, and then lowering the now whole, sealed vault, with Jenny and her casket inside, to the floor of the grave. The truck with the trailer bed full of excavated dirt pulls back up to the site and, after the crew rolls up the fake grass sets, dumps some of its earthen load into the grave, the crew directing the dirt onto and around the vault. When the grave's completely filled in, one of the workers moves over the dirt with a gas-powered industrial tamper and over it lays mats of sod scrapped off the site yesterday.

Less than an hour after the Johnson family drives away from the cemetery, the funeral and burial of their young daughter is complete. In just three days, Tom Fielding has orchestrated for his clients the best of modern memorialization: embalming and casketing of the dead. The viewing of a corpse made so lifelike it imparts a soothing "memory picture" to help mourners "come to terms" with their loss. A fitting funeral service. And now, interment within industrial structures expressly designed, despite the priest's consignment of Jenny's own "dust to dust," to prevent contact with the earth and the elements that surround her on all sides.

Fielding is back at his office as the last of the sod is returned to the soil on Jenny's fresh grave. The funeral director can now finish the paperwork on this successful burial, but it's far from over. Belowground, the American way of death continues to play itself out.

By the time Fielding closes out the Johnson account, the sewage treatment plant in town had processed the one hundred twenty gallons of untreated "funeral waste" the mortician sent directly down his sink during Jenny's ninety-minute embalming. In addition to the water from the hose running onto the embalming table, the waste held a mix of body fluids—whole blood, fecal matter, liberated contents of internal organs—and the potentially carcinogenic chemicals in the embalming solutions, including formaldehyde, phenol, and menthol. The flow might also have carried down the drain pathogens of any disease Jenny's body might have unknowingly harbored, perhaps tuberculosis.

Like many municipalities, Fielding's city allows funeral directors to release their embalming effluent into the sewer system, untreated. The concentration of contaminants and caustic embalming chemicals flowing from the funeral home is generally low, according to the superintendent of the wastewater treatment plant, and, when mixed with other waste at the plant, is diluted to levels that allow for its safe release into area waterways. Other municipalities around the country are more circumspect. The wastewater treatment facility that serves northeast Rhode Island, which includes the city of Providence, for example, requires that funeral homes pretreat their effluent before releasing it. One method it approves involves setting an IV bag filled with bleach to drip directly into the drain when embalming waste is flowing. Concern is for the health of both the public and treatment plant employees. After city sewer workers in Bangor, Maine, saw "a large gush of red blood" pouring into a sewer near a funeral home, the superintendent of the wastewater treatment plant and area funeral directors agreed that funeral homes would refrain from discharging embalming wastes into sewers anytime city sewer workers were engaged nearby.

Twenty years ago, Fielding might have been allowed to discharge into a septic system if, as is true of some twenty percent of funeral homes, he were connected to one. Since then, state and federal regulators have begun cracking down on the practice. Massachusetts, for one, classifies funeral home effluent as a nonsanitary waste and expressly forbids its release into any septic system in order to protect groundwater it might seep into—and any drinking water it may constitute—from contamination. The EPA, likewise, regulates against the release. "Embalming waste includes formaldehyde and other contaminants that may not be released into groundwater," says Karen Johnson, chief of the EPA's Safe Drinking Water Act in the region covering Virginia, West Virginia, and Pennsylvania. "Septic tanks have no capacity for breaking them down into nontoxic materials. They pass right through the septic system and leach field, endangering ground- and drinking water." For that reason, Johnson requires funeral homes on septic systems in her region to pump embalming wastes into a holding tank that's then hauled to the sewage treatment plant (which may require the concentrated contents to be pretreated before allowing them into its system).

The casket the Johnsons purchased for their daughter is one of nearly two million that are sold in this country every year. To keep up with demand, the Batesville Casket Company, the world's largest manufacturer of caskets, alone rolls one burial casket off the assembly line of one of its seven manufacturing plants every minute.

Like any other manufacturing industry, casket-making is an industrial operation and, for an industry this large, demands large inputs. The manufacture of Jenny's Damask Rose required a share of the almost twenty-seven hundred tons of bronze and copper that's annually poured into those caskets. That's but a fraction of the ninety-thousand-plus tons of steel that's stamped, welded, ground, sanded, and painted in the process of turning out metal caskets. (All-wood caskets, which account for not quite twenty percent of all caskets sold, consume some forty-five million board feet of lumber every year—most of it oak, cherry, and maple—enough to fully build more than thirty-five hundred homes.)

The end product isn't just the casket. The major casket manufacturers make the EPA's biennial list of each state's top fifty hazardous waste generators, and they are required to post to the agency's toxic release inventory the quantities of chemicals they release into the atmosphere: methyls, xylene, and other regulated emissions generated in the spraying of coatings onto casket exteriors.

When viewing caskets in Fielding's display room, the Johnsons had chosen the Damask Rose largely because the funeral director spoke of the superior "protection" it would offer their daughter. The shell's naturally rust-resistant bronze material confers some of that benefit, but it's a thin piece of rubber that runs along the casket's lip that accounts for much of the casket's protective quality. Caskets that boast this neoprene strip are known in the trade as "sealer" models, because the gasket creates a tight seal when the casket lid is lowered to the base and locked. Batesville, the company that introduced the caskets to the industry in the early 1940s, outfits the majority of its metal caskets with these gaskets, and tests the ability of each to hold a vacuum seal. Caskets that fail the vacuum test are pulled off the assembly line and inspected under a blacklight for microscopic holes.

The rubber seal typically adds hundreds of dollars to the price of a metal casket, the choice of bronze many thousands more. Like all materials, both will eventually degrade, a fact implicitly acknowledged by the Damask Rose's fifteen-year warranty. In a period after death, however, when the funeral director locks the casket for the last time, that gasket can for a time perform as advertised—though at the body's expense. Sealing lid to base, the gasket can transform a natural, inevitable decay into a gruesome process and the corpse into what one consumer advocate dubs a "smelly stew."

Various microbes are involved in the breakdown of the human body. In the airless environment of the sealer casket, it's the anaerobic bacteria that thrive. Unlike their oxygen-fueled aerobic counterparts, these agents attack the body's organic matter by putrefying it, turning soft body parts to mush and bloating the corpse with foul-smelling gas. In entombment in the aboveground mausoleum, the buildup of methane gas has been sufficient enough in some cases to blow the lid off caskets and marble door panels off crypts. To address what became known in the industry as the "exploding casket syndrome," manufacturers added "burpers" to their sealer caskets, gaskets that release—or "burp" out—accumulated gases. The gaskets may have reduced the incidents of exploding caskets, but they don't change the conditions that fuel the production of methane. Anaerobic decomposition continues apace, and inside the sealed casket, the result is a funereal version of the decay that's found in swamp bottoms and the bowels of unturned compost piles.

Barbara Osborne has seen the human effects of anaerobic decomposition firsthand. In the spring of 1997, the Mississippi native bought a $4,000 "protective" casket for her father, who'd died suddenly of a cerebral hemorrhage. Made from rust-resistant copper, the sealer casket carried a seventy-five-year warranty. The mausoleum where Osborne planned to place her father's casketed remains hadn't yet been finished at the time of the funeral, so the funeral director offered to hold him until then. A mere two months after the funeral, Osborne went to the funeral home's holding facility to lay flowers on her dad's casket. Inside, Osborne recalls how she could "smell the horrific odor of rotting flesh" wafting off the casket, which was "stinking to high heaven." She placed her flowers and fled. Months later, in an effort to prove her father was indeed deteriorating inside the "protective" casket, Osborne had it opened. "There was rot, fungus and mold," Osborne told members of a U.S. Senate subcommittee hearing on funeral industry abuses in 2002. "His clothing was soaking in his own fluids, with a white, hairy-looking fungus growing everywhere." Osborne sued the casket's manufacturer for consumer fraud. The company settled the lawsuit out of court.*

Had Osborne entombed her father directly in the aboveground mausoleum, chances are the staff there would have taken measures to ensure the fetid conditions inside the casket never produced detectable odors. According to Darryl Roberts, a former cemetery owner, the protective caskets families pay hundreds of extra dollars for are "routinely unsealed after the family leaves" by the mausoleum in order to "relieve the inevitable buildup of gases within the casket." Mausoleum staff may use other strategies to deal with sealed caskets, including leaving the casket lid unlocked (thus not creating a seal between lid and base, allowing air in), sprinkling odor- and fluid-absorbing powder inside the casket before entombing, and zipping the entire casket into a huge plastic bag, which itself may sport a gas-releasing burp valve.

No matter how it's sealed inside the coffin, a corpse, even an embalmed one, will eventually decompose. Just how decomposition proceeds depends on any number of factors, such as the condition of the body at death, the kind of preparation it receives for burial, and the environmental conditions of the grave itself. However it occurs, the break-

---

* A company spokesperson says its metal sealer caskets are designed to "resist graveside elements for a specific period of time," not to prevent the decomposition of human remains. Today the company no longer advertises its sealer caskets as "protective" and has reduced the warranty of upper-end metal caskets, like the copper model Osborne purchased, from seventy-five years to fifteen. The gasket seal still remains, and the caskets are marketed as having been "tested for resistance to entry of outside elements." The warranty now carries this explicit disclaimer: no burial product prevents the decomposition of remains.

down of an embalmed body like Jenny's is likely to release combined body fluids, liquefied tissue, formaldehyde, bacteria, and corporeal acids that collect at the lowest spot of the casket, pooling in a rancid, toxic soup.

The porous wood casket offers little resistance to this corrosive mix, which may then easily trickle out. Metal caskets are more resilient, but the remains' acids work to breach them as well.* Danell Pepson discovered that even the $4,500 solid copper casket she'd bought for her embalmed grandmother wasn't strong enough to withstand them. Visiting the mausoleum crypt where her grandmother's remains had been placed seven years earlier, the Pennsylvania woman noticed a "thickened fluid" oozing from the crypt's outer ledge and running into the mausoleum grounds. Thinking the malodorous substance was merely decomposing grass clippings, Pepson scraped it off with a garden trowel. When the substance reappeared, Pepson contacted the funeral director who'd handled the interment. The "fluid," she eventually learned, was her grandmother's rotting, formaldehyde-laced remains, which were leaking from her copper casket. Opening the crypt, she found the remains had also run into the adjoining crypt where her grandfather lay and had begun rusting out his steel casket as well. Pepson subsequently had both grandparents disinterred and cremated.

Pepson's is no isolated incident. The leaking casket is a common enough occurrence that mausoleums may take steps to prevent it from happening or control it when it does. When a casket arrives for entombment, staff may place it on a lipped tray in order to prevent oozing body fluids from running onto the crypt floor; others may sprinkle powder or prop "pillows" inside the crypt to absorb liquids and odors. The structure of the mausoleum itself may be designed to address leaking and smelly caskets. Ventilation systems in some mausoleums pump fresh air (and, in some cases, liquid pesticides to control infestations) into and out of individual crypts, both carrying off the odors of decay and helping to speed the desiccation of casketed remains. Floors may also be sloped toward fluid-capturing drain holes.

As fluids leak out of aboveground crypts, they may also leak from

---

* To counteract the corrosive effect of ground- and rainwater washing over the exterior of the casket, one manufacturer outfits many of its stainless-steel caskets with the same kind of "cathodic protection" that keeps "water heaters, electrical transmission towers and the Alaskan pipeline" from rusting out. The protection consists of a magnesium anode bar attached to the bottom of the casket, which draws would-be rust from the casket to the rod itself. Like the anode rod sitting in hot-water heaters, the rod's lifespan is limited.

buried vaults. For all the resources and effort—and for the Johnsons, the financial investment to the tune of $2,000—that went into its manufacture, purchase, and installation, the Clematis burial vault will fail Jenny eventually. The weight of the soil, the running of backhoes overhead, rainwater percolating through the soil, the freezing and thawing of the ground will all conspire over time to create openings in that shell; the gasket will weaken and break the seal between lid and base. Water may be the first element to intrude. In witnessing the disinterment of vaults during his career, Darryl Roberts says more than three dozen vaults billed as "waterproof" had to be drained before the cemetery crew could raise them out of the ground. "Often," he writes, "they were full of water." For forensic scientist Bill Bass, the "wet" casket is a common sight in the vaults he's been asked to open in investigating murder cases. Of the caskets he's viewed in unlined but sealed concrete vaults, some eighty percent have been wet.

We call our cemeteries parks and lawns and fields and greens. Yet the American graveyard hardly qualifies as a natural environment. For all their landscaping aboveground, our cemeteries function less as verdant resting grounds of the dead than as landfills for the materials that infuse and encase them. Over time the typical ten-acre swatch of cemetery ground, for example, contains enough coffin wood to construct more than forty houses, nine hundred-plus tons of casket steel, and another twenty thousand tons of vault concrete. To that add a volume of formalin sufficient to fill a small backyard swimming pool and untold gallons of pesticide and weed killer to keep the graveyard preternaturally green.

Like the contents of any landfill, the embalmed body's toxic cache escapes its host and eventually leaches into the environment, tainting surrounding soil and groundwaters. Cemeteries bear the chemical legacy of their embalmed dead, and well after their graves have been closed. In older cemeteries, arsenic may be the longest-enduring contaminant. A highly toxic and powerful preservative, arsenic was a mainstay of early embalming solutions in the pre– and post–Civil War years. Druggist, surgeons, and emerging chemical companies of the period mixed anywhere from a few ounces to many pounds of arsenic into their new preservatives, but, as they'd soon discover, at great risk to the embalmers' health. By 1910, enough embalmers had themselves perished from their efforts to preserve the dead with arsenic that the federal government stepped in and banned its use in embalming solutions.

Cemeteries that date back to the turn of the twentieth century may yet show traces of that long-banned preservative. Nearly a quarter of the water samples that John Konefes of the University of Northern Iowa drew from hand-pump wells on the grounds of some dozen Civil War–era cemeteries scattered around the state tested positive for arsenic, an element not common to Iowa groundwaters. Two samples contained arsenic at levels above the then-proposed drinking water standards. Konefes says his limited 1990 research only suggests the potential for arsenic contamination of older cemeteries, but believes it's strong enough to warrant further study. The toxic element "will not bioremediate, it will not break down," he says. "Exposed to water seeping through the grave, some of the arsenic in an embalmed body will leach out and it has to go somewhere." Konefes's work suggests that nearby groundwater, which may supply individual families or communities with their drinking water, is a logical place for arsenic to run.

No one has launched the large-scale study Konefes has proposed. In the mid-1990s, a geology professor and some of his students at New York's Hamilton College did, however, conduct small-scale research into graveyard contamination. Testing groundwater down-gradient of a tiny, 1820s cemetery on college property, the group found trace amounts of arsenic and other lesser-used ingredients of early embalming compounds, such as zinc, lead, and mercury. A sampling of groundwater above the cemetery showed no arsenic contamination. Those upper groundwaters flow beneath the cemetery in the direction of the lower groundwaters, so the appearance of arsenic in the latter suggests the toxic element came from the cemetery and its arsenic-embalmed bodies.

More recently, two geologists at the University of Toledo detected arsenic not in groundwaters but in cemetery soil. Testing the soil of graves in a large, mid-1800s cemetery in northeast Ohio, Alison Spongberg and Paul Becks recorded "dramatic increases" in readings for arsenic in a number of samples taken from depths at which coffins lay and had eventually decayed. Lacking burial records, the researchers could not definitively trace the arsenic's source to embalmed bodies interred there. But given that the samples were taken near graves dating back to the period of arsenic embalming, they "may indicate contamination from previous embalming practices and/or wood preservatives," according to the study's authors.

Spongberg and Beck also found their cemetery soil contaminated with a number of elements that are major components of another common burial product: the coffin. In soil samples taken at coffin depth, they detected elevated concentrations of copper, lead, zinc, and iron, the very metals used in casket construction. Noting the high levels of both arsenic and coffin metals in their cemetery soils, the authors assert that their study warrants "concern for the quality of soil, groundwater, and nearby surficial water systems" in and around cemeteries. Archaeologists take the potential of arsenic contamination seriously, for their own health's sake. For fellow archaeologists conducting digs within historic cemeteries, one contractor advises testing soils before starting and, in those sites that boast high arsenic readings, consulting with HAZMAT experts to map out a strategy that ensures the safety of workers, from requiring the use of protective eyewear to keeping down arsenic-laced dust.

Arsenic is less likely to taint the environs of the newer grave. In the decade before arsenic was banned from those first prep rooms, formaldehyde emerged as the embalmer's preservative of choice and today is the prime ingredient of practically all embalming solutions on the market. Yet like its more poisonous forbear, formaldehyde, too, leaves its mark on the environment.

Though safer for embalmers, formaldehyde is nonetheless a human carcinogen, and because of its potentially toxic effect when released into the environment, the Environmental Protection Agency regulates it as a hazardous waste. The funeral industry, however, legally buries over three pounds of the formaldehyde-based "formalin" embalming solution every time it inters an embalmed body. As the vast majority of casketed burials involve embalmed bodies, funeral directors oversee the burial of millions of gallons of formaldehyde-laced preservative into cemetery grounds every year.

Little research has focused on the potential environmental consequences of depositing such large volumes of hazardous substance into cemetery grounds. Two, non–peer reviewed Canadian studies that examined the issue found traces of formaldehyde in groundwaters either beneath or down-gradient of seven cemeteries in Ontario. The amount of formaldehyde that turned up in the waters was small, both authors report, indicating, as the 1992 study issued by the Ontario Ministry of the Environment states, "that cemeteries are not a significant contributing source of formaldehyde to groundwater" in that country. No one is systematically testing cemetery groundwaters for formaldehyde pollution in the United States and the U.S. government has no established safety standards for the amount of formaldehyde in drinking water.

One side effect of the funeral industry's use of formaldehyde that has received more attention concerns the health of embalmers who handle it. The Occupational Safety and Health Administration (OSHA), which classifies formaldehyde as a potential occupational carcinogen, strictly regulates its use among the funeral trade based on evidence that regular exposure to the toxic gas may harm its workers. Numerous studies have found that embalmers and funeral directors exhibit a higher incidence of leukemia and cancers of the brain and colon, as well as a severe and persistent skin condition known as "embalmer's eczema," all presumably caused by formaldehyde. Other agents in embalming compounds pose yet additional health risks. One study traced a noted loss of sex drive and breast enlargement among embalmers to estrogens in the massage creams they apply to the dead.

The kind of send-off the Johnsons bought into for their daughter likely plays out more than a million times every year in this country. On any given day then, some twenty-seven hundred licensed embalmers like Tom Fielding will wheel a newly deceased family member into their prep rooms and there ply their trade, plugging orifices, letting blood from veins, pumping formaldehyde into arteries, wiring jaws shut, puncturing inner organs. Twice nearly every minute on average, one of those preservative-filled bodies will then be sealed inside a casket that's sealed inside a vault and topped with a ton of dirt that's all but prevented from ever reaching them. The burial's many environmental effects—the leaching chemicals, the consumption of resources, and the resulting pollution—live on.

The funeral industry has taken to calling this final undertaking the "traditional" American funeral service, to suggest that its many ministrations on behalf of the dead are in keeping with a long and honorable history that's worthy of continuing. In fact, today's typical funeral is but a modern construct, and one that bears little resemblance to the way earlier generations cared for, paid tribute to, and buried their dead.

The truly traditional American way of death took a simpler and more personal approach. Expected deaths in the early years of the Republic took place not in hospitals but in homes—those who died elsewhere were returned there, sometimes borne on wooden planks—with the family attending to and "watching" its dying member to the end. After death, women of the community gathered to wash and dress the body, sometimes enshrouding it in a gownlike cloth quickly sewn for the occasion, or, if poor, in a plain winding sheet. A family called the local cabinetmaker to fashion the octagonal wood coffin, usually from pine; into the twentieth century, the family might purchase a coffin ready-made at the furniture store and transport it home themselves.

The cleaned and groomed body was laid into the finished coffin and, often, moved into an unheated front room or parlor, attended around the clock by at least one family member. Friends and relatives dropped in to pay their respects to the dead and comfort the living. In some traditions the community gathered to wake the dead, staying with the corpse until burial, and, in the process, renewing the communal bonds shaken by the loss of one of its own.

If the funeral service weren't held in the home, pallbearers carried the coffin to the church on their shoulders and, after a service there, to the cemetery, where they'd lower the coffin into a grave the family might have dug themselves. There was no vault or coffin hermetically sealed against the elements. No chemical embalming of the remains. A body consigned to the earth would return to the earth and, shortly thereafter, decay and become part of it.

The exact form of the funeral varied by locale and the status of the deceased. Rural burials tended to be plainer than urban; the rich might be placed into coffins fashioned from handsomer hardwoods and decorated with elaborate hardware. Still, death in early America retained for most of its citizens a largely spare, earthy, and family-centered focus.

Marked changes to those burial traditions began to appear in the mid-nineteenth century, laying the groundwork for the more lavish, modern burial we observe today. Spurring them was the same confluence of cultural, social, and economic forces that wracked the age, including an emerging industrialism, the Civil War, and the entrenchment of a genteel code of conduct.

The latter espoused a civility that flourished among the British upper middle class. Adopted by the colonial elite in this country, the refined life hewed to a set of courtly values that were literally spelled out in conduct manuals circulating among high society of the times: polite behavior, fashionable clothing exhibiting a restrained elegance, handsomely appointed estates, and fine possessions. The funeral, as historian Brent Tharp documents, demanded no less a display of good taste. For the mannered gentry, that meant sending off a loved one in a "neat" coffin fashioned from a handsome hardwood (such as black walnut), which was then burnished to a high sheen and adorned with silver handles, escutcheons, breast plates, and other hardware. At the funeral the genteel mourner might wear garb of black crepe bought especially for the occasion, and leave gloves, scarves, rings, or other presents with the bereaved family.

The growing middle class worked to emulate the refined lifestyle—and the more involved funeral etiquette—of its "betters." The industrial engine beginning to drive the economy made it possible, mass-producing the trappings of the tasteful funeral that could increasingly be had in the growing marketplace of goods and on a workingman's wages. When it came to elaborating on the simple funeral, capitalism and gentility proved a winning combination. "The commercial revolution provided the accoutrements for gentility," notes Tharp, "and gentility provided the demand for goods."

One such capitalist enterprise—the manufacturing of metal cookstoves—produced the first radical change to America's burial traditions: the metal coffin. Pounded out in the factories of an industrializing North, the sturdy metal coffin promised the dead greater protection from the elements. Yet with its high finish, curved lines representing drapery, and floral embossments, the metal coffin was clearly fashioned to appeal to the refined aesthetics of the living. By the end of the nineteenth century, a utilitarian pine box no longer sufficed for the respectable funeral. Now the coffin needed to be handsome as well as functional, an object beautiful (and expensive) that reflected the bereaved family's good taste and status to the greater community.

A final alteration to the coffin aligned it with the demands of the truly gracious funeral. To some manufacturers, the metal coffin's octagonal, form-fitting shape suggested too graphically the decomposing corpse inside, producing in viewers a "disagreeable sensation" that worked at cross-purposes with the neat coffin's refined aesthetic. In the 1850s, manufacturers consequently altered the coffin's form, trimming and straightening the sides to create the nondescript rectangular box that's common today. The re-formed coffin was christened a casket, a word that referred then specifically to a jewelry box. Like jewelry, the corpse was becoming a precious object, one worthy of the goods and services a nascent funeral industry would encourage families to lavish on their dead. To further protect the valued remains from both grave robbers and the natural elements, concrete and metal producers crafted sturdy and handsome "burial cases," or vaults, to hold the casket. Concern about grave robbing was waning at the beginning of the twentieth century, but most cemeteries began to require vaults for their ability to prevent the manicured grounds from sinking into grave sites when the buried wooden coffins collapsed.

By this time, the casket-building carpenter had evolved into the full-time undertaker who would arrange—or, undertake—services a family needed for the proper funeral: the carriage and hearse, the grave digging and funeral service, as well as the "casket" he now infrequently produced himself. For those with means, the assistance of the undertaker was a welcome convenience in time of need. It would take an event no less cataclysmic than the Civil War to transform him into the seemingly indispensable funeral director he is today.

The bloody, half-decade conflict raged mostly across battlefields of the rural South. Per military tradition, dead on both sides were buried where they fell (or close by), often hastily and sometimes covered in nothing more than their blankets or the uniforms on their backs. For Union families, such rudimentary burial on enemy soil compounded a grief already denied the balm of a traditional funeral, with its final gaze of the dead and casketed burial in the family plot. When they could, Northerners endeavored to spare their beloved this foreign and ignoble burial, dispatching relatives, friends, and even undertakers to battleground grave sites or hospital morgues with instructions to locate and ship remains home. Early in the war, the slain soldier's fighting unit might shoulder that responsibility itself, and take up a collection to fund his return.

North-bound trains carried slain Union soldiers to their families, but at more than financial cost. Battle-torn remains actively decomposed inside their railcars on the long journey home, and during the sweltering summer months, they might putrefy rapidly, making for an unpleasant arrival. Encasing a corpse inside an airtight metal casket might delay its decay, but, as Gary Laderman, author of *The Sacred Remains* and *Rest in Peace,* notes, the caskets were expensive and even when procured offered no guarantee against the effects of putrefaction. Gases from the decaying corpse could build up inside the airtight container and eventually blow it—and the remains inside—apart.

As a consequence, Northerners found themselves exploring an ancient strategy of preserving their dead for the long rail ride home: embalming. At the time, only anatomists embalmed the dead, and then only those bodies bound for use as cadavers in medical research. Spurred by the demands of grieving families, surgeons and the "embalming undertakers" who learned from them now set up operations outside Civil War battlefields and morgues, where they worked to preserve the many thousands of slain soldiers for the sole purpose of the funeral. Using a liquid solution of arsenic, mercury, and a variety of chemicals, those first embalmers produced well-preserved and natural-looking corpses that satisfied bereft families and impressed onlookers, including the media. Stories of successful embalmings of military generals circulated widely in the newspapers of the time, and helped to advertise—and sell—the new technology to the public.

The funeral of Abraham Lincoln brought the practice more fully into the embrace of the mainstream. As was his son before him, the body of the slain president was embalmed and, after a brief viewing in the White House, loaded onto a funeral train bound for Oak Ridge Cemetery in Springfield, Illinois. The trip, which covered more than sixteen hundred miles and took nearly two weeks, stopped at some dozen Northern cities along the way, where Lincoln's wood coffin was transported to central locations and opened to public view. In all, some million mourners filed past the open casket of the sixteenth president. Most Americans had seen the face of death up close before; this embalmed one, with an expression so peaceful and natural-looking that viewers would reach out and touch it, compared more favorably to the ones they'd gazed upon in the parlor rooms of their hometowns. Lincoln's corpse proved the "viability" of embalming to its viewers, says Laderman, and showed that, unlike the "laying out" practiced by most families, it could enable a viewing well after a death had occurred.

Up to this point in time, Americans had largely opposed the idea of embalming. To a mostly Christian population, embalming represented a pagan/Egyptian practice that involved the grotesque mutilation of the body, a kind of desecration of the human temple of God that was condemned in the New Testament. The pleasing face that Lincoln and other Civil War dead put on the ancient art, however, softened popular resistance, as did the embalmer's adoption of the trocar, an arrow-shaped tool that allowed him to rid the corpse of bacterial colonies in the gut through a small incision in the abdomen, an approach less visibly gruesome than the typical evisceration of the bowels. Embalming had, in fact, so impressed itself on the country during these war years that, as one historian notes, "by the time the last shot [of the Civil War] had been fired, it had secured for itself a permanent place in the American funeral customs."*

The Civil War didn't just sanction embalming, it elevated the importance of the undertaker who could perform it. Families could wash and dress a body themselves, lay it out in their parlor, perhaps cobble together a coffin. They couldn't, however, embalm their dead. The surgical procedure required a knowledge and skill that only the undertaker possessed, learned at the side of Civil War surgeons and through firsthand experience on the battlefield. It also required the use of often patented embalming fluids. When death came calling in the Reconstruction era, families who wanted their loved ones prepared for viewing (via embalming) now had to contract with—and pay—a third party to do it.

With a corner on embalming and a full range of funeral goods and services at his command, the undertaker began to usurp the family as the primary agent in matters relating to postdeath care, and the full-time funeral "director" was born. At first he performed his embalming duties in the family's home. But by the early decades of the twentieth century, he increasingly conducted them in his own funeral "parlor," a cozy replica of the family home with "slumber" rooms for corpses on view and a handsomely appointed living room for arrangement conferences. Some directors retrofitted their onetime dining and living rooms into chapels where funeral services could be held, making the funeral home a one-stop shop for care of the dead. A few decades after Lincoln's funeral train, death had moved permanently outside the home. Americans began to die not in bedrooms but in hospitals then springing up; after their death, the funeral director embalmed, dressed, and, finally, laid out their remains in his own parlor. Stripped of any meaningful engagement with the corpse, the family was left to assume the passive role of observer and mourner, invited to view its loved one in someone else's "home" at prescribed hours and at fixed cost.

By the turn of the nineteenth century, a new American way of death—

---

* Opposition to the practice, though in the minority, has never ceased. Various religious leaders, consumer advocates, and, most famously, the funeral critic Jessica Mitford have all railed against embalming, deeming it an unnecessary mutilation of a corpse that not only adds many hundreds of dollars to the modern funeral but literally lays the foundation for a host of other goods and services a funeral director can then confer upon the embalmed body, from cosmetics/dressing ($250) and rental of "slumber" rooms for viewings ($300) to handsome caskets (to as much as $20,000). Both Judaism and Islam object to embalming on the grounds that it constitutes the abuse of a corpse.

with remains embalmed, put on view, casketed, and buried in the cemetery plot—was firmly entrenched. An industry devoted to the new funeral practices quickly appeared, and was soon churning out an expanded array of goods and services for its bereaved clients, from caskets of sixteen-gauge steel to "floral tributes" so elaborate they'd require a separate "flower car" to transport them to the church. Today, the cost of a standard funeral may easily run to $10,000, to the shock of families new to the business of funeral-making in the modern age.

For almost a hundred years Americans have been handing their dead over to the care of an industry that's turned the funeral into a too standard, expensive, resource-intensive, and, to many families, sterile act. The modern funeral has become so entrenched, so routinized, in fact, that most families believe it's all but required when death comes calling.

It's not. The chapters that follow profile some dozen families from across the country who looked—and found—more meaningful memorialization outside the slumber rooms and ersatz parlors of their hometown funeral homes. In some cases, they've simply reclaimed and breathed new life into old tradition; others have embraced fresh alternatives that offer a unique and life-affirming take on dust to dust. All of them are part of a growing movement that's changing the face of death and burial in this country, creating a new—and more truly natural—American Way of Death.

*It's hard to celebrate someone's life at a service when his dead
body is sitting there in the room. It's the big pink elephant you
just can't get around.*

Bill Sucharski,
owner and operator of Philadelphia
Crematories Incorporated

☙

CHAPTER THREE:

Cremation

Alice Benson may have died sometime shortly before her son came to sit
at her bedside in Philadelphia's Roxborough Memorial Hospital. But
Brian likes to think his eighty-year-old mother waited until he held
her hand one last time that morning before slipping away. "Mom's
hand felt warm when I first took it," recalls Brian, a native of the city's
northeast side. "But when I turned back to her bed after trying to hang
a stained-glass butterfly in the window—which I couldn't get to stick to
the glass—I looked at Mom and thought, 'She's not breathing.'" A
nurse he called in from the hallway couldn't feel a pulse. The doctor she
paged checked Alice's vital signs and, finding no life in them, pronounced her dead. "I'm sorry for your loss," he told Brian at that bedside. "Take all the time you need to say good-bye."

As the medical staff cleared the room, Brian phoned his wife, Janice,
with the news and then sat alone with his mother, now gone, as he had

every day in the week since paramedics had rushed her to the hospital. "It's a lonely and confusing place to be," Brian tells me in a quiet, halting voice months later. "I'm fifty years old and feeling like a vulnerable little kid all over again." From the hallway he heard the laughter of hospital employees at work, which at this hour of death simultaneously infuriated and yet reassured him that life does go on. The grief of losing a parent he adored was mixed with the solace of knowing that the woman who suffered such mental and emotional turmoil in her final years had died quietly in her sleep and was now, at last, at peace.

But if Brian couldn't quite fix his emotions the morning of his mother's death, or know for sure he'd been with her in her final moments, Alice Benson's only son was very certain about how he wanted to handle her burial and funeral. Not long after embracing Janice when she came into the hospital room, and once they'd shared a final good-bye with Alice, Brian looked at his wife and said, "Let's go see Bill."

Bill Sucharski owns and runs Philadelphia Crematories Incorporated (PCI), one of seven crematories licensed to operate within the Philadelphia city limits. Brian had met Bill for the first time the day before, when he'd called PCI—which he'd found in the Yellow Pages under "crematories"—and drove down that afternoon for a tour. By that time Brian knew his mother was near death. The brain injuries she'd suffered after collapsing in the home where she was living were severe, doctors had told him, and they didn't expect Alice to last out the week. Brian wanted to make arrangements for her cremation before she died and to see the people—and the place—he would entrust his mother to. "I didn't think the crematory would look like a burning funeral pyre," says Brian, whose family had always chosen burial. "But I needed to know that it was clean and efficient, and that the staff would handle Mom's remains with care and respect." Though he thought it unlikely, he also wanted as much as possible to reassure himself that he wasn't handing over his mother to some rogue crematory like the one in Noble, Georgia, where hundreds of bodies sent for cremation were found rotting on the grounds instead.

As for deciding on cremation for his mother in the first place, Brian knew that's what she wanted. "Mom hated the pomp and dog-and-pony show of the standard funeral," he says. A former nurse to the terminally ill, Alice had always taken a somewhat detached, unsentimental view of a corpse. "My mother thought that having people see her dead body laid out in a funeral home wasn't going to do her or anyone else any good." Burial she found equally objectionable, in large part because it needlessly took up so much real estate and at such high cost. Cremation, by contrast, just seemed simpler, cheaper, and "a whole lot more conserving."

The tour Brian took of the Philadelphia crematory the day before Alice's passing lasted less than fifteen minutes. But the brief walk-through proved sufficient to dispel any reservations he held about the facility's cleanliness or the efficacy of cremation. Far from the smoky, sooty environment he'd somewhat expected to step into, the warren of rooms that comprise PCI's street-front building—urn display room, chapel, staff office, receiving paddock, the cremation area itself—were brightly lit, neatly ordered, and, in Brian's words, "absolutely spotless." Andrew, the genial Gen X staffer who shepherded Brian around, explained the paper trail that follows the body from arrival to final processing, showed him where ashes were collected, bagged, and held for pickup or delivery. On the way out he introduced Brian to Bill, who explained how PCI handles arrangements for families that work with him directly instead of going through a funeral home. "Just let me know when the time comes," he said. "We'll work with you on the final arrangements."

Less than twenty-four hours later, Brian and Janice return to do just that. Bill, outfitted in the standard company dress—blue jeans and black polo shirt with Philadelphia Crematories Incorporated stitched above the left breast in white—greets the couple at the door. Janice has never been inside a crematory, so he leads her on the same tour Brian took yesterday. PCI offers this tour to anyone who shows up, announced or otherwise. "We want people to know we're not doing anything we're ashamed of," Bill says. "They'll feel confident and comfortable with our service if they see it up close."

This time Bill's short tour ends in a bright conference room. Taking a seat at a long table, Brian notes the refrigerator in the corner, a sink, cabinets, microwave oven. "I realize we're sitting in a kitchen," he says. "You think of all the important conversations you've had sitting around the kitchen table. It seems right to be making arrangements for my mother here." The intimate, familiar setting also makes for a welcome contrast to the funeral parlor Brian visited to handle his father's burial more than a decade ago. "The funeral director's office was darkened, the only light coming from a couple of low desk lamps," says Brian. "The atmosphere was just so heavy and gloomy."

Bill joins the Bensons around the kitchen table and explains his service. After the Bensons leave, he'll contact Roxborough Hospital to collect Alice's remains, return them here, and handle all the paperwork required for a death. If the Bensons prefer, they may handle those arrangements themselves. Among other options relating to the care of the dead in Pennsylvania, as among a large majority of states, is that families are allowed to retrieve a body from the place of death and, in this case, deliver it to the crematory themselves. The Bensons would first need to gain the signed death certificate and cremation permit and then file a copy of the death certificate with the department of health. If they did that and transported Alice here on their own, Bill would accept the body and handle the cremation. Like most other families, however, the Bensons pay PCI $735 to take care of those arrangements for them. The cremation itself runs an additional $215.

No local, state, or federal law mandates that a body be cremated in a casket; some local crematories, in fact, will cremate bodies that are covered in nothing but the winding bedsheets a nursing home may send them out in. Not PCI. "No one would want to come into our holding room and see his mother uncovered with other bodies," says Bill. "We require a container to at least preserve the dignity and privacy of the deceased." The containers need not be substantial, though. The six containers/caskets pictured on the brochure he shows the Bensons are somewhat plain models fashioned from either fiberboard or common woods like pine, and lined with mostly crepe interiors. Prices range from $55 to $2,750. As is true in eighty percent of all cremations nationwide, the casket Brian picks out for his mother is made of plain cardboard ($55), whose simplicity and low cost, he believes, best squares with her philosophy of life.

PCI's display room showcases a bigger selection of urns. On shelves and tabletops sit scores of urns in various shapes and sizes, built from a wide variety of materials. Birch-veneered hardwood boxes ($95). Fully biodegradable paper pots ($175). Blown-glass vases ($615), and one reef-shaped urn that supports a pod of dolphins cast in bronze ($1,025). Again for simplicity's sake, Brian selects a basic model, a sheet bronze cube with a walnut base and cap ($95). When Bill tells him PCI offers engraving, Brian asks to have the face of the urn inscribed with his mother's full name and birth/death dates ($35, which Bill doesn't end up charging Brian).

The big questions answered, Bill quickly runs down other merchandise and services he offers. Brian purchases the guest book, prayer and acknowledgment cards ($55). He passes on the use of the on-site chapel where some families hold services prior to the cremation ($350) and on the ocean scattering of Alice's ashes off the New Jersey coast by boat ($150). Janice says she'll write an obituary for Bill to place in the *Philadelphia Enquirer* and *Philadelphia Daily News* ($298). All these directions Bill notes on his arrangement sheet. When the Bensons depart, he'll plug that information into his computer, generating a worksheet that will follow Alice's remains from the arrival of her body in his paddock to her final committal as ashes into the cubical urn. When Brian receives his mother's cremated remains, they'll be no question they belong to Alice Benson.

For PCI to act on his wishes, Brian must sign a form that states he is Alice's next of kin and that he authorizes PCI to cremate her remains. The form also asks Brian if his mother's remains harbor any foreign objects: cardiac pacemaker, prostheses, silicon implants, or radioactive cancer "seeds." "All of these have to be removed before the cremation because incinerating them can damage the cremation chamber and threaten the safety of the staff," says Bill. "There are also pollution issues." Pacemaker batteries explode inside a hot retort and could injure staff when they open the chamber door to check on the cremation's progress. Cremated remains can stick to bits of silicon that survive incineration, while certain plastics in prosthetic limbs and such may generate a visible black cloud when burned. Incinerating bodies containing radioactive seeds used in some cancer therapies—including radium-226—may spew radiation into the atmosphere.

Brian initials the section indicating that his mother's remains contain no such contaminants. If they had, Bill would have made sure the hospital staff had removed them before releasing Alice to his facility.

Finally, Bill asks if Brian would want to view his mother before her cremation or be present at the moment she's committed to the cremation chamber. In a mechanized version of the traditional cremation rite observed at open-air funeral pyres in parts of India, a number of PCI's Hindu clients have gathered around a deceased family member as the body entered the retort; the eldest son, who by tradition would have lit the pyre, had then pressed a button on the control panel to start the cremation. Brian, who was raised Baptist, feels no such compunction to participate so fully in this final moment. "I spent every day with my mother when she was dying," he says. "I said all the good-byes I needed to say then."

As the hour-long conference comes to a close, Bill tallies the cost of Alice's cremation, which comes to $1,453, payable, he tells Brian, following the cremation itself. As they all rise from the table and shake hands,

Bill says he'll send a staff member to pick up Brian's mother shortly and schedule the cremation for sometime tomorrow afternoon or early evening. Her ashes will be ready at the end of the day. Brian lives a couple of miles away and says he'll stop in and pick them up.

Brian Benson's decision to cremate his mother puts him at odds with an unbroken tradition of burial on both sides of his family. But it's one that other families—and entire cultures—have been making as far back as the Stone Age.

Archaeologists have unearthed from that period special cremation sites in certain river valleys of what is now the Ukraine, and turned up cremation "urn fields" dating back to 1,500 B.C.E. throughout much of greater Europe. Farther east, religious texts suggest cremation may have been practiced in India as early as the second millennium B.C.E.

In the ancient world, the Greeks at first only burned their dead to stop the spread of plague or to prevent enemy troops from desecrating slain warriors. By the time of Homer's epics, cremation had spread to the larger populace, who saw it mostly as a means to purify the soul and liberate it from its tainted mortal shell. Romans took up the practice for similar reasons, laying corpses atop altar-shaped pyres and throwing into the fire clothing, ornaments, and other objects the deceased valued in life. Cremations occurred so frequently in Rome that they were banned from taking place within city limits, for fear that roaring pyres might torch nearby homes and foul the air.

The tradition of body burning held strong in large swaths of Europe well into the first millennium. In the Scandinavian north, the elite were often cremated to release their departed spirits to the afterlife and thus prevent them from tormenting the living; exalted warriors were given a more cinematic if less common send-off, set to sea on burning "fire ships." From the Continent, cremation spread to areas of Anglo-Saxon Britain, where the dead were burned upon the "bone fires" from which we inherit the less funereal English word *bonfire*.

On this continent, various Native American tribes, many of them from the Southwest, cremated their dead. Among the reasons for observing the practice were a desire to release one's spirit into the afterworld, prevent the ghost of the deceased from haunting the burial ground, and to protect remains from wild animals (and, in some cases, from sorcery).

It took the spread of a religion no less powerful than Christianity to tamp the flames of cremation. Early Christians adopted the Hebrew tradition of burial (and took inspiration from Christ's entombment), and came to view cremation as a pagan practice that desecrated the physical creation of the Maker. In 789, the Christian king Charlemagne enforced that view by law, declaring cremation a crime punishable by death.

For the next thousand years, burial prevailed as the common method of body disposal throughout much of the Western world. In the mid-nineteenth century, cremation got a second look. As in ancient Greece, concern for public health provided the spur. Overcrowded graveyards, said a growing chorus of medical and scientific authorities, were leaching pathogens into waterways and emitting noxious vapors into the air, spreading disease to the masses. With its purifying fires, cremation would effectively neutralize these vectors of contagion, its proponents argued, by reducing its major contaminant—the poorly buried, decaying human body—to sanitary ash. And unlike the funeral pyres of old, newly designed retorts would do it in an enclosed environment and with an efficiency befitting an emerging industrial age.

The first of these "modern" cremations took place in Europe in the late 1800s. In the United States, the first occurred in 1876 in a homemade, coal-fired retort just south of Pittsburgh. The practice was slow to take hold in the mostly Christian nation of the time, but grew steadily. The Catholic Church, which officially banned cremation in 1886—Pope Leo XIII called it a "detestable abuse" of the human body—eventually came around to the practice, if reluctantly. It wasn't until 1963 that the Holy See finally approved cremation for Catholics; it took another thirty-four years for it to allow U.S. priests to officiate at funeral Masses where cremated remains were present.

Today, some thirty percent of all Americans are cremated. By 2025, the percentage will jump to forty-five percent, predicts the Cremation Association of North America (CANA), an industry group based in Chicago; five years later, the number of cremations will outnumber burials for the first time in our history—and stay there. "In most countries where cremation has been introduced and taken hold, cremations eventually surpass burials," says Jack Springer, director of CANA, noting the examples of Japan (where ninety-eight percent are cremated), India (ninety-plus percent), Switzerland (seventy-five percent), Great Britain (seventy percent), and, increasingly, China (forty-seven percent). "We have every reason to believe the same thing will happen here."

Religious preference and/or approval for body burning fuels cremation's popularity in some countries, such as Hindu India; a shortage of cemetery space helps drive it in others, like Great Britain. Surveys show Americans choose cremation largely because it costs less ($1,400 on average, versus $10,000 for the standard funeral) and is simple to arrange and carry out.

We're also concerned about the environment, says Jack Springer. Cremation trims much of the thirty million board feet of lumber that's diverted to coffins annually, the million and a half tons of concrete funneled into burial vaults. Cremated bodies also leach none of the 800,000 gallons of formaldehyde that are injected into embalmed remains every year. But when it comes to the environment, it's land that matters most. "The second most popular reason Americans choose cremation is because it preserves land," says Springer. Cremated remains obviously need not be buried in a cemetery (or anywhere else); if they're not, one's cremation may play no role in the loss of the two square miles that are turned over to new grave space every year, according to the calculations of Kenneth Iserson, author of *Death to Dust*. Even if ashes are buried in a cemetery, they may take up less space than the average thirty-two square feet for a single coffin (depending, however, on cemetery policy, as some cemeteries allot the same size burial plot for either urn or coffin).

On the afternoon following Alice Benson's death, Andrew pulls the company van into PCI's parking lot and backs into the receiving paddock at the rear. In the van's hold, zipped into a body bag and strapped to a gurney, lies Alice's remains, which he had signed for at Roxborough Hospital and removed from its in-house morgue.

Andrew slides the gurney out the van's back doors and wheels Alice to the front of a deep, neck-high refrigerator that faces this receiving area.

Like a few states, Pennsylvania prohibits cremators from immediately cremating a body, in order to give authorities time to investigate any questionable cause of death. The waiting period in Pennsylvania is twenty-four hours, which means that PCI won't be able to legally cremate Alice until tomorrow morning. To hold her until then, Andrew will place Alice onto one of three shelves inside the refrigeration unit.

Andrew could slide the body bag holding Alice into the unit as is, but he finds it easier to maneuver remains if he refrigerates them in the coffins in which they'll be cremated. To learn what kind of coffin he'll need for Alice, he pulls the copy of the worksheet Bill had generated from the Bensons' arrangement conference.

As happens in more than sixty percent of all cremations the company handles, Alice, Andrew sees, will be cremated in one of the company's corrugated cardboard coffins. A dozen of these "alternative containers," as they're known in the trade, sit stacked in the far corner, the flattened forms of hundreds more rise next to them on wooden pallets, ready to be folded into shape. A local cardboard maker manufactures the plain containers for Bill in elongated rectangles measuring six feet six inches by two feet.

The container is fashioned from mere cardboard, but this particular fiber is engineered to support a three-hundred-pound body without buckling. For heavier remains, the staff first inserts a plywood tray into the coffin for reinforcement. No matter what its occupant's weight, every container is fitted with a bottom liner made from more cardboard, which traps any leaking body fluids.

Andrew pulls an assembled coffin from the tall stack and lays it onto a flatbed dolly he's positioned next to the gurney; the coffin lid he lifts off and sets aside. A coworker named Jay, whom he waves over from the office, comes out to lend a hand. From a box stationed outside the office door, each man grabs and slips on a pair of latex gloves and then positions himself on opposite ends of the gurney. Grasping the bag's corners in each gloved hand, they lift Alice off the gurney and lay her into the coffin.

PCI cremates bodies without taking them out of the bags, hospital shrouds, or bedsheets they come enclosed in, mostly to limit its workers' exposure to any pathogens the remains may harbor. Andrew does, however, briefly unzip Alice's body bag so he can determine if it contains any object whose incineration could damage the cremation chamber or produce noxious emissions.

The hospital may have already removed the most common of hazards, the pacemakers and such. It's everyday glass Andrew's more concerned about. "Anything that's made out of glass can melt and stick to the bottom of the cremation chamber," Bill tells me. "The glass could trap bone fragments when it cools and you can damage the chamber lining trying to pry them out." Glass can lurk in any number of objects that might accompany a body into the retort—jewelry, certain clothing buttons, eyeglasses—although looking over Alice, who's dressed in the simple hospital gown she died in, Andrew finds nothing of concern.

Cremators are more likely to come across a potential hazard with casketed remains that come directly from a funeral home. "Sometimes families put items into the coffin at the funeral home that could be problematic," says Bill, noting industry examples of shotgun shells and bullets slipped into the pockets of avid hunters and police officers that have exploded inside the retort. Among the banned items Bill and his staff have plucked from caskets headed into his retorts are bottles of champagne, wine goblets, and glass picture frames.

Sometimes, the casket itself constitutes a threat. PCI removes coffin handles and trim that are made from zinc, because burning the soft metal can produce a thick, white smoke that's hard to control. Staff also strips off excessive amounts of plastic hardware, whose incineration can send dark plumes billowing out crematoria smokestacks in violation of clean-air guidelines, and generate temperatures hot enough to damage cremation chambers. The funeral homes PCI works with know to steer their cremation clients away from coffins made from plastic, Styrofoam, or fiberglass, all of which PCI bans from its retorts.

PCI's trio of cremation units can accommodate metal coffins, but Bill thinks cremating remains casketed in noncombustible materials is neither necessary nor worthwhile. "First you have to take the coffin lid off before the cremation and afterward sweep up the remains from inside the charred shell. It's a real messy process," he says. The still-intact casket then has to be crushed with a backhoe and buried.

With the exception of metal, PCI will cremate most of the other standard models sold by funeral homes, as long as they fit into the retort. The company prefers, however, to handle caskets designed expressly for cremation. Such "cremation caskets" are stripped-down versions of traditional models. The few PCI sells itself boast softwood framing, plastic-free accessories, fiberboard lining, and fabric coverings, all of which make for a cremation that generally consumes less time and fuel, and generates less heat (and emissions) than standard caskets.

Finding no problematic objects in Alice's possession, Andrew zips up her body bag and returns the lid to the coffin. In his brief inspection, he'd made sure to take note of Alice's average size and weight. If she'd weighed in at three hundred pounds or more, he would have had to adjust the cremation accordingly, since incinerating bodies with large amounts of fatty tissue can generate as much as twenty times more heat than leaner bodies. "At that point the unit can't efficiently cremate the body, so you get black smoke coming out of the chimney," says Bill. In those cases, he schedules the cremation to take place first thing in the morning in a cold unit (to keep chamber temperatures down) and sets the unit's timer to a longer burn, by as much as an hour per every hundred pounds over two hundred.

If Alice's cremation were scheduled for later today Andrew would now wheel her coffin into a nearby holding room. Instead, he opens the door of the refrigeration unit and, with Jay's help, slides Alice's coffin onto an open shelf. Set to a constant thirty-five degrees, the fridge is cool enough to delay a body's decomposition for weeks, though PCI generally holds remains here for no longer than a single night.

To identify the container's occupant, Andrew peels from the worksheet a stick-on label that's printed with Alice's name and the "cremation number" the computer had assigned her and puts the sticker onto the end of her coffin. The rest of the worksheet he slips under the clip that's affixed to the fridge and shuts the door.

The Power-Pak II is a 24,000-pound cremator made of mostly concrete, fire brick, and carbon steel. When fully heated to standard cremation temperatures of between fourteen hundred and eighteen hundred degrees, the unit can reduce a normal-size body and its casket to a couple of pounds of bone and ash within two and a half hours.

Bill Sucharski operates three Power-Paks. The units sit side by side in an open room opposite the office, their gleaming steel fronts together stretching some thirty feet, the tops nearly skimming the ten-foot, steel-beamed ceiling. When all three units are running, their fans and burners fill this room with a dull roar you can just talk over.

By early afternoon on the day following Alice's death, the number two unit has already cremated two bodies. It's still radiating heat when Bill and Andrew wheel Alice's casketed remains to the lip of its shuttered door. On the coffin top rests her worksheet, which Bill had pulled off the fridge and now slips under a clip riveted to the front of the retort.

The Power-Pak's control panel—a display of dials, buttons, and colored lights—sits on the right side of the unit, facing out. Bill twists the power dial to the "on" position and watches the digital readout as it climbs upward from five hundred degrees, the temperature of one of the unit's two chambers. Some ten minutes later, when it registers eighteen hundred degrees, Bill presses a green button on the panel, and the door to the retort retracts, revealing the darkened, rectangular hearth where Alice's remains will be cremated.

The men move quickly now, in part to keep heat from escaping the unit. Andrew positions a cardboard dowel in at the front of the hearth, and then, standing to the side of Alice's casket, grasps the far end of the container and pushes it into the retort. The "loading table" on which the casket sits is fitted with spinning pins, so the casket slides forward swiftly when Andrew pushes, the dowel rolling the foot of the casket to the back of the hearth. As soon as the head of the coffin clears the lip of the hearth, Bill presses another green button and the door descends.

Almost immediately there's a faint burning smell. "That's the coffin catching fire," says Bill, who now dials the master cycle to one hundred twenty minutes. If he'd started this cremation in a "cold" unit, Bill would have set the timer closer to two and a half hours. But because the hearth's already hot from its previous cremations he can cut the length of Alice's cremation by a fifth.

The cremation's on autopilot now. At this stage of the process, the program introduces "throat" air into the unit to help burn off combustion gases and maintain temperatures; shortly it will trip a burner that sits on the roof of the hearth, directing flames down on what's left of the coffin and the remains inside. An hour and a quarter from now a set of jets along the hearth will begin blowing air onto the remains, like a bellows pumping air into a fireplace, accelerating the cremation.

Andrew now rolls the loading table back to its station. Bill heads into the office. Every now and then Andrew will check the display panel or a corresponding one in the office to make sure operating temperatures stay at or above eighteen hundred degrees, and to look up through the skylight punched into the roof above the unit to see that no visible smoke pours from the stack.

The first "modern" cremation in the United States was conducted over a century ago in a clay-lined furnace sited within the rural hamlet of Washington, Pennsylvania. Fueled by forty bushels of a dirty coal residue, the cremation took almost ten hours—seven to preheat the retort, another three to do its deed—and sent its smoke straight up the chimney.

Improvements in retort design since that successful trial run have made for cleaner and more efficient cremations. Today's cremators run on cleaner-burning fuels (usually natural gas, propane, or oil), burn hotter and thus cleaner, and scour combustion gases before releasing them into the atmosphere. Some designs funnel cremation after-gases into separate machinery known as wet scrubbers, where they're sprayed with water, which clings to pollutants and literally weighs them down, or into filters sometimes larger than the units themselves. Like most cremators produced in North America today, the Power-Pak II that Bill Sucharski operates directs its emissions into an "after-chamber." Positioned below the hearth, the after-chamber runs so hot that much of the pollutants are burned off before they can escape up the smokestack.

But not all. Scrubbers, filters, and after-chambers can reduce but not entirely eliminate the raft of pollutants generated by the incineration of a human body. Carbon monoxide (a common product of combustion) and fine soot comprise the primary emissions, but sulfur dioxide (from combustion of the natural gas fuelant) and trace metals (from body parts, among others) may also be produced. Of all emissions, however, mercury poses the biggest threat to the health of the living.

The toxic metal, which is linked to brain and neurological damage in children, is found in dental amalgams. The cremation retort's high temps vaporize any mercury in dental fillings of the deceased, sending the metal up the stack and into the atmosphere. From there it's carried by prevailing winds, some of it falling into lakes and streams, where it's taken up by fish and other aquatic life—and eventually by humans who consume them.

How much mercury crematoria contribute to the environment is a matter of some debate. The New England Zero Mercury Campaign, a coalition of six environmental and health organizations, contends that all crematories in the United States emit some five thousand pounds of mercury every year. In the United Kingdom, where some seventy percent of the population is cremated, annual mercury emissions from crematories total about four times that, a revelation that recently prompted the government to require all operators to outfit the country's crematories with filtering equipment sufficient to cut mercury emissions in half by the year 2012.

The U.S. EPA asserts that mercury emissions are significantly lower. A joint test project between the EPA and the cremation industry found that total annual cremations account for the emission of less than two hundred forty pounds of mercury. As a consequence, the EPA in 2005 declared that levels of mercury and other air pollutants from crematory smokestacks are so low that the agency need not establish the federal emission limits it has imposed on other types of incinerators.

Many state and local agencies, however, impose their own pollution caps. To run his Power-Paks in Philadelphia, Bill Sucharski must meet emission standards established by the city's department of Air Management Services (AMS). AMS limits the emissions of, among others, visible smoke, hydrogen chloride (from the burning of plastic body bags and coffin components, mostly), and a number of metals, including mercury. A continually running monitor on his smokestacks shows the city if Bill's in compliance; he also has to pass a "stack test" every five years to keep operating.

Around three-thirty, ninety minutes after he and Bill had started Alice's cremation, Andrew looks up from his desk in PCI's staff office and checks the temperature gauge on the wall for unit B. The red display reads 1,825 degrees. That's normal operating temperature for this point in the cremation, but to get a better sense of just how far along Alice's cremation has progressed he'll need to peek inside the retort.

Walking out to the second unit, Andrew slips on a pair of leather gauntlets, and then slowly raises the crematory door.

He cracks the door only a couple of inches, to keep heat from escaping and to limit his exposure to any explosive pacemaker and the like that might have inadvertently passed into the retort, although they would probably have burst by now. Still, the gap's wide enough to afford Andrew a view of the cremation's progress.

The entire coffin is gone now, he sees, and all but a part of Alice's torso has been reduced to skeleton, still outlining a human form. With a long-handled hoe, Andrew pushes the torso forward so it sits more directly under the chamber's burner, and closes the door.

The unit automatically shuts off thirty minutes later. The cremation's complete, but Andrew lets the retort cool another half hour before raising the door. When he does, the roar of the cremator's fans fills the room, and a cloud of heat, enough to bring a flush to Andrew's face, billows out. In the air is the slightest burning smell, reminiscent of a snuffed fire.

All that's left of Alice's body now is a low spreading pile of bone fragments and some ash. In some cremations, select bones may be stained yellow, green, or pink, from their contact with the melted metals forming the coffin or from jewelry that accompanied a body into the retort. If the body contains medical implants—hip joints, back braces—the cremated remains may be mixed with sizable, glowing pieces of metal, many of them strong enough to survive this searing immolation fully intact.

But the bone fragments here, mostly phosphate and calcium in makeup, are gray and white, and free of implants.

Andrew grabs a long-handled brush and extends the bristled head into the far end of the hearth. With deliberate strokes, he sweeps the fragments and ash to the front, spilling them into a chute that empties into an aluminum pan at the base of the unit.

When the chamber's swept clean, Andrew pulls out the pan and carries it to a "processing station" directly behind him; returning to the retort, he pulls Alice's worksheet and slips it under a clip fixed to the station.

The bone fragments filling the pan don't amount to much. Cremation reduces a fully grown human to a mass of bone that accounts for a mere four percent of a person's weight in life. In this case, it's about five pounds, within the industry average of three to nine pounds. The cremation of newborns, who have formed little or no firm bone structure, may leave behind no fragments at all, a point PCI makes clear to parents beforehand.

Freshly cremated remains radiate too much heat to be handled immediately. Bill, who takes over from Andrew now, waits twenty minutes before donning a pair of insulated gauntlets and, with a pair of tongs, picking out pieces of metal, possibly once hairpins. As he does with all the foreign matter that turns up among cremated remains—hip screws, the sliver of a heart valve, pacemaker wires—he drops these pieces into a tin pail nearly brimming with metal parts culled from prior cremations. Once a year the staff bags the contents of its pails and deposits them inside a concrete vault that's buried in nearby Beechwood Cemetery. "These pieces of metal were once part of a living person," Bill tells me. "We don't throw them away like they were garbage." A number of European countries—the Netherlands, Sweden, Germany, and Denmark among them—take a more pragmatic view of this postcremation material and simply recycle it, a practice that hasn't been adopted here.

To capture bit metal, Bill dredges a hand-size electromagnet through the bone pile. The shards it attracts are hard to identify. He guesses one slender tine may come from a staple that held the cardboard casket together, a small disk was perhaps a piece of the body bag. Sometimes he finds small pellets that are created when dental gold is burned. The pellets are too miniscule to have much value, so instead of returning them to the family (unless they request otherwise), he deposits them into his metal bucket.

A few crematories may bag the fragments at this point and hand them to a family as is. PCI prefers to first pulverize the bone into the grainy powder most of us recognize as "ashes." In the past, cremators accomplished this by smashing bone fragments with a hammer or board, or by pushing them into hand-cranked grinders. More recently, they've employed motor-powered "processors"—sometimes referred to as cremulators—to do the job. The one at Bill's station consists of a stock-type pot into whose bottom a pair of rotating blades has been fitted, somewhat like a kitchen Cuisinart. Raising one end of the ash pan, Bill shakes the bone fragments into the open pot and inspects them. He looks to pick out any charred pieces from the cardboard coffin (or in other cases, wood), which could darken the ashes during the pulverizing.

Finding none, he secures the lid to the processor and turns it on. There's a whine, as blades pulverize bone. Grabbing the end of a vacuum hose now, Bill begins to vacuum in and around the station. "The vacuum captures any cremation dust we've raised," he tells me over the din of vacuum and processor. "This dust is vacuumed into a bag, which we bury in a cemetery." A vent on the station itself also draws in airborne ash dust and sends it through a filter, which is likewise buried.

A minute later Bill clicks off the processor and lifts the lid. The pile of bone fragments has been reduced to a two-inch layer of fine, white grain that looks as if it might have been scooped off the beach. These new ashes Bill shakes into the pan. Again, he drags a magnet through the ashes, this time picking up and brushing into the pail mere traces of metal.

Alice's ashes are now free of debris. Bill picks up the pan and pours its contents into a nearby canister that's lined with a heavy-gauge plastic bag, filling half the bag. Bill then lifts the bag out of the canister and carries it—and Alice's worksheet—over to a tabletop laden with kraft paper, tape, boxes. There's also a heat sealer—into which Bill slips the open end of the bag, presses the warm ironing arm down on it, and closes it—and the urn Brian had picked out for his mother. During her cremation, Jay had inscribed the urn's face with her name and dates with the help of an in-house engraving machine. Bill lifts the walnut lid off the urn, works in the bag of Alice's ashes, and returns the lid, snapping it shut. He then slips the urn into a thin, form-fitting blue box. To the front of the box he adheres a second stick-on ID tag from the bottom of the worksheet.

A metal bookcase in Bill's office holds half a dozen other boxes of ashes that await pickup by either family members or funeral homes. If a family requests, Bill can also mail remains, via registered U.S. post. (Federal Express and UPS refuse to ship ashes, because unlike most other goods they handle, ashes can't be replaced. The U.S. Postal Service requires that remains be packed in "sift-proof" containers and be signed for upon delivery.) Consulting the worksheet before he files it away, Bill sees that Brian had requested to pick up the remains, so he sets Alice's boxed urn on the bookcase next to the others ready to go out.

At eleven o'clock on the second Saturday in April, some fifty friends and family gather at the Holmesburg Baptist Church to celebrate the life of Alice Benson. Years ago Alice had lived in this northeast Philadelphia neighborhood, a five-minute drive from where Brian lives today, and played the organ at the church's Sunday services. At the front of the sanctuary there's a framed color photo of a younger, smiling Alice playing the piano aboard the *Queen Elizabeth 2,* on an Atlantic cruise she had treated herself to. Beside it sits the burnished brass urn Brian had picked up the day before. "It did feel a bit strange holding it, knowing my mother's remains were inside," says Brian of the moment Bill first handed him the boxed urn, a little nervous at first that he'd drop it right there in the PCI reception room. The actual heft of the urn, however, had turned his mind to his own mortality. "In the end you're reduced to so many pounds of ash," he says. "We're all heading here someday."

Standing in the pulpit, the minister leads the congregation in singing one of Alice's favorite hymns, "How Great Thou Art." He offers a blessing and says a few kind words about Alice that her emotional son hears but won't remember. Brian then rises from his seat and offers a brief eulogy. "I'll tell you what I know about Mom," he begins, struggling to continue, as he reviews the facts of Alice's life—her nursing career in Philadelphia, the health care center she opened in Florida. "What I remember," he continues, is a caring woman who tended to friends in this very neighborhood when they were sick; a patriot who strung up Christmas lights every July 4, fitting them with red, white, and blue bulbs; a gifted musician who loved Henry Mancini and Sousa marches. It was for those qualities, Brian ends, "I am hoping she will be remembered most."

After the service there's a catered lunch in the church basement. Near the front of the hall Brian has posted pictures of his mother—her high school graduation portrait, a photo of Alice in her wedding gown—and set out a boom box that played a recording from the 1960s of Alice at the piano, filling this room with the sound of her favorite hymns. The service and this lunch, the hall alive with friends and family from different phases of Alice's life, have rekindled the feeling of loss Brian's been able to suppress in the bustle of making arrangements for this day. Buoying him is the knowledge that he has at least fulfilled his duty. "The memorial service was my last act as a son," he tells me later. "I'd done what I had to do for Mom, and it had gone well."

By two the last of the guests offer their condolences to Brian and trickle out of the hall. A smaller group of close friends and family helps Brian pack up the car with the leftover food, picture boards, the urn and photo from the sanctuary, and heads back to the Bensons' house. In the course of selecting photographs of Alice for the service, Brian had come across a box of pictures of the people assembled here and breaks them out now. Seeing these loved ones drinking, eating leftover sandwiches, cooing over the babies, and laughing over the pictures, Brian's struck anew with the rich community that surrounds him, and that will continue in his mother's absence.

When he'd first walked into his house after the service, Brian had placed his mother's urn on a side table in the dining room, where it remains—for now. "I'm not sure just what I'll do with Mom's ashes," Brian tells me, four months after his mother's death. "Mom loved to visit the shore and walk the beach in the morning, so I may scatter them at sea. Her family also had a home in the Poconos, so I may place them there," he says. "Whatever I do, it will be a simple affair."

Resource Guide: *Cremation*

What:
Reducing a body to some five pounds of sterile, grain-size particles by subjecting it to temperatures of between fourteen hundred and eighteen hundred degrees inside an enclosed furnace for two to three hours and pulverizing the remaining bones into "ashes."

Where:
You'll find crematories listed in the Yellow Pages (under "crematory"). The Cremation Association of North America (www.cremationassocia tion.org, click on "Member Directory") lists member crematories, which agree to abide by certain ethical principles. If you go through a funeral home, the cremation itself will probably be farmed out to a contracting crematory. The nearest nonprofit, volunteer-run funeral consumers group (sometimes known as a memorial society) may direct its members to local crematories it has vetted and gained lower rates from. For the memorial society in your area see the Funeral Consumers Alliance Web

page (www.funerals.org, click on "Find a Local FCA"); membership to the group ($20 to $50) is usually required. Cremation "societies," which are for-profit businesses, may own their own crematories or contract with others.

How to Choose a Crematory:

Some crematories work only with funeral homes; some will work directly with families. Either way, Bill Sucharski, owner/operator of Philadelphia Crematories Incorporated, recommends touring the facility before finalizing arrangements. "See if the company maintains a clean and orderly facility," he says. "And ask how it identifies and documents the processing of remains." If you'd like to witness or participate in the initial start of the cremation, make sure the crematory allows it. (A crematory is not likely to allow you to witness the actual cremation, out of respect for the dead and because few modern cremation units boast windows looking into the retort.) Ask if staff members have gained voluntary certification by the Cremation Association of North America (CANA).

Cost:

The average cost of a cremation is $1,800, which includes the pickup of remains from the place of death, a viewing prior to cremation, casket/container, urn, and cremation itself. You'll pay more for fancier caskets and urns, and interment of the urn in more desirable cemetery locales and columbaria niches. The cost of cremation runs closer to $1,000 if you choose what's called "direct cremation" (no viewing, with the body going directly from the place of death to the crematory) and if you go with a cardboard casket and cardboard urn.

You may pay less if you make arrangements with a crematory directly, instead of working through a funeral home. Through special arrangements with local crematories or funeral homes, funeral consumer groups can sometimes offer members no-frills cremations at rates as low as $500. You may be able to get a lower price if you deliver the body to the crematory yourself (see below) and select a cardboard urn.

Improving the Cremation:

A crematory will typically consume less fuel and release fewer pollutants if a body is cremated in a shroud or cardboard container versus a standard casket. If you prefer a casket with a more traditional look, choose from among the so-called cremation caskets, which are stripped-down, quicker-burning, and cheaper versions of the standard casket. If you want the body to be viewed in a standard casket, you can rent a temporary "rental casket" for the viewing and then cremate the body in a shroud or cardboard casket afterward.

Some crematories may boast filters that lower their release of pollutants, including mercury, into the atmosphere. The nonprofit Green Burial Council (www.greenburialcouncil.org) plans to issue a "Green Certified" seal of approval to crematories that have fitted retorts with emission-scouring scrubbers.

What You Need to Know:
No local, state, or federal law requires that a body be cremated in a casket, but some states and crematories themselves may require an "alternative container," such as a cardboard box. Most states allow you to remove remains from the place of death and deliver it to the crematory yourself, but you'll generally need to gain a number of documents, including a death certificate from the attending physician, disposition and transit permits from the county registrar, and a cremation permit (sometimes from a coroner). For the specific requirements of your state, see Lisa Carlson's book, *Caring for the Dead* (1998, Upper Access Books).

Scattering Laws and Regulations:
You may legally scatter cremated remains on your own land. Scattering on private land requires the permission of the owner. Check with the appropriate government entity before scattering ashes on public lands. The National Park Service leaves permission to the discretion of individual parks and monuments (see policy of individual parks at www.nps.gov/parks.html). Those that allow it generally ask that you gain a permit beforehand from the park superintendent (for anywhere from $25 to $50), and then scatter in areas away from trails and bodies of water. The National Forest Service does not regulate the practice on its lands (though individual states may regulate scattering on national forest lands lying within their boundaries). For laws pertaining to scattering ashes at sea, see chapter four.

You're on this wide open sea on a beautiful day. Birds are flying overhead, sometimes porpoise are swimming alongside the boat. Only once in the eight years that I've been leading scatterings at sea has a family ever returned to the dock afterwards with tears in their eyes. It's just a totally different atmosphere than you have at a land-based funeral.

Ken Shortridge,
founder, Ashes on the Sea

↺

CHAPTER FOUR:

Burial at Sea

A calm overspreads the Pacific where it meets the waters running out of San Diego Bay. Waves lap at the yacht Bill Whalen has piloted out from Shelter Island, a band of pelicans streaming silently off the starboard port, just skimming the sea. In the distance, a lone, single-masted sailboat tilts to the horizon, retreating inch by inch into the ocean's vast green.

Standing on the flybridge of a Hatteras yacht named *Bay Watch*, its bow pointed to sea, a handful of passengers takes in the full grandeur of the Pacific. If they hadn't before, they can't help but feel from here the pull this ocean must have had on Leonard Nutter, and why on a bright, almost sultry afternoon in early August, his sister has come to these waters to scatter all that's left of his earthly remains.

"My brother, Leonard, always loved the water," says Janet King aboard the *Bay Watch,* surrounded by her grown children and their young families. "He often went out deep-sea fishing, and later in life fished commercially, sometimes working out of Santa Barbara or Dana Point." Janet's oldest daughter, Cheryl, remembers the battered boat behind the garage her uncle was always working on, his funny Popeye routines. So when the confirmed bachelor died of heart failure in the winter of 2004 and was cremated, Janet knew she'd cast his ashes over the ocean that had long held his affection.

It took a year for her to gather the will do it, to give up the last of a brother whose loss she deeply mourns. She's needed even more time to let go of another loved one whose ashes she's also come to scatter here today: her second husband, Ted, a recreational angler and sea lover who slipped away in his sleep three years ago.

"When people you love pass on, you have to eventually close doors and move ahead with your life," she tells me shortly before the *Bay Watch* glides into the Pacific Ocean and her family begins to gather in the bow. "I'm ready to do what I have to do now. I'm ready for closure."

Janet had never performed, or even witnessed, a scattering at sea. Before embarking on this one, the seventy-year-old mother of five looked into what was involved. There was more to it than she'd have thought. For one, the state of California requires families to scatter ashes no closer than five hundred yards from the nearest point of land. That mark had originally sat three miles offshore, where international waters officially begin. But in 1999, California brought it in, partly for safety's sake. "Go three miles out and you can find yourself in some mighty rough seas," says Ellis Kjer, an analyst with the state Cemetery and Funeral Bureau. "Allowing scatterings to happen closer to shore means boats don't have to go out into potentially dangerous sea conditions." The shorter distance also permits scatterings to take place legally within more of scenic San Francisco Bay, and it brings into compliance one California community whose traditional sea burials take place close to shore: surfers who paddle out into the Pacific and scatter friends' ashes from their boards.

There are other state requirements. Janet had to acquire a scattering permit from the county office of vital statistics, and then, when the time came, she had to remove Leonard's and Ted's ashes from their maple urns before scattering. "Before that law you used to hear about fishermen finding urns in their fishing nets," says Kjer. "Making families take the ashes out of their containers keeps urns from being inadvertently pulled out of the water or from washing up on shore." Within ten days of the scattering, Janet would also need to file the completed permit, noting the date and the general location of the "disposition." The Environmental Protection Agency requests that a similar notice be sent to a regional office within thirty days.

Rules are more strict for the burial of whole bodies at sea. EPA regulation permits this age-old practice but requires that bodies be taken out at least three miles and then consigned only to waters that are at least six hundred feet deep. In addition, families need to ensure that the body sinks to the seafloor "rapidly and permanently," typically by enclosing a body in a metal casket that's been punched through with holes (to facilitate its sinking) and weighted with concrete.

Before Janet knew all the laws involved, she'd planned to simply rent a boat and scatter the ashes of her husband and brother off Dana Point, a coastal suburb of Los Angeles where she and Ted had bought a condo three blocks from the beach. Two weeks before the big event, her son John advised her to hold off. He'd just read the brochure of a small outfit that conducted sea burials off the coast of San Diego. Called Ashes on the Sea, the company handles all the arrangements for a scattering, John told his mother, from providing and piloting boats to filing the necessary paperwork. Moreover, it knows—and follows—all the laws involved in a sea burial and is even licensed by the state to conduct scatterings. "Here's the number, Mom," he said. "I think you should call. It would make things a lot easier."

In this corner of the Golden State, Ashes on the Sea is one of scores of pleasure cruisers, boat-rental companies, sport-fishing charterers, and even individual boaters that will ferry families offshore to scatter ashes, for fees of varying amounts. Unlike most of them, however, "sea burial is not something we do between fishing trips or bay tours," founder Ken Shortridge tells me one evening at his hillside home northeast of downtown San Diego, Anya, his wife and business partner, sitting beside him. "It's been our main business from the beginning."

That beginning dates back to 1997. Like many, it was inspired by personal experience. "After my dad died of cancer that summer and was cremated, Mom told me it was always his wish to be scattered at sea," says Ken, a fifty-something dive master. "I lived closer to the water than my siblings, so she asked me if I'd do it." Ken didn't own a boat at the time.

At a dock in San Diego Bay not far from home he rented a twenty-one-foot powerboat for $140 and, on a mid-morning at the beginning of August, piloted it out into the Pacific. Like most days in this sunny crescent of southern California, this one was a beauty: clear skies, temperatures rising into the mid-eighties, low to no humidity. The seas, Ken remembers, were "absolutely flat." He'd never attended a sea burial, let alone conducted one. But he'd learned from his diving cohorts that state law at the time mandated that ashes be scattered no closer than three miles from the nearest landpoint. Eyeballing the distance to Point Loma, the fingertip of coast that crooks along the mouth of San Diego Bay, Ken figures he motored out four miles before cutting the engine.

The Shortridges had already held a memorial service a month earlier. On his drifting vessel Ken simply observed a moment of silence in honor of his dad and said a quiet good-bye. From the plastic urn on board, he pulled out the bag that held his father's cremated remains and, bending over the side of the craft's starboard quarter, poured the five pounds of ashes into the ocean, like he was "tipping a water pitcher." As ashes spread and sank beneath the sheen of sea, he tossed out a bouquet of long-stemmed red roses he'd stowed for the occasion.

And then it was over. From the moment he'd shut down the engine to the last rose floating out of sight, the scattering of his father's ashes had taken less than five minutes. But for Ken, that brief sea burial proved cathartic. "I was overcome with this huge, profound feeling of release," he recalls. "I still felt the loss of my father, but scattering his ashes took away that crushing grief. It was almost like, 'It's OK now.'" The emotional high came in part, he knew, from having successfully carried out his father's last wish; more affecting, though, was the watery environment itself. Floating on the vast Pacific, surrounded on all sides by the original source of life itself, Ken felt the smallness of the human condition and his connection to the larger, natural world. "It put my grief into perspective," he says, "and brought me to a new appreciation of the simple beauty of life."

Ken's spiritual uplift at sea contrasted markedly with the dejection he had experienced after leaving regular funerals back on land, whose mournful ceremonies put families into what he dubs a "corridor of sorrow." Drifting along the San Diego coast, Ken began to consider other benefits to this singular sea burial: scattering returns to nature what remains of a human body, its dust and minerals, and without tying up a plot of ground in perpetuity. As he had proved, the event itself is also fairly easy to arrange and carry out, and can be done inexpensively, particularly when compared to the average $10,000 price tag for the standard funeral. And then there is the opportunity the burial presents to spend a beautiful day at sea, to remember the deceased but to also glory in the pure majesty of the ocean. By the time he tied up at the marina later that afternoon, Ken had decided he would share the experience of sea burial with other families, and the idea of a company was born.

Back on shore, Ken researched the laws that regulate burial at sea. Looking at the regs, he couldn't believe that many of the thousands of families that scatter ashes every year off the California coast know—and thus follow—them: gaining the scattering permits, going out beyond the then-mandated distance of three miles, filing paperwork afterward. The best service he could offer families, he realized, wasn't just transport out to sea but conduct of a sea burial that followed the letter of the law. To make compliance easy on families, he'd even apply for and file their permits and report the scattering to the proper authorities after the fact. The state wasn't patrolling the high seas looking for violators of its ocean burial laws, Ken knew. But if someone complained to the state of an illegal scattering—maybe an angler who objected to ashes being strewn near a favorite fishing spot close to shore—officials from the Cemetery and Funeral Bureau and/or EPA might be compelled to investigate. For Ken, that possibility, though slight, wasn't worth the risk. "The last thing you want to do in memory of a loved one is something that can come back and cause a problem," he says. "By following the law, I'd make sure that doesn't happen."

A single legal hurdle remained. If Ken wanted to be able to legally scatter ashes himself, such as those a family might send him in the mail, he had to get licensed as an official "cremated remains disposer" (CRD). Granted by the Cemetery and Funeral Bureau, the license is the state's attempt to track the movement of cremated remains, ensuring that ashes sent to scatterers actually find their way to the sea. The licensing requirement rose out of the discovery in the early 1980s that one scattering company had repeatedly dumped ashes in a landfill; a decade-plus later, the pilot/owner of an air-scattering company was found to have stashed more than five thousand cartons of cremated remains in a storage unit, instead of scattering them. "We need to have control over people who do this as a business, so these kinds of situations don't repeat themselves," says Ellis Kjer of the Bureau. To gain the license, Ken agreed, among other things, to store any ashes he received in a place "free from exposure to the elements" and to scatter them within sixty days of receiving them. Once a year he was required to report each scattering to the Bureau in detail. At any time he was subject to unannounced inspections.

In early September, Ken filled out and mailed in the CRD application with a check for $100. Around the same time he incorporated a company he decided to call Ashes on the Sea. "I wanted a name that would tell anyone who saw it exactly what we do," he says. "I also made sure it started with an 'A' so it would be listed first in the phone book." Four weeks later, Ken received a letter telling him his application had been accepted. For the state's purposes, he was now CRD #399.

Ken Shortridge's summertime scattering of his father's ashes at sea evokes the Viking ship burials of Old Norse sagas. In the belief that the land of the dead lay across the waves, storied Scandinavians sent departed kings and warriors adrift on burning ships, simultaneously cremating and burying them at sea. Archaeological evidence suggests that the dead (with their possessions) were more commonly laid to rest in the hold of boats or ships that were then buried in the earth, the sea vessels serving as immense, open coffins.

Various islanders of the South Pacific have perhaps the richest tradition of water burial. So-called sea gypsies of the Philippines were known to weight their dead with heavy rocks and fishing nets and throw them whole into the sea. Some native peoples of the Solomon Islands observed a similar practice, while other indigenous tribes there laid bodies onto reefs to be consumed by sharks. Firsthand accounts from Borneo in the 1800s describe "death boats" in which corpses were sent to sea in an effort to land them in the afterlife. Canoes were used to launch the remains of some Samoans into the Pacific, though the crafts were also used as coffins in land burials.

Another form of water burial continues to be followed throughout much of India. Following the customary cremation of a Hindu, relatives cast the resulting bone and ash into the Ganges or any of the country's other holy rivers in the hopes of freeing the soul from its cycle of reincarnation. Portions of Mahatma Gandhi's ashes were immersed in the Ganges, as were those of Nehru and Indira Gandhi. Following the 2001 cremation of ex-Beatle George Harrison in a cardboard casket, his wife and son are believed to have scattered some of his ashes into the Ganges and the rest at the confluence of three rivers in India considered most holy in Hinduism.

Burial at sea was once standard practice in the maritime trades, mostly because ships lacked facilities (such as refrigerators) needed to hold decomposing corpses until their return to port. Following his death from dysentery in 1596, British explorer Sir Francis Drake was dropped into the Caribbean Sea off the coast of Panama, sealed inside a lead coffin. The remains of common sailors were more typically sewn into their sleeping hammocks or other sailcloth, the foot weighted with enough shot to sink them to the depths. The enshrouded body was placed on a plank at the quarterdeck, draped with a flag, and after a brief service presided over by the captain or chaplain, tipped into the ocean, where it was to remain until the "resurrection of the body, when the sea shall give up her dead," according to the traditional Anglican sea burial rite.

High seas burial was most often conducted in times of war; it was given to unknown numbers of U.S. troops as recently as World War II. Modern transports now make it possible to return home the remains of soldiers killed on battlefields anywhere in the world. Nonetheless the U.S. Navy continues to offer burial at sea for any active duty, retired, and veteran soldier, of all service branches, as well as their spouses and dependent children, free of charge. Today, it conducts some thousand sea burials a year, aboard U.S. naval ships. All but twenty-five to fifty are burials of cremated remains.

The most famous—and unusual—of naval sea burials in recent times was held when the ashes of John Kennedy, Jr., his wife, and sister-in-law were cast from a warship positioned off Martha's Vineyard in the early afternoon of July 22, 1999, almost a week after the plane he was piloting crashed into the Atlantic. Normally reserved for military personnel and their families, the military sea burial was allowed for the civilian Kennedy on account of his "service to the nation" (in part, for his role on the President's Commission on Mental Retardation). Also out of the ordinary was the nonmilitary service on board. Instead of following the traditional sea burial rite afforded to military dead, a Catholic priest and two Navy chaplains led a private funeral Mass during which Kennedy's sister, Caroline, and uncle Ted offered short eulogies.

The brief event took place out of the public eye, but unlike sea burials of other famous personages—Albert Einstein (whose ashes were scattered in an unknown New Jersey river), Janis Joplin (over the

Pacific), Jerry Garcia (into both the Ganges and San Francisco Bay)—Kennedy's renewed interest in the tradition of water burial.

The U.S. Navy, EPA, and Ashes on the Sea itself all noted a spike in the number of burial-at-sea queries coming into their offices that year. California, over half of whose dead are cremated every year, may be among the states most likely to see the effects. Already the northern California offices of the Neptune Society scatter at sea nearly thirty percent of the five-thousand-plus cremations it handles every year. The EPA region that includes California has recorded some eight thousand sea burials annually in recent years. Entrepreneurs with boats at their disposal clearly expect those numbers to climb as the state's population ages. In the last five years the number of CRD licenses the Cemetery and Funeral Bureau has issued jumped by more than three-quarters.

Ashes on the Sea had conducted more than two thousand scatterings when Janet King called into the Shortridges' home office at the end of July. By then Wendy Werner, the assistant who fielded the call, could offer Janet a number of different options.

The simplest—and at $155, the cheapest—Wendy told her, is to box the ashes in a padded, siftproof container and mail them via registered U.S. post directly to Ken, who would cast the ashes a mile off the San Diego coast. Neither Janet nor any of her guests would be able to accompany Ken on the boat. The staff could, however, videotape or photograph the scattering for her (for an additional $125 and $75, respectively). Wendy could even arrange for what the company dubs a "virtual scattering," where Ken would call Janet from the boat and narrate the event over the phone as it took place.

If Janet tended to get queasy at sea, she might prefer to take up a position somewhere along the coast—at the Ocean Beach pier ($350), say, or Point Loma Lighthouse ($500)—and watch Ken scatter the ashes just offshore. She'd get the best view from the Torrey Pines Glider Port ($550). Since the pier there extends more than five hundred yards into the Pacific, Ken could pull his boat to within a hundred feet of the pier's end and legally sprinkle ashes into the water right there, offering anyone stationed nearby a view nearly as good as anyone's in the boat.

When Ken first launched Ashes on the Sea in 1997, he mostly went out alone and scattered the ashes families sent him through the mail. Today, thanks in part to people finding the Ashes Web page (www.ashesonthesea.com), ninety percent of his business comes from ferrying families to scattering sites and helping them conduct their own, private services. These "attended scatterings," as the company calls them, are more expensive—running anywhere from $500 to $1,700— though they are obviously more meaningful for the family.

The prices here vary widely, Wendy explained, depending on the kind of boat that's used and the number of passengers. The least expensive scatterings take place on board the company's "regular fleet," the half-dozen dive boats that Ashes on the Sea rents from private owners. For parties of six or less, for example, one of these boats can be chartered for as little as $535; larger parties require larger boats, which rent from $700 (for up to twenty-three passengers) to over $1,000 (to a max of fifty passengers).

For families looking to travel in comfort, Ashes on the Sea can book them into one of its fleet of luxury yachts. Cost of passage ranges from $900 to $1,700, again depending on the length of the passenger list.

Janet knew before she called that she wanted to participate in the actual scattering of Leonard's and Ted's ashes. She was less sure about the choice of boat. At first she told Wendy to book one of the regular vessels, but soon changed her mind. "I thought, 'I'm only going to do this once, so I might as well go classy,'" she says later. "That's when I decided to hire the yacht." Because Janet planned to bring along a dozen family members—three of her grown children, plus their families—Wendy said the cost would be $1,200. That would gain her not just the yacht and flowers for scattering, but two hours at sea, which would include a leisurely bay tour after the scattering.

Ten days from when she called, Janet's family would converge for its annual, weeklong vacation at her condo in Dana Point, a beach town an hour north of San Diego. Ideally, the scattering would take place sometime during that week, she told Wendy. Consulting their schedules, the women agreed on the second Tuesday of August. Wendy wouldn't know exactly what time and from what marina the yacht would depart until Ken hired a boat that was free that day. As soon as he did, she'd send out an information packet detailing those and other specifics.

In the meantime, Wendy said, Janet should mail in a certified copy of Ted's and Leonard's death certificates, and a check for $600, half the total cost of the scattering. Before hanging up, she reviewed Janet's selection of services and encouraged her to call anytime with questions.

One option Wendy didn't tell Janet about: the burial of a whole body at sea. Ashes on the Sea is among the few companies that will perform the service, but, says Ken, "It's not our first choice, because it's just a lot of work." Per EPA regulation, a body must typically be placed in a coffin that's weighted with concrete, riddled with holes, and bound shut; maneuvering the many hundred pound behemoth on and off the boat without damaging the coffin or boat is "a real challenge." To then release it into waters that reach the required six-hundred-foot depth means motoring out beyond the Continental Shelf, the voyage there and back requiring the better part of a day at sea. Given the time, effort, and even fuel needed, Ken charges $10,000 for the service. So far, the sum has been high enough to scare off the half dozen callers who have inquired about it.

Ken's not a licensed captain, so he can't legally take families out on his boat. After learning about Janet's request, he calls around to his stable of licensed captains, eventually contracting with one who pilots a yacht big enough to accommodate a dozen passengers. Because of a work conflict, he also arranges to have one of his part-time associates, Jerry Heath, handle Janet's scattering.

Wendy, meanwhile, prepares an information packet for Janet. Many of the company's clients have never stepped foot on a boat, so the packet offers suggestions on how to prepare for a sea journey: eat only light meals before boarding, take motion sickness tablets as a precaution, wear soft-soled shoes, bring a jacket. Included are street directions and a map to the marina where the yacht will be moored. Departure time is one o'clock on the ninth, but Janet and family should arrive fifteen minutes early.

A few days later, Ken's wife, Anya, receives Leonard's and Ted's death certificates, which she needs in order to apply for the scattering permit. On the permit applications she notes, among other things, the birth and death dates of both men, the general location of the scatterings (off the coast of San Diego), date of disposition (08–09–05), and name and license number of the cremated remains disposer (Ken Shortridge, CRD 399). She then faxes the completed forms and death certificates to the local registrar of the vital records office, and mails in a check for $22. The next day, the registrar, who deems the forms and death certificates in order, faxes Anya an approved permit. Anya will have ten days after the scatterings to return the completed permits, with Ken's signature, to the registrar. She'll return the death certificates to Janet when she arrives for the scattering. Per state law, Anya will modify the death certificates first, indicating the new location of the men's "final disposition." The only other paperwork that's required is the boat captain's report of the scattering to the EPA.

Zuniga Point is a mile-long jetty of ballast rock that extends into the Pacific from the far southwest edge of Coronado Island. Bill Whalen, the captain Ken hired, ferries the King party past the light station at the jetty's tip and pulls the *Bay Watch* in behind the bank of rocks. For scatterings, this locale's ideal. The jetty knocks down any sea swells coming in off the Pacific, leaving the waters here so becalmed that it's the rare passenger who gets seasick. And when Bill turns the boat's bow inland, he's able to offer the stately San Diego skyline as a backdrop.

During the trip out, Jerry had taken Leonard's and Ted's urns belowdecks to prepare their ashes for scattering. In a typical sea burial, a family may reach into an urn and strew ashes by the handful or, as Ken had done with his father's remains, simply tip the urn (or bag) upside down, pouring its contents into the water. Though simple, both methods have their risks. "The winds swirling around a boat can change directions suddenly, and blow ashes right back onto the deck if you're not careful," says Jerry recalling a recent outing in which two black-clad men who tossed ashes overboard had returned to shore wearing gray, their tuxes visibly lightened with ash. (When scatterings go awry, families tend to take them in better humor than you'd think, Ken tells me later. "They'll say, 'That was just like Uncle Charlie' or 'Aunt May was always one to cause a fuss,'" he says with a chuckle. "They always blame the mishaps on the dead.") To make sure cremated remains actually reach the water, Jerry and Ken coach families to kneel at the gunwale and extend the arm that holds the urn down toward the water's surface before pouring. In more recent years, Ashes on the Sea has devised an alternate scattering method that's proved even more reliable: lowering ashes into the water by basket.

The basket Jerry has brought aboard is woven from wicker reeds, its basin lined with a plastic sheath. Removing the lids of the two urns by his side and then untying the bags inside that hold the cremated remains, Jerry pours each man's ashes into the basket, one set of remains next to the other. Per one family's wishes, Jerry had handed over the basketed ashes just like this, each person scooping out and then scattering a spoonful of ashes. It's more often the case that the company first covers the ashes with flowers. For this scattering, Jerry sprinkles the petals from a dozen red and white roses over the ashes, completely covering them with a soft quilt of color. The petals make for a handsome presentation and, more functionally, prevent any breeze from blowing the ashes away. Yet they're mainly intended to serve as a kind of blind. "The sight of the ashes, particularly if they include recognizable bone fragments, can freak some people out," says Ken. "The petals give them something else, something beautiful, to focus on."

Ken and his staff will help families conduct a committal ceremony, but it offers no preset version of its own. "People have different values and beliefs about what that should be," says Ken. "We let them do what they want, as long as it's legal." In their eight years in business, Ken has consequently witnessed a striking, and moving, array of services. During one recent outing, a family passed around a bowl of ashes, each person speaking a few words of remembrance in turn before scattering; in another, friends and relatives wrote notes to the deceased on rice paper and then strewed the notes after the ashes.

Clergy from all faiths have been on board to consign the dead to their watery graves, Anglican ministers sometimes uttering the prayer most popularly associated with sea burial: "We commend to Almighty God our shipmate and commit his body to the depths. . . . Ashes to ashes, dust to dust." Just as many services have been less overtly religious, with some families reading a favorite poem or passage of literature or, in one case, old love letters. (For such readings, Ken recommends printing out copies in large type, which is easier to make out on a rocking, windblown boat.)

Among the more stunning send-offs involves the release of a flock of doves during or after the actual scattering (a service the Shortridges offer, for $300). The most memorable event, however, had one family loading up a miniature version of a Viking ship with keepsakes and sending the vessel out to sea (though not, as in the Nordic sagas, in flames).

Unlike most standard funerals back on land, sea scatterings rarely take on the atmosphere of formal affairs. On the deck of the *Bay Watch,* Janet's family is mostly outfitted in slacks or blue jeans, short-sleeve shirts, and canvas walking shoes; they carry on cheerfully, catching up with each other, someone every now and then breaking away to partake of the spread Janet has set outside the cabin—croissant sandwiches, a platter of fruit, chips, soft drinks, and bottled water she'd ordered from a local grocery store. Enough time has elapsed since the passing of these two men to keep this boat from being weighted with grief. This family's not here to mourn, but to honor the lives of two special people and to return their remains to a place they deemed special in life.

Around two-thirty, forty-five minutes after the *Bay Watch* had left the Shelter Island marina, later than they had planned, Jerry appears at Janet's side with the rose-covered basket of ashes and tells her she may begin the service any time. Word spreads around the boat and family members begin to converge at the bow, taking seats along the bulkhead. Days earlier Janet had asked her daughter Cheryl to prepare a eulogy. When everyone's assembled, Cheryl steps up to the gunwale and turns to face her family. At her feet lies the basket filled with her beloved uncle's ashes and those of her mother's second husband; at her back the Pacific stretches to the white beaches of Coronado, the San Diego sky-line rising beyond. "As a family, when we think of Ted a word pops out like a banner behind an airplane—adoration," she begins, recalling the abundant love the onetime merchant showed to and received from family and friends, the worldly goods he willingly gifted away in life. As Cheryl reads, and shortly ends by reciting Psalm 144, Janet, who has elected to stand off to the side, alone, silently weeps, daubing her eyes behind her sunglasses. "At that moment I know that this is really the end, and that I'm going to miss two people who were very important in my life," Janet tells me later. "We're finalizing the end of their lives."

The boat is mostly quiet now, the only sound is of water against the hull, an occasional horn sounding from distant boats. Again, Cheryl begins to read, this time in honor of Leonard, the long-distance trucker who was "tough on an engine, tender with a kitten," one who tended the sea above and below the surface as a commercial fisherman later in life. After ending with a prayer from the Book of Proverbs, Janet reaches for her mother and enfolds her in a long embrace.

The moment has come to scatter the ashes. After he'd covered the ashes with petals, Jerry had knotted one end of a ten-foot length of rope through the handle of the scattering basket; to the bottom he'd attached a tag line, which he'd tug to tip the basket. Earlier he'd shown Janet how to maneuver the basket, but she'd ask him to do it when the time came. "Handling the scattering would have taken me away from fully experiencing it," she says. "Jerry knew how to do it better anyway."

Now, after mother and daughter embrace, Jerry nods to Janet, who meets him at the prow. Family members find positions along the rail as Jerry holds the basket over the port side of the boat and slowly lowers it. Sometimes the Ashes on the Sea staff will lower the basket all the way into the ocean, allowing water to fill it up and carry off its contents. For this scattering, Jerry stops the basket's descent a foot or so above the water and then tugs on the tag line. When he does, a gray plume bursts from the wicker basket as the two sets of ashes spill into the air and rain into the water. Red and white petals follow, floating a moment before they, too, land on the waves.

The cloud of ashes spreads across the Pacific, sunlight here and there glinting off flecks in the water. Within minutes the ashes sink out of sight beneath the waves, but not the petals, which fan out from the boat and slowly trail off into the distance. They're still yards off the bow when Jerry tosses after them a wreath woven from red carnations and white lilies, a gift from Ashes on the Sea. Janet's son John follows with more petals, and then from a dozen other family members comes a shower of tiny white cymbidium orchids that Cheryl's husband had sent down for the occasion.

Standing along the rail, family members watch the floral tributes float out to sea, some of the adults wiping away tears. Janet's weeping, too, though not so much from sadness as from relief. "It's over now. It's finished. I did what I came to do—and after all those years of holding these ashes I'm free," she says. A peacefulness she hadn't expected comes over her. Later she'll attribute much of that feeling to her having fulfilled her duty to Leonard and Ted, and having done it well. Yet a sense of peace also comes from the sea itself. "Water is very soothing," she says. "Just being on the ocean on a beautiful day makes me feel calm and relaxed, even though we're out here for a burial."

Petals continue to ride on the water but Janet turns back to her family. Cheryl comes over to kiss her mother; Janet, seeing her daughter-in-law in tears, goes over to hug her. Janet's children call her over for a group picture in the bow, and then, as Bill begins to navigate the boat bayward, most of the party heads back to the circle of chairs set out in the stern. There's some talk now of Leonard and Ted, but the attention is mostly focused on Janet's living, vital family. A granddaughter's plans for graduate work. The happy, year-old great-grandson in the middle of this circle whose playful antics make him literally the center of attention. This is her future, Janet knows, and although missing two men she wishes were here, it's yet a good one.

Two hours later, after its leisurely tour through San Diego Bay, the *Bay Watch* pulls into Shelter Island marina. Janet's one of the last to disembark. In keeping with Ken's experience that few families ever return from a scattering with tears in their eyes, Janet's feeling upbeat. "I did a good thing today, and I'm at peace," she thinks to herself as she steps off the boat. There will be hard times ahead, but Janet knows she's turned a corner on her grief, and with her life, on these seas. "That part of my life with Leonard and Ted is done with. I know I can get on with my life now. I feel ready to go forward."

Resource Guide: *Burial at Sea*

What:
Scattering the cremated remains over or consigning a corpse to the Atlantic and Pacific Oceans, and the Gulf of Mexico.

The Laws:
According to regulations based on the Marine Protection, Research and Sanctuary Act of 1972, the EPA requires that you scatter ashes at sea at least three miles from the nearest shoreline, except in California, where ashes may be strewn as close as five hundred yards. Any memorial flowers and wreaths tossed overboard must readily biodegrade. You have to report the burial's date and location, among other information, to the nearest regional EPA office within thirty days of the scattering.

Individual states and localities may impose their own regulations. California, for example, requires would-be scatterers to gain a permit beforehand, while New York allows ashes to be dropped right off docks jutting into Great South Bay. Consult local officials before heading out.

Scattering anywhere in the country's inland waters—lakes, rivers, and streams, which are protected under the Clean Water Act—may require a permit from the local and state governing body. Local prohibitions against scattering may exist in some waters.

If you're looking to cast an entire body into the sea, the EPA will make you go out three miles and then into waters that are at least six hundred feet deep (which usually lie off the Continental Shelf, even farther offshore). You'll then need to prepare the body in a way that "ensure[s] that the remains sink to the [sea] bottom rapidly and permanently." The regulation doesn't expressly demand that you place the body in a coffin that's weighted with concrete, drilled through with holes and bound, but that's what most companies and the U.S. Navy do. Again, you'll need to report the event to the EPA within a month's time.

Providers:

No federal or state law prohibits you from performing either type of sea burial yourself, as long as you obey the pertinent laws. Any number of fishing guides, boat rental companies, individual boaters, and the like can do it for—and with—you, as can hundreds of companies that advertise themselves expressly as sea scatterers. When selecting a scattering company, make sure the boat and captain are licensed, and check with the better business bureau for any complaints. In California, choose a company whose principal is a licensed cremated remains disposer (CRD), signifying that the company knows all the federal and state laws and has agreed to follow them. Check the state funeral board and local officials for laws pertaining to sea burial in your waters of choice and ask the company how it meets them. The San Diego company profiled in this chapter, Ashes on the Sea, can be found at www.ashesonthesea.com.

If the person you want to bury at sea is active-duty, onetime, or retired military of any branch of service (not dishonorably discharged), the U.S. Navy and Coast Guard will do it for free (the same holds true for a spouse or dependent child). Both cremated remains and whole bodies will be returned to sea via vessels involved on active maneuvers, so families may not attend the sea burial. Bodies and ashes must be forwarded at the family's expense to one of six ports of call in the Gulf and both oceans. In the case of whole bodies, a nearby funeral home must prepare the corpse for sea burial according to military instruction, which includes embalming and casketing in a metal coffin that's punctured with twenty two-inch holes, banded with six nylon or metal straps, and weighing at least three hundred pounds. Ashes are scattered only; the casting overboard of urns is not allowed. For more information, contact the U.S. Naval Mortuary Affairs program (866-787-0081; www.tricare.mil/MMSO, click on "Navy/Marine Corps Mortuary Affairs").

Cost:

Depends on a number of factors. You'll pay in the neighborhood of $100 to $200 if you mail ashes to a scattering company and ask that they be scattered without your being on board. Hiring a company to take you out for a scattering can run from $300 to nearly $2,000 depending on your choice of boat (such as a dive boat or yacht), number of passengers (the greater number usually requiring a bigger—and more expensive—boat), and length of the journey.

What You Need to Know:
Biodegradable containers are designed to disintegrate in water. California, however, which requires that ashes be removed from their urns before scattering, bans the casting overboard of biodegradable containers on the grounds that no independent authority has yet proved they work as advertised, according to Ellis Kjer of the state Cemetery and Funeral Bureau. The U.S. Navy would consider casting a biodegradable urn overboard, if requested, according to an official at the Navy Mortuary Affairs office.

All this said, there are no "ashes police" who are actively enforcing existing scattering laws, and it's highly unlikely that you'll be cited for an illegal sea scattering.

When I dived on my father-in-law's memorial reef a year after I'd sunk it, it was teeming with grouper, snapper, goliath fish and the whole wide range of sea life he wanted to join when he asked me to add his ashes to the artificial reefs we were building.

Don Brawley,
founder, Eternal Reefs

When you boil it all down there are just three things you can do with someone's ashes. You can inurn them, whether in an urn, niche, columbarium, or just up on a shelf. You can scatter, and that can be blasting the ashes in fireworks or sprinkling in the ocean. Or you can reef them.

George Frankel,
CEO, Eternal Reefs

CHAPTER FIVE:

The Memorial Reef

On a blustery morning near the end of May, cloudy skies overhead, waters at a light chop, a sixty-foot towboat named *Defiant* slips out of Ocean City, New Jersey, and heads to the open waters of the Atlantic. Her destination: the Great Egg, an artificial reef seven nautical miles offshore that the New Jersey Department of Environmental Protection created to attract fish and other marine life to this quiet crescent of coast. It's here that the crew will wind a sling around each of the nine perforated domes that sit on its deck, raise them onto a wooden plank jutting from the stern, and, with a hearty tug, commit them to the deep.

Defiant's crew has sunk such "reef balls" before, hollow concrete modules that resemble igloos someone's punched a dozen holes into. Since launching its artificial reef program in 1984, the state has deposited some four thousand of them into coastal waters, stretching from Sandy Hook in the north, down to Cape May at the southern tip, in an effort to create the hard, reeflike substrate that draws ocean life. But the ones being deployed today are no ordinary reef builders. In addition to the sand, silica, and microfibers that comprise a typical reef ball, each of those sitting on deck also contains the cremated remains—the ashes—of a person. On this late spring morning, the crew of the *Defiant* isn't just sinking reef material to the depths; it's burying at sea what's left of nine human lives.

One of the "memorial reefs" being deployed this morning is for John Slowe. On a bitter cold January afternoon two years ago, the New Jersey native collapsed in his living room after carting in firewood for a party the Slowes were throwing for an Eagles play-off game. A fireman who lived upstairs tried to revive him, an ambulance came, but to no avail. Slowe had died almost instantly of a massive heart attack. He was fifty-six. "John loved the water. He often dived the shipwrecks off Long Island, and was always taking diving trips down to the Caymans or out to Hawaii," his wife, Carrie, tells me aboard the *Miss Beach Haven,* one of three charter boats that's following the *Defiant* out to Great Egg, ferrying passengers who have come to witness the placement of their memorial reefs into the Atlantic. "He hadn't heard about this concept, but I know he would have loved the idea of returning to the sea, and creating a place for life there."

Carrie, a fortyish court stenographer who lives almost thirty miles northeast of Ocean City in Beach Haven, had first learned about memorial reefs a month after John's cremation. She'd been aimlessly clicking through TV stations one night when she came across a Discovery Channel program about an Atlanta-based organization called Eternal Reefs. The show followed the group as it helped a couple of families mix the cremated remains of their loved ones into a concrete slurry that was poured into dome-shaped forms and then hardened into what the company dubbed memorial reefs. A month later, the cured domes were sunk into coastal waters, as families watched from charter boats circling the deployment site. Underwater video of older sites showed pods of memorial reefs on the ocean floor teeming with life, each ball sprouting coralheads, sponges, and other sea creatures, schools of fish darting in and around its open portals. The memorial reefs the Georgia company cast into southern waters of the United States were clearly no mere watery tombs; here the remains of the dead literally lay the foundation for new life under the sea. "I saw that show and thought: 'Oh, my God,'" says Carrie, who had placed the wooden box holding her husband's ashes on his bedside nightstand and later transferred them to an old-fashioned diving helmet. "'This is just what I have to do with John.'" Two years later, heading out to sea aboard the *Miss Beach Haven,* she's on the final leg of a journey to do just that.

The idea of using human remains to create habitat for marine life has its genesis in the coral reef beds of the Florida Keys. "When I was a student at the University of Georgia in the mid-1980s, my roommate and I would take diving trips to the Keys," explains Eternal Reefs's founder, Don Brawley. "Todd Barber and I would take off from Macon at six or seven at night, drive twelve hours straight and arrive at the Keys around sunup. We'd pile out of the car at one of the first bridges we came to, pull on our diving gear, and do a dive right there." Those Florida roadtrips, funded on just enough pocket change for a cheap motel and a case of beer, made for outstanding diving in a tropical hot spot not so far from the hordes of other spring breakers. But those trips also brought the college diving buddies face-to-face with an environmental catastrophe in the making. "Every time we went back, the reefs looked worse," Don recalls. Fungal poxes stained more of the coralheads, plastic bags and other debris smothered others; heavy objects—dropped anchors, the propellers of passing motorboats—had simply sheered off or smashed large chunks of reef. The coral reefs, both men could see for themselves, were deteriorating. And it wasn't just happening in Florida. Reefs around the world were in trouble and for many of the same reasons.

Back at home, the friends went on to graduate and launch their careers, Don in the computer field, Todd in management consulting. But the two couldn't shake what they'd seen in the Keys. At a party in the fall of 1990, they committed themselves to doing something about it. The plan they landed on was ambitious. Instead of merely protecting the natural reef from abuse, as some had done, they'd increase the reef's undersea footprint by creating more of it. The structures they'd make to do that would be artificial, formed from man-made materials. But unlike some other "design" reefs, which were crafted mostly to attract fish for anglers, theirs would so closely mimic the real thing that the coral-creating polyps, anemone, sea fans, and other plant and animal life inhabiting natural reefs would literally take hold. "Our goal was to create the substrate that would support the whole ecosystem that revolves around a reef," says Don. "We wanted to actually create habitat for the microlife that everything else in a reef depends on."

The structure he and Todd designed for the task was a chin-high honeycombed dome they called a "reef ball." Cast from a ton of concrete, the broad-bottomed module was sturdy enough to stay put on the ocean floor (its portals further dissipating current flows that might otherwise carry it adrift), and it offered plenty of rough structure, both inside and out, onto which encrusting organisms could attach and grow. The concrete itself the pair engineered for an underwater environment. They tempered its alkalinity to match that of saltwater (thus boosting its life span and simultaneously encouraging marine life to latch on), and added microfibers and silica for strength. When dropped to the depths, their reef ball was built to last five hundred years.

After securing permits from the state of Florida, the team deployed its first reef balls onto an established artificial reef off Fort Lauderdale in 1991. A year later they founded the Reef Ball Development Group (later reincorporated as the Reef Ball Foundation), a nonprofit organization that works with government and private marine groups to sink reef balls into waters around the globe. Since then five hundred thousand have been deployed worldwide in more than thirty-five hundred projects. The artificial reef structures have more than met their founders' expectations. Within five years of their deployment, reef balls attract eighty percent of the species found on nearby natural reefs, in both population and diversity; over a longer period and with some fine-tuning that takes local factors into consideration—by, say, placing balls farther apart or closer together—they can reach one hundred percent.

All this time, Don's father-in-law had been following his son-in-law's passion for reef building with keen interest. A retired mechanic and deep-sea fisherman from Atlanta, Carleton "Petey" Palmer at first saw reef balls mostly as a way to improve his catch at sea. But when he was diagnosed with liver cancer in the mid-1990s, he asked Don to put his reef ball technology to an entirely novel use. "When I die, I want you to take my ashes and put them into those artificial reefs you're building," he told Don over supper one night late in 1997. "I'd rather spend eternity down there with all that life than in a field full of dead people." When Don, in jest, asked if he'd rather be laid into the Gulf or the Atlantic, Petey said it didn't matter, as long as the spot had "lots of red snapper and grouper." Both men chuckled at the idea, and Don forgot all about it until Petey died a few months later and a funeral director handed him the cardboard box containing his father-in-law's ashes and said, "I understand you're supposed to get these."

As it happened, the reef group had scheduled a placement of reef balls off Sarasota for that spring. In May, Don flew down and, with Todd watching, added Petey's ashes to the cement mixer that poured thirty reef balls. A month later, he ferried his father-in-law's memorial modules six miles off the white beaches of Sarasota and dropped them into the Gulf.

News of Petey's singular sea burial spread. Soon people were asking Don if he'd "reef" their loved ones, too, and Eternal Reefs was born. Getting permission to sink cremains-containing reef balls proved easier than Don had anticipated. The EPA, the government entity that oversees the deployment of materials into U.S. waters, deemed that human ashes so completely mix with concrete in the casting that the resulting memorial reef ball does not, strictly speaking, constitute human remains, and is thus not subject to laws regulating burial at sea. Placing memorials in the ocean proved no problem, either, as long as they were put down onto established artificial reef sites already approved by federal, state, and local governments.

The reef building community was quick to see the potential of the underwater memorial concept. "We're helping them build reefs for the community at no cost to the taxpayer," says George Frankel, the Eternal Reef CEO who partnered with Don to form the company in 1999. "And because of our history and affiliation with the Reef Ball Foundation, we know what we're doing."

When Carrie called Eternal Reefs to request an information packet in the spring of 2003, the company had already sunk three hundred memorial modules onto some dozen reef sites, thirty of them containing only the ashes of pets. By that time, Don and George had honed an approach that melded the business of a construction project with the ceremony demanded of a memorial event. After a family has chosen from a list of upcoming deployment sites, it's invited to participate in the actual casting of its reef ball, to physically add and mix the ashes of its loved one into the concrete slurry that fills out a module. A month later, the family comes to a "viewing" of its cured module, and on the following day, boards a charter boat to watch it be "buried" at sea.

The sites themselves are mostly established reefs in southern waters of the United States—off Corpus Christi, Miami, Charleston, among others. Don and George had chosen these locations because they are relatively close to the Atlanta home office and to the construction yard in Sarasota where the majority of modules are cast. The Reef Ball Foundation had also paved the way in those places, having already secured permits to sink standard reefs there.

That the nearby locales are great places to visit is no accident. "We've tried to establish memorial reef sites near vacation destinations, because we want to give a family every reason to come back and visit," says George. With more and more families moving away from their hometowns, fewer relatives return to the ancestral cemetery, according to George, an Atlanta resident who has never visited his own mother's grave site on Long Island. "Place memorial reefs near beach attractions and families are more likely to come back and remember their loved one," he says.

Carrie would have preferred to inter John in one of his favorite diving sites off the Cayman Islands. But Eternal Reefs had no immediate plans to move outside the country. The company did tell her, however, that it was surveying sites farther up the northern coastline. As it turned out, Eternal Reefs was exploring the possibility of placing modules onto a popular site outside Ocean City, New Jersey. For Carrie, the location would be ideal. The beach resort lay just south of the Slowes' barrier island home, and John had often dived shipwrecks not far from there. Carrie decided to hold on to John's ashes until Eternal Reefs came north. When it did in the spring of 2005, she was ready.

To get John into those waters, however, she had to first take him to a dusty construction site a thousand miles away in Sarasota, Florida.

Even without an exact street address, it's hard to miss Reef Innovations. One of a handful of contractors licensed to produce reef balls, the company cures its marine modules outdoors, along a roadside edge of property just north of downtown Sarasota. Drive up Center Avenue and you'll spot them a good block away, stacked two, sometimes four to a row, their honeycombed forms rising behind a chain-link fence that rims the company grounds.

Most of the time the rubble yard just inside the fence is where Reef Innovations casts the patented reef balls that are deployed throughout U.S. waters. But on a bright, balmy morning in April recently, as it does some dozen times a year, the company crew joins a band of volunteers from a local diving outfit to help families add the cremated remains of their loved ones to the funereal version of the standard module, the memorial reef.

It's nearing ten o'clock when Carrie Slowe, outfitted in jean shorts, a loose blouse, and running shoes, enters the yard. In her hand, she clutches a five-pound plastic bag that holds the remains of her husband's ashes. Before flying down from New Jersey last night, Carrie buried a handful in her backyard flower garden; a couple of months after John died, she scattered some on the Maui mountaintop where they'd exchanged wedding vows and in the Caribbean waters they'd both dived off Grand Cayman Island.

Carrie is one of twelve clients who are casting today. The event's not scheduled for another hour, but already the yard's full of other casually dressed families, who inspect the fiberglass molds into which concrete will be poured or who mill inside an expansive, airportlike hangar near the entrance. Most have flown in from New Jersey or Maryland, into whose coastal waters these finished reefs will be placed a month from now. There must be some two dozen people in all, a mix of middle-age sons and daughters of the deceased, white-haired siblings, a few friends.

Many, like Carrie, are widows or widowers. There's Mary Simpson, a retired schoolteacher whose late husband used to skin dive off Key West in the days before oxygen tanks. And Dave O'Ferrall. An arthritic condition known as Still's disease had kept his thirty-three-year-old wife out of the surf in her last years, but she loved the sea and asked Dave to add her remains to a memorial reef after seeing a TV show about the idea.

Don and George, both decked out in T-shirts and baseballs caps bearing the Eternal Reefs logo—a memorial reef ball resting on the ocean floor, undulating waves and full moon overhead—stand in the yard. They greet families as they arrive and direct them into the hangar, asking them to place the remains they hold into the bucket inside that bears their loved one's name.

By the time Carrie enters the hangar, most of the twelve buckets lined up on the concrete floor already contain a box, bag, or canister of ashes. Each also holds a numbered tag, a two-foot-long metal pike, and a hand-size bronze memorial plaque that bears the inscriptions families ordered in advance. The one in Carrie's bucket reads: "The flight is eternal . . . enjoy. John V. Slowe. 1946–2003." "John enjoyed life more than anyone I've ever met," she tells me. "The inscription means that his life goes on forever and that he'll continue to enjoy a life after death."

Don calls families into the hangar and, after they've settled onto folding chairs, welcomes them. As he finishes reviewing the casting process, a ten-wheel concrete mixer, its tumbler spinning, turns into the yard. On Don's cue, families grab their buckets and head outside, seeking out the assembled molds that carry their names. Carrie finds John's quickly. She's the only one who bought the largest of the three modules the company offers, a four-foot-high by six-foot-wide model called the Atlantis ($4,995). About the size of two washing machines pushed together, it's twice as tall and broad as the Aquarius ($1,995) and a third bigger than a Nautilus ($2,995), the most popular choice today. None of the families decided on the company's lowest-cost option ($995), which entails mixing remains with those of other deceased into a multitude of modules that comprise an entire "community reef." For Carrie, the Atlantis was the obvious choice. "I had to get the big model," she tells me in the yard, with a laugh. "John was a big man, and he lived his life big, very big."

Eternal Reefs has positioned the molds in a straight row atop plywood platforms, John's at the far end. Depending on its size, each is fashioned from either two or four fiberglass panels that are punctured with fist-size holes. When pinned together, the panels enclose an empty core, which is then stuffed with a rotund, air-filled bladder and, into the opening of each hole, volleyball-like balloons. During the casting, concrete flows and eventually hardens around those inflated forms. A day later, the forms are deflated and removed, leaving behind a hollow center and portals through which both marine life and water can travel.

The cement mixer, its revolving hopper producing a steady grumble, is ready to pour. George instructs families to empty remains into their buckets. At the end of the line, Carrie opens John's plastic bag inside her white pail, turns it upside down and shakes her husband's ashes into the basin. In the two years since John's cremation, this is the first time his entire remains have been released from their container. It's also, Carrie understands, the last time this will happen. "I know I'm saying goodbye," Carrie says of that moment. She takes this final opportunity to sink both of her hands into what's left of the physical part of her husband and slowly sifts them through her fingers. "I needed to touch them one last time," Carrie explains later. "I'm not sure I could have let them go if I hadn't."

George appears at her station, hose in hand, and directs enough water into the pail to cover the ashes. With both hands Carrie grasps the metal pike that came with her pail and begins stirring. She's still at it when George returns with a quarter-bucket of concrete, which he shakes into Carrie's pail. This time she stirs more vigorously, until she can no longer tell the difference between John's ashes and the concrete.

With a louder churning sound, the truck starts to pour concrete into the first mold and moves quickly up the line. When it rolls to Carrie's station, two crew members maneuver the chute leading from the mixer directly over her mold. The casting moves quickly now. The door to the hopper opens, and concrete begins to flow down the chute and into the mold. George tells Carrie to grab her bucket and stand to the side of the chute. On his signal, she overturns her bucket into the running stream of concrete, a crew member reaching into her pail with a gloved hand to help scoop all of it out. Residue clinging to the bucket George flushes into the chute with his hose.

Concrete runs quickly into the mold. Minutes later it reaches the brim, and the mixer moves on. George comes by to tag the freshly poured reef with a label that reads: "Slowe. NJ." Tomorrow afternoon his crew will pull the forms from the hardened module and cement Carrie's plaque into one of its portals. They'll then scoot the ball to the edge of the yard to cure with the others. Next month the finished memorials will be lifted onto a flatbed and trucked up to their final port of call in either Maryland or New Jersey.

It's just after one o'clock when John's reef is cast. The cement mixer pulls out of the yard soon after that, the staff hoses down buckets and pikes and returns them to the hangar. This once bustling, noisy construction zone is quiet. Up and down the line of stations families gather around their newly poured reefs for group photographs they'll share with those back home who, surely, can't quite picture what happened here. An elderly man stands silently before his wife's reef, arms crossed at his chest; two daughters embrace by another module, weeping quietly.

Families are free to leave, but they linger under the hot Florida sun to participate in one final rite of casting. Twenty minutes later, it arrives: the visible rim of concrete at the module's top firms and, in an act that symbolically joins the living who created it with the dead who comprise it, family members sink the flat of their palms into the concrete. When they lift their palms out, their handprints remain behind.

Reaching over the lip of John's module, Carrie Slowe smoothes its wet surface with a card and in large block letter etches the word *EXCEL-LENT.* Following it she pushes an imprint of her hand, tracing the outline of a heart into the palm. "John would say that things were, 'excellent,'" Carrie says. "Writing that was my way of saying that John and the reef he was part of were excellent, too."

Families snap final photos and begin to leave. Carrie's one of the last to go. She hugs Don and George on the way out of the yard.

Carrie's hotel is a thirty-minute drive north from here, and she cries all the way back. The short morning's been a continual and exhausting process of letting go—of first shaking John's ashes out of the bag that's held them for two years, of stirring them into concrete, and then, finally, releasing them into the reef mold. For two years, Carrie alone has held her husband's remains, this bit of bone she calls not "remains" or "ashes" but simply "John." Now, as she pulls her rental car onto Center Avenue on the way out of town, she's leaving him behind—in another state and in someone else's care—for the first time since his death. Tomorrow morning she'll catch a return flight to Atlantic City. When she walks into the beach house they once shared, she knows that this physical part of John will no longer be there.

And yet, Carrie finds some comfort, and some very small joy, in today's leave-taking. Having participated in a process she'd witnessed only on television, Carrie's even more certain she did right by her husband in this rubble yard. "I'm leaving knowing that John would be proud to be involved with this project. He'd love the idea of giving something back to the earth," Carrie says. "I also know he would be proud of me for following through with it."

It's not done yet. Almost exactly a month from today, she'll have one more chance to see her husband's remains in their final form. Aboard a charter boat with family members and friends, she'll see just where he's going—and watch his "flight."

The Great Egg Reef lies just off Ocean City, a bustling beach retreat on the lower arc of New Jersey's barrier islands. The reef is a mile-long site fashioned from mostly concrete pipe, Vietnam-era army tanks, a two-hundred-foot Navy barge, and five hundred reef balls that were manufactured by inmates at the state correctional facility in Delmont. Since the fall of 2004, however, in an area set apart from other sunken material and labeled on new diving charts as the Eternal Reefs site, Great Egg has also been home to ten memorial reefs. In late May, nine more of them, including one for John Slowe, will be added to it.

A natural reef is technically any shallow structure rising from the sea floor. What little natural reef New Jersey harbors is limited to a small outcropping of granite rock in the far northern waters off Long Branch. Great Egg is one of fourteen artificial reefs the state has created to extend that natural sliver—and its ecological benefits—farther down its one-hundred-thirty-mile-long coastline. "Reefs are tremendous producers of marine life," says Bill Figley, a marine fisheries biologist with the N.J. Division of Fish and Wildlife who has been involved with the reef program since its inception in 1984. "By placing material like rock, concrete, ships, and fabricated reef balls on our part of the seabed, we're trying to create structures that will serve as aquatic nurseries where there are none."

Fish and other ocean organisms will colonize artificial structures just as readily as natural ones, says Figley. When divers recently hauled up ten sample reef structures that the state had sunk offshore over a period of seven years, biologists found that each one supported eight hundred times more marine life than the surrounding sandy seafloor, providing hard substrate habitat for more than one hundred forty-five different species, from snails and anemone to lobster and sea bass. Reef balls have proved particularly fertile structures. "Each reef ball functions like a little microreef, with it own independent population of fish and marine life," says Figley. Encrusting organisms, like blue mussels and a stone coral indigenous to northern waters, latch on to the ball's hard, nubby exterior, as do sponges and anemone. Starfish and sea snails roam its surface; crabs and lobsters trench into sandy alcoves around its footprint. The ball's perforated dome provides protection and habitat for a variety of fish, eighteen of which on average populate each reef ball.

New Jersey's reef-building program now ranks among the most active in the country. So when Eternal Reefs looked to offer its clients memorial placement into Atlantic waters farther up the east coast, the Garden State seemed a natural choice. "The Ocean City site met all our criteria," recalls George, who first approached Figley at an annual Atlantic States fisheries conference in 1998 and broached the idea of teaming up. Most important, Figley had already gained the local, state, and federal permits needed to sink artificial material into the ocean, and the reef's purpose—to provide habitat and create locales for diving and fishing—squared with the company's mission. "We won't put our memorials into beach retention projects or into harbor development, for which regular reef balls have been used," George says. Ocean City also provided the infrastructure that's critical to a marine deployment of this kind, including the heavy machinery (like cranes) and fleet of vessels—tugs, barges, passenger boats—that Eternal Reefs rents.

For the company's clients, Ocean City—with Atlantic City beckoning a mere ten miles up the road—would prove one cemetery site that boasts plenty of other, nonfunereal draws. "Families have every reason to come back here," says George.

Bill Figley, New Jersey's reef builder, took an even more pragmatic view of the site. Established in 1995, Great Egg is the least developed of his artificial reefs, and George's memorial reefs provide him with valuable infill at an unbeatable price: free. As for using human remains to help build up reef structure, Figley says the notion doesn't bother him. "The fish don't care," he says. "They'll come equally to reef balls that do and don't contain someone's ashes." Figley does acknowledge the specialness these concrete urns have to some among the human population. He therefore sinks them together in a unique life-producing, aquatic graveyard away from other material, in an isolated corner of the reef at coordinates 39°14.N/74°21.W.

Traveling ten knots into steady headwinds, it takes *Defiant* nearly an hour to reach Great Egg. The three charter boats carrying family members arrive nearly in its wake and begin to circle the towing craft as its crew prepares to deploy the first memorial reef.

More than fifty friends and relatives of John Slowe crowd the deck and cabin of the *Miss Beach Haven.* They huddle in tight groups, catching up with each other, sharing stories of John, some disappearing into the cabin to dip into the spread of bagels, fruit, and assorted drinks Carrie has laid out there. A bag leaning against an ice chest holds a bottle of Jack Daniel's, John's beverage of choice. Just outside the cabin door, a clutch of John's diving buddies pull on fat cigars, in his honor. Aboard this floating funeral coach, the mood is anything but somber. These passengers tell me they have mourned the loss of a dear friend, fellow diver, and family man. But today, on these high seas, they've clearly come to celebrate the good life John lived and the life he'll continue to nurture in the waters he loved.

Many of these seagoers had attended yesterday's "viewing" of John's finished reef in a sandy marina just outside Ocean City. There, under an open sky, seagulls screeching overhead, fishing skiffs trawling the nearby channel, they'd joined the friends and relatives of the other eight deceased to pay last respects and to see the memorials. For the few who'd participated in the casting down in Sarasota, this was the first time they'd seen their finished modules. For Carrie, seeing John's reef—its plaque now cemented into a portal and her handprint and "excellent" clearly visible along the rim—is harder than she'd expected. The concrete form she'd helped fashion "looked strangely beautiful," she says, "but seeing it also renewed my sense of loss, particularly since I knew I was coming closer to letting it—letting John—go."

Eternal Reefs had distributed sidewalk chalk, which Carrie's elementary school–age niece had used to scribble over John's reef in pastels of blue and pink; a sister had placed a sheet of tracing paper over the plaque and rubbed out an impression with charcoal. An hour into the viewing, two teams of military personnel arrived and conducted military honors for a pair of veterans. For each veteran, a bugler played taps while his comrades folded an American flag over the module and handed the triangular national ensign to the widow. Soon afterward, families began exiting the yard. Carrie and her family were last to go. As they headed to their cars, Carrie lingered a moment at John's dome. Nearly leaning on the module, she'd placed her palm at a spot next to the plaque and, then, before joining her family, had kissed the vessel that would soon carry what remained of her husband to the depths.

The next morning, all the families reconvene at a dock in Ocean City and board the crafts to watch their memorial reefs be placed into the Atlantic. They're not long at the Great Egg site when George comes over a loudspeaker on the *Miss Beach Haven* to announce that the first reef—for eighty-nine-year-old Eleanor "Nonie" Baldwin—will be dedicated.

To sink each module, the *Defiant* employs a crane and a wooden plank that's balanced over the stern, like a playground seesaw. The crew winds a sling through Baldwin's module and attaching the sling to a hook at the end of the crane's cable, raises and then lowers the module onto the deck-end of the plank. The sling is removed and then the crane cable is attached to the boat end of the plank. The crew winches up the cable, raising the plank, and Eleanor Baldwin's module begins to inch toward the water. The cable rises higher and higher until the memorial reef slips down the plank and splashes into the Atlantic.

Prior to boarding, the Eternal Reefs staff had distributed flowers to each family. Now, as the Baldwin reef sinks below the waves, her family tosses red and white carnations into the water.

Between securing each module with rope, raising it onto the plank, and then tipping it into the sea, the *Defiant* crew needs a good fifteen to twenty minutes for each deployment. John's is scheduled last, so it's approaching noon when George comes over the loud speaker to announce the placement of the John V. Slowe memorial reef. Aboard the charter boat, Carrie begins to distribute the stemmed flowers she and Eternal Reefs have reserved for the occasion, yellow roses mostly, with a mix of carnations. In the bow someone brandishes the bottle of Jack Daniel's, and plastic shot glasses of whiskey are passed around the boat. All eyes turn to the stern of the towboat.

John's memorial has come to rest on the plank of the *Defiant* now, and in one of those implausible, indelible scenes that even doubters aboard this craft are hard-pressed to ascribe to pure happenstance, the sun emerges for the first time all morning. For a brief moment, the big dome that Carrie helped forge for her larger than life mate seems to bask in this newly arrived light, the pastel chalk drawing clearly visible, Carrie's garland of red and white carnations looping through the portals just in view.

And then it's gone. No sooner has the crane begun winching up the cable when the plank reaches its tipping point, and the two tons of concrete and five pounds of human ashes that is the John V. Slowe memorial reef shoots down the wooden slide and, with a crashing sound that can be heard over the drone of boat engines and waves slapping against the boat hull, splashes into the Atlantic. Within seconds, the heavy, perforated dome sinks out of view on its sixty-five-foot descent to the ocean floor.

From the *Miss Beach Haven* a loud cheer goes up. Someone shouts "To John!" and his friends and family, seniors and teenagers alike, raise their glasses to the late scuba diver and onetime high school teacher, and drink. Flowers fly overboard. From her perch in the bow, Carrie, standing between her mother and father, tosses into the water a single, golden bloom, a dried Hawaiian exotic from a bouquet John had once given her.

Months later, Carrie will recall the mixed emotions those moments evoked. "When his dome sank so fast in the water, I felt the loss of John all over again. It just seemed so final," she says. "At the same time, I knew John would have loved this, being such a sea lover. So I couldn't help but celebrate."

Its cargo deployed, the *Defiant* slips into the circuit of boats ringing the reef site. All that's left now is to dedicate the site. Over the intercom George reads the names of the nine persons whose memorials were sunk to the depths this morning. After each name is read, the three charter boats sound their horns in turn. At the sound of John's name, another toast is raised and more flowers are committed to the waves.

For the last time comes George's voice as he recites John F. Kennedy's famous musings on the sea: "I really don't know why it is that all of us are so committed to the sea. . . . We are tied to the ocean, and when we go back to the sea—whether it is to sail or to watch it—we are going back from whence we came."

The boats pull out of formation now and turn toward shore. There's more talk, but a kind of quiet has settled over the *Miss Beach Haven*. Up at the bow Carrie stands surrounded by her family and friends, her mother's arm around her, her father at her side. At some point, most everyone finds a moment to embrace her and share an observation about John's poignant sea burial. For Carrie, the forty-minute ride back to Ocean City passes too quickly. "There was a lot of love on that boat, for both John and me, and that helped with the loss I was feeling—and still feel," she says. And for the first time in the two years she's watched over her husband's ashes, she begins to feel a sense of relief. "I'd done what he would have wanted me to do. John was such a man of the sea, and I had brought him back to the place he loved."

Resource Guide: *The Memorial Reef*

Eternal Reefs
P.O. Box 2473
Decatur, GA 30031
Toll Free: 1-888-423-7333
Outside USA: 404-875-1876
Email: info@eternalreefs.com
www.eternalreefs.com

What:
Adding cremated remains to concrete "memorial reef" balls that are sunk onto one of more than a dozen existing artificial reefs in the

Atlantic Ocean and Gulf of Mexico, augmenting existing reefs and creating habitat for marine life.

What Happens:
You are invited to participate in the casting of your memorial reef ball, which involves adding cremated remains to the concrete slurry as it's poured into a mold. Staff can do this for you, if you prefer. A month later, the cured reef is transported to its deployment site, where an outdoor "viewing" of the reef is held. The following morning, you'll board a charter boat and observe the "placement" of the memorial reef into the water.

Where:
Memorial reefs are deployed onto a dozen established reef sites every year, mostly in waters of the Southeast. Past deployment sites include waters off the coast of Florida (Sarasota, Fort Lauderdale, Miami, Tampa Bay), South Carolina (Charleston), Texas (S. Padre Island), North Carolina (Topsail Beach, Morehead City), and Virginia (Norfolk, Chesapeake Bay). Northern sites include Ocean City, Maryland, and Ocean City, New Jersey. Eternal Reefs is looking to add locations in the New York City area and in the Pacific Northwest.

Most castings take place in Sarasota.

Cost:
Determined by the size of the reef ball. The smallest, a two-foot-high by three-foot-wide model called Aquarius runs $3,995. A slightly bigger Nautilus is $4,995. Twice as large as the Aquarius is the Mariner ($6,495). The lowest-cost option ($2,495) involves mixing remains with those of other families' into a pod of reef balls that comprise a "community reef." Cost for all options includes casting, viewing, and placement. Each ball is fitted with a bronze plaque, with your own inscription, at no extra charge.

If you choose to participate in the casting of a memorial reef, you'll need to travel to the casting site, typically in Sarasota, at your own expense.

Miscellaneous:
A funeral home can handle arrangements with Eternal Reefs, if you prefer. A list of participating homes is available on the Eternal Reefs website.

When my 7-year-old daughter Alison [died in the hospital],
there was one thing that I knew for certain in all the turmoil and
tumult that surrounded my family: I was not letting her out of
my sight; I was not surrendering the last vestige I had of her
vibrant and loving being to the care of strangers. I [would] con-
tinue to care for her myself as I h[ad] always done.

Beth Knox,
founder, Crossings: Caring
for Your Own at Death

∽ℳℳ∾

CHAPTER SIX:

The Home Funeral

If you had wanted to pay your last respects to Mary Barnsley the day after she passed away, you'd have had to come to her apartment in Austin, Texas, to do it. There you would have found her lying on her own bed, dressed in a favorite pastel blouse and matching slacks, a turquoise comb pinning back a wave of white hair. From the chest down she'd have been covered with a homemade quilt and a sprinkling of rose petals; in her hands, crossed at the chest, there'd have rested a single pink rose.

Taking a seat next to her bed, you'd have noticed the burning candles and tiny, white lights strung over the window frame, the photographs of Mary set out on the dresser, maybe detected the fragrance of rosemary and lavender. Like the dozen friends and family members who came to visit with Mary during the three days she lay in this room, you would have had all the time you needed to sit in this quiet, private place and say good-bye—to remember, to pray, to mourn, to thank. And then, like those others, perhaps come away better prepared to accept the death of this ninety-eight-year-old mother, wife, and former schoolteacher, and to let her go.

Such a close, personal, and ultimately healing encounter with a loved one at death is just what Sally and James Barnsley hoped for when they conducted a home funeral for James's mother in the summer of 2005. "We wanted to care for Mary ourselves when she passed away," says her daughter-in-law Sally. "We'd had her at home with hospice in the last months of her life, and it just seemed fitting that we'd continue to take care of her after death with the same love and attention we'd shown her in life, not hand her off to some stranger" at the funeral home. The Barnsleys knew it was possible. Like the vast majority of states, Texas allows families to care for their own dead, in their own homes, and Sally had learned how to do it. With other friends in the area she'd taken a workshop that taught the basic strategies of home death care—how to bathe and dress a body, pack it with dry ice, file the necessary paperwork—and had cofounded a group of local volunteers willing to help one another conduct home funerals for their own loved ones when the time came.

So, on the afternoon in July when Mary drew her last breath, surrounded by her family, in her own bedroom, no one rushed out to call 911, the doctor, or the local funeral home. "We sat there quiet and reverent, and let her spirit go in silence," says Sally of the end of her mother-in-law's often difficult, two-month decline. At some point, someone stepped out to call the hospice nurse. Later, after the nurse had come and gone, Sally made two calls of her own. "Mary passed away this afternoon," she told each of the volunteers who were on call for just this occasion. "Can you come now?"

The Barnsleys' decision to handle the after-death care of one of their own, on their own, is in keeping with a once long-held tradition in this country. For more than a century Americans cared for their own dead as a matter or course. Mostly the women of the house (or other women who advertised themselves as professional "Layers Out of the Dead") washed, dressed, and laid out a body in the dining room or the home's unheated front parlor, where it lay in repose for any number of days, often under constant vigil. Visitors stopped in to offer condolences to the family and pay last respects to the deceased. In the absence of a local coffin shop, men crafted a coffin themselves or hired a local cabinet- or furniture maker to do it. Death was a constant, if not welcome, part of life, and like many duties in the early years of the Republic, families shouldered those involved in caring for the dead themselves.

This truly traditional American way of death began to change in the mid- to late-nineteenth century, when a nascent funeral industry offered to "undertake" those after-death care responsibilities on the family's behalf. First in the home, and then in private funeral parlors that served as replicas of the real thing, a rising class of morticians was soon directing all aspects of a death, from washing, dressing, and, starting around the turn of 1900s, routinely embalming the deceased, to laying out the remains for viewing in reposing rooms, at specific hours and in caskets they sold themselves. That assistance of the funeral director has unburdened the family since then of the myriad arrangements that need attending to in time of death, freeing it to more fully grieve and accept its loss. In theory, at least. When a loved one dies, Beth Knox is among a number of home-death-care advocates who believes it just doesn't always work out that way when death comes calling.

"When you allow the funeral director to whisk away a body, you miss out on the rewards that come from having a home funeral," says Beth, who is the founder and director of Crossings, a Maryland-based nonprofit that helps families conduct home funerals. "There's a comfort and healing that comes from physically caring for the dead and from spending quiet, private time in the presence of death. It's a tremendous help in the bereavement process, and helps you see death as a natural part of the cycle of life."

Beth speaks from hard experience. In 1995, this mother of three held a home funeral for her daughter, Alison, who'd died from the impact of an air bag that deployed during a low-speed auto accident. Alison was seven years old. Beth had spent the last evening of Alison's life sleeping with her child in the hospital bed of the Baltimore hospital she'd been transferred to, had been at Alison's side when she passed away. By then, she'd decided that she couldn't—wouldn't—leave what remained of her vibrant, loving daughter to the care of the hospital staff and funeral director. "I'd brought Alison into this world, had nursed her, seen her through nursery school and into first grade," says Beth. "I couldn't turn my back on her and just walk away, surrendering her to the cold hospital morgue and handing her over to strangers. I wanted to take her home and care for her there, just like I had done when she was alive.".

With the reluctant assistance of a funeral director, to whom the hospital administration would only release a corpse despite state law that allows families to take control over their own dead, Beth brought her home. In Alison's own bedroom, Beth dressed her daughter in a soft white dress, placed a wreath of flowers around her head, laid her in a simple pine casket padded with dry ice and surrounded by pictures, favorite toys, and stuffed animals. And then opened her house to the community. For the next three days, Alison's schoolmates, teachers, babysitters, friends—several hundred people in all—came into this room to say good-bye. They came bearing gifts—food, flowers, and homemade cards; the children played with Alison's young brothers, filling the house with laughter and helping the boys find some comfort and distraction from their loss. Family and friends came and sat with Alison, as did her brothers themselves, who came to understand that the spirit of the sister lying in the coffin, on her own bed, had gone and would not return. Beth calls that vigil both "terrible and beautiful." At the end, she was able to find the will to let her daughter go. "To the degree that death can be ameliorated by love, that's what happened," she says. "The community lifted us and carried us, helping us bear and even find beauty in a very large loss." For herself, having Alison at home allowed Beth to follow a mother's instincts. "I was able to continue to love my daughter by caring for her, and by doing that I could begin to accept what had happened and begin to heal."

A couple of years passed. Walking in the woods one day, Beth had an epiphany that would lead to the founding of Crossings: she'd turn what she learned from her own personal tragedy to the benefit of others in their time of loss. Incorporated two years to the day of Alison's death, Crossings "empowers people to care for their own dead," says Beth. "We show families that home funerals are possible and legal, and then teach them how to do it." To that end, Beth speaks to hospice workers and hospital staffs, and consults directly with families who are caring for their own dead at home. Much of her effort goes into running workshops around the country in which this death-care midwife, as she's often referred to, teaches the nuts and bolts of conducting a home funeral. It's the kind of knowledge earlier generations once passed down, when the home funeral was de rigueur, Beth notes. "I'm just helping families remember how to do it."

*   *   *

Early Saturday morning in mid-October 2003, some two dozen people, including Sally Barnsley and the two women she'll call on two years later to help with her mother-in-law's home funeral, assemble inside a Waldorf school on the west side of Austin to participate in Beth Knox's "Caring for Your Own at Death" workshop. The night before, most of them had attended her public screening of Elizabeth Westrate's *A Family Undertaking,* a documentary film that follows a number of families who conduct home funerals. Now they've reconvened in this spacious classroom to learn how to do what those families undertook, or, as Beth puts it when she welcomes the group, to gain "the courage, confidence, and connections to do what our hearts want us to do when a loved one dies: to care for them at home."

To show just how possible that is in this very community, Beth introduces an official from the state health department. Susan Rodriguez, who works with the state's Bureau of Vital Statistics, starts by reviewing state law, which essentially allows residents to act as their own funeral directors, with many of the same rights and responsibilities a funeral director has. For the families assembled here, that means they may legally keep the deceased in their own home (or, had the death occurred in the hospital, bring the remains home), lay out the body, and transport it to the cemetery or crematory afterward themselves, though with some restrictions. To hold a body longer than twenty-four-hours, for example, families are required to either embalm, seal in a leak- and odor-proof container, or cool the remains (via refrigeration, dry ice, or some other unspecified method). They also have to wait forty-eight hours before the dead can be cremated, in order to give state medical examiners time to investigate any questions they might have about what caused the death.

A fair amount of paperwork is involved, Rodriguez says. A person acting in lieu of the funeral director has ten days to fill out and file the completed death certificate at the vital records office. A "report of death" form must also be completed and filed at the same office within twenty-four hours of the death. In the case of cremation, the family needs to gain from the state medical examiner a "burial transit permit" to transport a body from the home to the crematorium. The cremation can't happen at all unless the medical examiner, who reviews all deaths occurring in Travis County (where the workshop was taking place), issues a form allowing the cremation to proceed. At first glance, the reporting process seems straightforward enough. In an actual death, it can turn out to be much more complicated, admits Rodriguez, given the multiple forms needed, each of which must be filled out perfectly, and the "number of people who have to lay their hands on them."

Much of the rest of the morning is devoted to addressing issues related to home death care. Embalming, Beth tells the group, is not required by law, though some states do require that remains held longer than a day be refrigerated in some manner. Dry ice is an allowed form of refrigeration in Texas, and can delay decomposition for extended home funerals. Odors from a corpse are "almost never an issue" largely because of the dry ice, says Beth, but those that arise can be masked with flowers and heated defusers filled with the oils of sweet-smelling herbs. The easiest home funerals are those where an expected death has occurred at home. In the case of an autopsy, in which the body is opened and then sewn back together, a funeral director can be helpful in presenting the body for a home viewing. Autopsies can sometimes be avoided if the family voices opposition for religious reasons. Islam, for one, considers the autopsy an abuse of a corpse, forbidding it except when required by law; Judaism, likewise, disapproves of the practice for similar reasons.

After lunch, the group reconvenes for a session on the how-to of the home funeral. "Caring for the dead is a lot like caring for a bedridden invalid," says Beth, as she sets out hand towels, clean sheets, and a basin of warm water infused with aromatic lavender oil. To demonstrate how it's done, she selects one of the women to serve as a stand-in for a corpse, who then lies face up on a raised bed in front of Beth.

There's no need to rush into preparations, Beth begins: "The body doesn't decompose or start leaking right away." It is, however, a good idea to undress a body within two hours of death, before rigor mortis begins to stiffen limbs into position, and to then involve more than one person in the actual shifting and moving of remains, which tend to lengthen and become unwieldy.

Depending on the cause of death, the actual washing of a body may be thorough or more ritual in nature. Taking a cue from Jewish custom, early Christians washed the bodies of their dead, to ritually cleanse them of their spiritual impurities. Members of the Jewish burial society known as the Chevra Kadisha continue that long tradition, washing their dead and covering the remains with a white cloth prior to burial, a practice similar to that observed by Muslims. The washing, Beth says, can done with the deceased in the bed, using wet sponges or hand towels. Before starting, towels or absorbent "chucks" pads should be placed under the deceased, to absorb water and/or body fluids. Pressing down gently on the lower abdomen will release any waste that might otherwise appear later when the muscles in the bladder and bowel relax.

At this point, Beth invites her audience to come up in groups of six and begin to bathe the dressed "corpse." Dipping hand towels into the basin of water, the participants wash the feet, hands, face, and neck. When they're finished, Beth helps the last group roll the volunteer onto her left and then right side, and change the sheet under her, replacing old sheets for new, one side of the bed at a time.

Families might now want to move a body to another bed or into a coffin for the viewing, and they can use the sheet to do it. Given the heft—literally the "dead weight"—of a corpse, Beth recommends involving half a dozen people when transferring a body. To give this group a sense of just how heavy a body can be, Beth directs the six participants to ball up the ends of the sheet on which the volunteer rests, and then raise her off the bed. When they do, Beth has them carry the volunteer to the end of the room and back, making sure to keep the head elevated to prevent fluids that would collect in the deceased's lungs from discharging.

In an actual death, the body would now be dressed and laid out. Remains don't break down immediately upon death, Beth assures the group, but noticeable effects of disintegration, such as leaking body fluids and odors, will eventually occur if no steps are taken to retard decomposition. Just when those effects will show depends in large part on the condition of the deceased at death and the temperature/humidity in the room. In many cases, a body may be safely laid out as is for a day, particularly if the room temperature is cool. Remains laid out for a longer period should be cooled. The Texas Department of State Health Services has laid down specific rules regarding this, requiring that any unembalmed body held beyond twenty-four hours be cooled to a temperature between thirty-four and forty degrees. Just how a family must meet that requirement isn't spelled out. According to an official with the state funeral board, however, acceptable methods would include laying the deceased onto a bed of frozen gel pacs or plastic bags filled with ice cubes. Another accepted, and easier, method, says Beth, is to undergird a body with dry ice.

A frozen form of carbon dioxide, dry ice is three times colder than regular ice and, for death-care givers, has the advantage not only of lasting longer but of "melting" via evaporation, not by reverting to liquid (and, in the process, wetting bedsheets and clothing it comes into contact with).

Blocks of the ice should be wrapped in towels or pillowcases, says Beth, and then placed under the deceased's abdomen, pelvis, and chest, and if the body is very warm, on top of the stomach. Sixty to eighty pounds of the ice, which can be bought at some supermarkets or package stores, should suffice for a three-day vigil. Families should use enough at any one time to slow decomposition but not so much that the body freezes; the ideal amount, says Beth, keeps the body cool but still soft to the touch. And because dry ice releases carbon dioxide gas, which can cause headaches and hyperventilation when breathed in for too long and at high concentrations, windows should be cracked in any room in which it is used.

With daily changes of dry ice, a body can be laid out for several days. In Beth's experience, the traditional three-day wake works well for the purposes of the home funeral. "The body is often beautiful that first day," she says. "By the third day, the deceased begins to look like an empty shell, and it's often at that point that a family may be ready to let go."

About an hour after Mary passes away, Joyce Ahlert, a nurse from Hospice Austin, arrives at the Barnsleys' home and, after checking Mary's vital signs for the last time, officially pronounces the death. She records the time of death as four forty-seven—the time of her pronouncement, which is common practice, not of the actual death itself—and phones it in to Mary's physician.

Joyce leaves shortly afterward, knowing the Barnsleys will be handling arrangements from here. She's gone by the time Sally's two helpers—Lisa and Donna—arrive around five-thirty, ready to help Sally and her twenty-four-year-old daughter, Laura, prepare Mary's body for the vigil. When they show up, Sally's husband, James, and his brother Howard head out to purchase dry ice.

The women collect in Mary's bedroom and begin assembling the supplies they'll need to prepare her body: washcloths, towels, soap, sheets. Into a basin of warm water they pour fragrant oil of lavender and sprinkle rose petals. With the exception of Donna, none of these women have laid out a body before. Before starting, they circle Mary's bed to prepare themselves for the task ahead. "By washing Mary this afternoon, we're stepping into the long lineage of women who have cared for their loved ones for thousands of years," Donna begins. "Let us fill our hearts with appreciation and love for Mary as we do this work." Addressing Mary directly, Donna says in a more lighthearted tone, "We might be awkward and clumsy. Please be patient with us!"

Taking up positions on either side of the bed, the women gently work off Mary's nightgown; one of them unties the scarf Laura and Howard had earlier looped around Mary's head and jaw to close her mouth (had her eyes been open at death, they'd have closed them as well, perhaps laying plastic sachets weighted with rice on top of the lids). One side at a time, they wash the body with wet, soapy cloths, and towel it dry. Hospice had been bathing Mary every day, so this washing takes on a more ritual nature. No one presses on the abdomen as Beth had suggested in her workshop, since the ninety-eight-year-old had eaten and drunk little in the weeks preceding her death and what waste there was had already flowed into a catheter the hospice nurse had removed before leaving. That's also why Sally doesn't slip a pair of disposable diapers onto her mother-in-law, deciding instead to later position the lower half of her body over a waterproof pad to prevent any discharge from soiling the bedsheets.

An inert body can be hard to maneuver. Working together, though, the four have little trouble fitting Mary into the clothes Sally had picked out: a summery, pink-and-turquoise blouse her mother-in-law was fond of and matching slacks, white socks but no shoes. The underclothes Sally doesn't bother with, preferring to keep the ensemble to "the minimum."

The women work quietly and calmly; there's no rushing about, no time frame. "It's all very peacefully done," Sally later recalls. "The whole feeling was that we were giving a gift to Mary, and while there are practical matters to consider, we're doing this slowly and reverently in honor of her."

Mary had died in the hospital bed hospice had supplied her. For the vigil, Sally wanted her mother-in-law to lie in her own bed, which the Barnsleys had relegated to a corner of the room during her decline. This other bed the women now make up with fresh sheets, laying the waterproof pad on top of the bottom sheet. James and Howard, who have just returned with the dry ice, step in to help with the transfer. They push the made bed over to the hospital bed and, with the women, ball up edges of the sheet Mary had been lying on. On cue, the four of them then pull the sheet—and Mary—onto the made bed, making sure to position her lower half over the waterproof pad. As Beth had showed them, they roll Mary onto her left side, then right, to remove the transfer sheet.

At a natural foods store James and Howard had bought thirty pounds of dry ice ($30), enough they figured to last the first day. The ice came in five-pound blocks (not in the pellet form it's sometime sold in), which the brothers had broken into smaller pieces by dropping the blocks onto the Barnsleys' back steps. Donning leather gloves—dry ice can "burn" skin on contact—they then wrapped the pieces into grocery sacks, and stuffed the sacks into half a dozen pillowcases.

In the bedroom, the women turn Mary into positions that allow James and Howard to place the dry ice–filled pillowcases at the warmest areas of her body. A single pillowcase goes under Mary's head and another on top of her stomach, a pair of pillowcases goes beneath both the shoulder blades and hips. The Barnsleys will need to replenish the dry ice once every twenty-four hours from now on. They'll go through the most today, when Mary's body is warmest, somewhat less every day afterward. Considering Mary's advanced age, size, and protracted illness, the Barnsleys start with twenty-five pounds. To extend the life of the ice and keep the room cool, they turn up the air conditioner that had been running; they also crack the bedroom window to allow the dry ice's vapors to escape.

The dry ice in place, Laura combs her grandmother's hair, pinning back one wave with Mary's favorite turquoise hair comb, and then drapes a pink sheet around the head. Over the rest of the body Sally spreads a homey quilt and then positions Mary's hands over her chest, left crossing over right, slipping between them a pink rose. Laura plucks the petals from another rose and sprinkles them over the quilt, covering her grandmother in shades of the natural world. Remembering that Mary had wanted a family member to receive her wedding band, Laura tugs the ring off her grandmother's hand and sets it on a side table, atop a single rose petal.

During Mary's decline, Laura had placed candles and cut flowers around her room, and had strung the window and dresser mirror with tiny white lights. On the dresser top she now sets out a dozen framed photographs of Mary from various stages of her life. In one of them Mary stands before a towering cactus near the Arizona home she and her husband retired to; another black-and-white shot shows a young Mary posing for the camera on an expanse of lawn. More flowers are stationed about, irises Lisa had brought, pink roses from James, and big bunches of rosemary Sally clips from her garden. The bouquets brighten this place of final repose, but also serve to perfuse the room with a fragrance that could later mask any odors of death. When Sally lights an oil defuser sitting on a cedar chest by the window, a stronger scent of lavender fills the air.

By six-thirty, an hour after they started, the work of laying out Mary Barnsley is done. Looking at her mother-in-law, surrounded by flowers and lights and candles and pictures, Sally's struck by how beautiful the sight is. Later that night, she'll sit in this room on the chair she sets next to the bed. In the quiet of the night, alone with the woman she held such affection for, Sally will read Bible verses the devout Presbyterian liked and contemplate her passing. "I think of the people Mary knew and loved who died before—her husband, mother, brother, sisters," she later says of that night, "and how they're all greeting her into their world."

When the Barnsleys first brought hospice into the home and the attending physician told them that Mary might have as little as two weeks to live, Sally made plans to purchase a coffin. They'd planned a cremation for Mary, and Sally knew that any crematory in the state would require that a coffin or other minimal "container" be used. On a lead from Donna, she had called All Faiths Funeral Service, an Austin funeral home known for its willingness to help families make alternative arrangements, and bought one of the cardboard coffins it had in stock for $35.

For most of the summer the coffin had stood in the Barnsleys' garage. After Mary's death, Sally's two daughters carry it out into the backyard and lay it across two sawhorses. Artists by profession—Laura is an illustrator, Martha paints murals in private homes—the sisters spend the better part of an afternoon transforming the industrial, brown box into a parting gift for their grandmother. The entire coffin—lid and base—they color over in pastel blue for sky, punctuating it here and there with billowy, white clouds. On the lid, above where Mary's head will eventually rest, they paint the image of a golden eagle, its outstretched, tawny wings nearly spanning the width of the coffin, as if carrying away Mary's spirit.

Sally and James meanwhile handle the more clerical tasks associated with a death in the state of Texas. As the person acting in lieu of a funeral director, James fills out the top portion of a blank death certificate Sally had gotten from the vital records office, entering mostly factual information about his mother: Mary's full name, address, birth and death dates, social security number, as well as method of disposition (in this case, cremation) and place of disposition (the nearby Superior Mortuary Services crematory, which Sally knew worked directly with families). The couple then brings the death certificate to Mary's attending physician, who fills out the medical section, listing the cause of death as degenerative joint disease, since reduced mobility had caused the falls that precipitated her decline.

Sally and James now bring the completed death certificate to the vital records office in downtown Austin. There the registrar faxes it to the medical examiner, who reviews all deaths in the county. Because of a misunderstanding about what exactly's required in the case of a family caring for its own dead, the medical examiner requires the Barnsleys to present a new death certificate signed by a funeral director.* The request sends the Barnsleys scurrying around town to regain the attending physician's signature and the signature of a funeral director (which they get from a funeral director who works with the company operating the crematory the Barnsleys are using). After the Barnsleys refile the new death certificate, the medical examiner issues the burial transit permit the family needs to transport Mary from the Barnsleys' home to the crematorium, as well as the form that authorizes her cremation.

Back at the Barnsleys' home, half a dozen family and friends come throughout the day to visit Mary, many of them sitting quietly with her or reading Bible verses. A full day has passed since Mary's death, and the Barnsleys find that the dry ice has completely evaporated. They repack the pillowcases with twenty pounds of fresh ice, five pounds less than yesterday. "Mary's body was pretty warm because she'd had a slight fever in her final day, so the ice evaporated more quickly than we anticipated," says Sally.

The following morning, a Thursday, Sally calls Superior Mortuary to schedule Mary's cremation. The family-run funeral home operates a small crematory that abuts a historic, rural cemetery just east of town. When James tells John, one of the company's funeral directors, that he'll be transporting Mary there himself, John reminds him to bring the documents necessary for cremation: burial transit permit, authority to cremate form, and a signed copy of Superior's own form giving the company the Barnsleys' permission to cremate Mary. They've already pur-

---

* The medical examiner (ME) required the funeral director's signature on Mary's death certificate because the Barnsleys had missed one step in taking control of Mary's remains: no one had notified the medical examiner's office or the justice of the peace (JP) of Mary's death at the time of her death. Had the ME or JP been contacted, he/she would have come to the house and "verified" the death, enabling the Barnsleys to file the death certificate without incident and gain the medical examiner's required burial transit permit and "permission to cremate" form.

chased a fiberboard coffin, James says, and want Mary's ashes placed in a basic, cardboard urn.

Superior would normally charge a family $350 for such "basic cremation" services ($250 for the cremation, $100 for its help with the death certificate). But the company doesn't charge the Barnsleys anything, given the hassle the family had gone through obtaining the death certificate. Before hanging up, the men schedule the cremation for the next day, Friday, at noon.

James and Sally notify family and friends of Mary's death and invite them to attend a memorial service in the Barnsleys' home on Friday morning, two hours before Mary's cremation. The arrangements with Superior now made, James and his daughter Laura spend the evening putting together a program for the memorial, deciding on the sequence of events, picking out and practicing a few songs. In the living room where they'll hold the memorial, the Barnsleys set out sympathy cards and flowers they've received, more candles. On a side table they place pictures of Mary and a vase of red roses. There's also a photo album Mary put together years ago, with pictures from her teaching career, including those of many of her young students.

Among those planning to attend the service is James's cousin Regina, whom the Barnsleys have invited to stay with them. She had sat briefly with Mary when she first arrived that afternoon, but it's not until two A.M., when everyone's asleep and a quiet pervades the house, that Regina has a chance to sit quietly with her aunt. Regina had seen her a week before she'd died. Flicking on the light in Mary's room now, she's struck by how much more "pretty and peaceful" the woman appears, dressed in the handsome, color-coordinated outfit, with her hair styled. She takes a seat next to the bed and, on impulse, strokes Mary's cold cheek and hands. On a side table there's a Bible, which Regina picks up and reads silently, picking passages at random and, at the same time, praying for the woman who was more grandmother than aunt to her. Thoughts stray to her late father, and she wonders if he and Mary, brother and sister, are reunited at this moment. She also remembers her late mother, and how it pained her to leave her mom at the funeral home, in the company of strangers, especially at night, and is thankful that's not happening now to Mary. An hour later, when it felt "right to leave," she returns to her bed. "That time was very special to me," Regina says later. "I was prepared for Mary's death, but I was thankful to be able to have some quiet, one-on-one time with my aunt before she was really gone."

At ten the next morning James welcomes two dozen friends and family who gather in the living room to celebrate the life of Mary Barnsley. He and Sally had briefly considered whether to bring Mary into this room. But they'd decided against it, thinking the sight of her body or the closed coffin might make some guests uncomfortable; they also weren't sure the coffin would fit through the doorways leading to the room.

When Martha had thought of a song her grandmother would like, the Beatles's "Tomorrow Never Knows" had come to mind. In a strong, clear voice she now sings without accompaniment the words John Lennon had borrowed from the Tibetan Book of the Dead, in which he compares death to a relaxed, alternative state of mind that "is not dying." Sally then invites anyone to share a memory of Mary. Regina says she hoped Mary knew just how much she'd influenced her life; one friend improvises on a verse by Rudolf Steiner that Laura particularly likes: "Angels, Archangels . . . receive Mary's web of Destiny."

James had wanted everyone to sing together, so he and Laura pass out song sheets with the lyrics to "Going Home," a hymn set to the largo of Dvorak's *New World Symphony*. The mournful melody is often sung at memorial services, and enough people here know it for the singing to "sound pretty nice," Sally recalls. When it comes to the end, the group joins hands and recites the Lord's Prayer. There are no tears. Nearly one hundred years old when she died, Mary had led a good, long life, says Regina, and her passing was in some ways a welcome end to a protracted and often painful illness.

James now invites everyone to say any final good-byes to Mary. Following him into Mary's apartment, they circle the closed coffin that rests on the floor, in the middle of her living room. Earlier that morning, James and a friend had lain Mary into the newly decorated coffin and carried it here. They'd left the lid off before the start of the memorial service, so anyone who wanted could have one last look.

Mary's color had grown somewhat more pallid and her mouth had begun to open, but otherwise her appearance had changed surprisingly little since the midwives first washed and dressed her. Just that morning Sally had detected the first signs of what Beth Knox calls the "subtle smell of death." Most visitors probably didn't note it, but Sally decided to add more lavender oil to the defuser and refreshed the vases with rosemary.

When last views had been taken, James fitted the lid onto the coffin and tied it down for good with a set of plastic stays.

Now, following the service, Mary's friends and family circle her closed coffin, in silence. Standing at the head of the coffin, one friend who is trained in the movement art known as eurythmy begins to gesture with her hands and arms, acting out the nonverbal equivalent of the word *Alleluliah*. When Mary was still laid out in her bed, Laura and a family friend had carried the empty coffin from her bedroom to the backyard to make sure it would fit through the doorways en route. James and his cousin Greg now follow that same path with the occupied coffin, walking it out the living room, down a short flight of steps, and out to the driveway. There Greg's pickup truck sits parked, its tailback down. The men slide the coffin into the truckbed, where it rests on top of a thin foam mattress Greg has laid there to keep the box from sliding around on the drive out to the crematory.

The crematory sits over in Webberville, some twenty minutes away. James has invited everyone to join a procession out there, but most stay behind. James and Greg pull out in the pickup. Sally, Laura, Regina, and two other friends follow behind in Sally's car.

Superior Mortuary's crematory is housed in a small cinder-block building adjacent to the grounds of Old Jones Cemetery, a peaceful, historic graveyard overspread with shading oaks and cedars. James and Greg pull into the crematory just before noon and, after conferring with Robert, the facility operator, back the truck into the facility's open bay. Inside, James hands over the burial transit permit, authority to cremate form, and the crematory's own permission form, signed by both James and his brother Howard. Robert then maneuvers Mary's coffin off the truck and onto a flatbed dolly, which he wheels over to one of two retorts. Opening the retort door, he pushes the coffin inside, and shuts the door.

A few people—James, Sally, and Greg—stand inside this tight space, facing the retort; the others wait outside, lingering by the car or standing under the trees. There's no ceremony, nothing left to say. Having Mary at home these three days, all who wanted have had their time with her, have been able to say their final good-byes. So when Robert asks James if he's ready to start, Mary's eldest son says yes, and Robert presses the button that fires the retort.

For a moment, the family and friends of Mary Barnsley stand quietly as the muted roar of the retort fills the room. For Sally the occasion evokes mixed emotions. "The end is certainly sad, but my feeling was also that Mary was freed at last from the body that had been weighing her down and causing her pain for so long," she tells me later. "Like that bird my daughters painted on the coffin, Mary could now soar away to a better place."

The group lingers on the grounds another half hour, some talking with each other and with Robert, who relates the history of the cemetery, once part of a Civil War–era cattle ranch his wife's grandfather used to own. Laura, her arms folded, stands quietly alone. Regina leans against the car and looks up at the crematory chimney. Seeing the smoke issuing from the chimney, distorting the image of the clouds behind it, she reflects on Mary's passing. "That's my aunt Mary rising into the sky," she thinks. "And she's changing the formation of the clouds."

Research Guide: *The Home Funeral*

What:

Caring for the remains of a loved one yourself, in your own home. That care may include bringing a body home from a hospital or nursing home, washing and dressing it, laying it out for vigil, holding a memorial service, and transporting the deceased to the cemetery or crematory.

The Laws:

All states except New York, Connecticut, Nebraska, Indiana, Michigan, Utah, and Louisiana permit families to care for their own dead at home. You'll be acting as your own funeral director, and as such must follow state funeral laws. Embalming is almost never required, but in most cases you'll need to refrigerate or cool any unembalmed body you lay out for more than twenty-four hours, typically by placing it on dry ice. You'll also need to gain and file any number of documents, including death certificates and transit permits to transport the deceased. For a detailed description of your state's laws, see Lisa Carlson's *Caring for the Dead* (1998, Upper Access Books).

How-to:

Beth Knox, founder of Crossings, recommends planning as much in advance of a death as possible. It's vital to know exactly what your state requires in the case of death (see Carlson's book) and to have a group of helpers on call to come and assist you in what may be a physically and emotionally demanding endeavor. The actual preparation of the body Beth compares to caring for an invalid. For tips on how to wash, dress, and move a body, see Crossings's *Resource Guide* ($55, plus shipping) and Final Passages's *Complete Home Funerals* ($45, plus shipping), from the organizations below. Both Crossings and Final Passages offer workshops around the country on home death care ($150 for Crossings's, $350 for Final Passages's).

To retard decomposition, most death-care advocates suggest buffeting a body with dry ice. You'll find dry ice at many supermarkets, convenience and package stores, as well as Airgas outlets (www.airgas.com). Expect to pay about $1 a pound. You'll need anywhere from fifty to eighty pounds for a three-day vigil; start with thirty to forty pounds the first day. Dry ice comes in either pellets or square slabs. The pellets are easier to work with but evaporate more quickly. Slabs need to be broken into four- to five-inch square chunks. Dry ice will "burn" skin on contact so wear gloves when handling. Slabs or pellets should be wrapped in towels or pillowcases and laid under the deceased's head and torso, and, if the body is feverish, on top of the abdomen. Dry ice "melts" by evaporating, releasing carbon dioxide. Crack a window to vent vapors. You'll need to replenish the dry ice every twenty-four hours or so.

Beth suggests finding local funeral directors who are willing to work with families. You may want to hire them to handle certain aspects of the home funeral you'd rather not undertake yourself (such as paperwork), or you may need services only they can perform (preparing for viewing a body that's been autopsied, for example).

Resources:

Elizabeth Westrate's documentary film *A Family Undertaking* profiles a number of families who conduct home funerals (www.pbs.org/pov/pov2004/afamilyundertaking). You can rent the film via Netflix (www.netflix.com) or purchase it ($89, through Crossings). Beth Knox is featured in the film, as is Jerrigrace Lyons, founder of Final Passages. *Alison's Gift* (1999, NOISLA Publishing, available through Crossings), by Pat Hogan, tells the complete story of the passing and home funeral of Beth's daughter, Alison.

The organizations below are reviving the art of the home funeral. They offer assistance and information on many aspects of home death care via private consultations, workshops, and resource materials.

California
Lakeside
Thresholds
Barbara Kernan, 619-390-1411
www.thresholds.us

Placerville
Nancy Poer, 530-622-9302
E-mail: whitefeather@directcon.net

Sacramento
Heidi Boucher, 916-601-9134
E-mail: heidibouch@comcast.net

Santa Monica
Sacred Crossings
Olivio Bareham, 310-968-2763
www.sacredcrossings.com

Sebastopol
Final Passages
Jerrigrace Lyons, 707-824-0268
www.finalpassages.org

Colorado
Boulder
Natural Transitions
Karen van Vuuren, 303-443-3418
www.naturaltransitions.org

Maine
Auburn
Last Things
Klara Tammany, 207-786-7468
Chuck Larkin, 207-873-7854
www.lastthings.net

Camden
Crossing Circles of Maine
Dake Collins, Richard Ailes, 207-236-0505
E-mail: mainecrossings@aol.com

Portland
Our Sacred Passage
Lea Moon, 207-841-6510
www.oursacredpassage.com

Maryland
Takoma Park
Crossings: Caring for Our Own at Death
Beth Knox, 301-523-3033
www.crossings.net

Massachusetts
Cambridge
Threshold
Nancy Accola, 617-491-2368
E-mail: cfyod1@verizon.net

Great Barrington
Sacred Undertaking
Ann-Elizabeth Barnes, 413-528-1306
E-mail: annelizbarnes@gmail.com

Michigan
Ann Arbor
A Natural Undertaking Funeral Care
Erika Nelson
E-mail: erika.beth.nelson@gmail.com
www.anaturalundertaking.com

Minnesota
Minneapolis
Twin Cities Threshold Group
Linda Bergh, 612-927-0894
www.lindabergh.org

Rites of Change
Ellen Hufschmidt, 612-729-6817
www.ritesofchange.com

Portages
Jean Madsen, Michael Sorrell, 651-398-8172
www.naturaldeathcare.com

Roseville
Marianne Dietzel, 651-633-0432
E-mail: m_dietzel@yahoo.com

New Mexico
Santa Fe
Juliette Armstrong, 505-603-0432
E-mail: juliettesehee@aol.com

New York
Hillsdale
Sacred Undertaking
Jonathan Hasse, 518-325-7454

North Carolina
Asheville
Caroline Yongue, 828-676-9806
E-mail: cyongue@iglide.net

Piedmont
The Sophia Center for Life Studies
Crossings Care Community
Sandy LaGrega, 336-292-7947
Betty Hare, 336-621-6433

Ohio
Circleville
Pickaway Home Funeral Services
Ann Harr, 740-412-1752
www.pickawayhomefuneralservices.com

Oregon
Canby
Farewell Assistance
Janie Malloy, 503-651-2669
www.farewellassistance.com

Portland
Spiral of Life
Tricia Sweeney, 503-233-3383
www.spiraloflife.org

Pennsylvania
Philadelphia
A Natural Undertaking
Donna Larson, 484-880-7129
Jennifer Bingham, 610-688-4264
www.naturalundertaking.org

Texas
Austin
Crossings Care Circle
Donna Belk, 512-922-8043
Sandy Booth, 512-440-7979
www.crossingscircle.org

Washington
Olympic Peninsula
Ceremony for Life's Thresholds
Nora Cedarwind Young, 360-302-0197
www.thresholdsoflife.org

Seattle
A Sacred Moment
Char Barrett, 206-529-3803
www.asacredmoment.com

Wisconsin
Madison
Simple Wisdom Sanctuary
Mary Kateada, 608-442-0054
www.simplewisdomsanctuary.com

Viroqua
Threshold Care Circle
Charlene Elderkin, 608-606-8060
www.thresholdcarecircle.org

Webster
Northwoods Home Funerals
Lucy Basler, 715-866-7798
E-mail: lucybasler@gmail.com

One customer from Sioux City commissioned us to build him a simple, pine casket. Rope handles, no finish, no hinges, no interior. Just a bare-bones box. He told me he wanted to make a statement: the casket is simply a vessel for another vessel that we're done with. There's no reason to get carried away.

Loren Schieuer,
woodworker and coffin-maker

⟨∞⟩

CHAPTER SEVEN:

A Plain Pine Box

For nearly three years the casket Ed McKenna planned to be buried in sat up in the attic of his two-story home in rural Salix, Iowa. The casket was a simple make, a rectangular chest lumbered from knotty pine, unlined and unvarnished. A slender birch handlebar ran the length of all four sides, and the casket's flat lid was split into two sections, so Ed's wife, Evelyn, had to raise only one half of the lid whenever she wanted to get at the handmade quilts she stored inside.

"I always did like the idea of a plain wooden casket," Ed tells me at his kitchen table late one winter morning, the fallow fields just outside the farmhouse window still glazed with frost. For Ed, a retired farmer and meatpacker nearing his eighty-eighth birthday, the humble casket recalls the simple funeral services of his childhood in the early decades of the last century, when families in this remote farming community handled undertakings on their own and either hired a local carpenter to make the casket or bought one ready-made at the furniture store.

His grandmother Justina's funeral in 1925 was typical of the time. "I remember peeking into the bedroom where she was laid out," says Ed, who was then seven. "A couple of women were coming and going with basins of water, and they were fixing her hair." For the home wake, the women lay Justina in a wood coffin that her nephew, a carpenter, had built, and family and friends stopped in to pay their respects. On the third day, pallbearers carried her closed coffin to the church across the street and, after the service, loaded it onto a horse-drawn wagon, which mourners followed out to the cemetery on foot. At the cemetery gates, the pallbearers again collected the coffin, carrying it this time on its final leg to the grave a family member had dug. No lowering device stood over the grave, there was no burial vault to set the casket in. Straddling the grave site, the pallbearers simply lowered Justina McKenna, and the wood coffin in which she lay, directly into ground.

Decades later, after he'd retired from the Swift plant in Sioux City and over time began to more deeply consider his mortality, Ed found himself recalling his grandmother's simple funeral. With its straightforward arrangement, family focus, low cost, and basic, handmade casket at the center, that prairie burial of old "seemed to me just a natural way to do it," says Ed. He'd been moved, too, by the Jewish funeral rite he read about, in which the dead are buried in a plain, pine box, no matter what their station in life. Both traditions made so much sense that he told Evelyn he wanted a similar send-off when his own time came.

Ed saw an opportunity to acquire that plain coffin when he opened the Sunday paper and read about a furniture maker in nearby Pierson who built caskets on the side. In September 2002, he drove out to Schieuer Woodworks to see what Loren Schieuer had to offer. He didn't have to look long. When Loren opened the broad display case where a trio of his finished coffins sat on carts, Ed saw just the thing he was looking for: an unadorned chest made from pine boards, a split lid that opened one half at a time. Loren told his visitor he could lacquer the coffin's exterior if he preferred a finer finish, and upholster the bare interior with a crepe lining. "No," Ed said. "This is exactly what I'm after: a box made from plain lumber." At $700, the price struck Ed as reasonable for a piece of handcrafted woodwork, particularly when compared to the many thousands of dollars families at his church were paying for the metal caskets they bought from area funeral homes. Standing in the wood shop, Ed paid

Loren the casket's full amount in cash, and, after the woodworker loaded the purchase into the bed of Ed's pickup truck, drove the hour back to Salix.

Evelyn just laughed when she saw the coffin in the driveway. Married to Ed for almost sixty years by then, she'd come to expect the unorthodox from her quirky husband. She thought it handsome, though, and Ed said he'd go back to Pierson and buy her an even more attractive casket made from oak, if she wanted. Evelyn told him to hold off. "Instead of getting another one, why doesn't the one of us who goes first use the casket you've already bought?" she suggested. That was fine with Ed. Evelyn was seventy-eight, five years younger than he, and in good health. There was no doubt in Ed's mind that he would be the one to use this coffin, freeing Evelyn to buy that oak one for herself after he was gone. "That was the plan," says Ed. "But it didn't work out that way."

The woodworking shop where Ed McKenna bought his pine coffin is housed in a turn-of-the-century brick building that fronts Main Street in downtown Pierson, Iowa, a small farming community half an hour due east of Sioux City. On a crisp, January afternoon, the open, high-ceilinged shop on the first floor is filled with an array of custom furniture in various stages of completion—sections of office cabinets, kitchen chairs, a fireplace surround, and, resting on a flatbed dolly tucked inside a display case by the front door, a single coffin. "This is our standard model," says Loren Schieuer, the fiftyish woodworker and owner, rolling the rectangular box out of the display case and opening the upper section of the raised, split lid. "It's made from solid red oak that's milled in northern Minnesota. The design is pretty basic, and with the raised lid and deep finish the casket's reminiscent of what you might find in a funeral home."

The oak is one of nearly fifty caskets Loren has constructed since adding caskets to his main line of handcrafted furniture eight years ago. At the time, the fourth-generation Schieuer carpenter hadn't intended this detour into the dismal trade. "A local farmer commissioned me to build a horse-drawn hearse, which I worked on in here over a two-year period," Loren tells me in his shop office, the finished hearse pictured in a framed newspaper article hanging on the wall. Struck by the singular funeral carriage, visitors would invariably ask if Loren were going to build old-fashioned coffins as well. The cabinetmaker had no interest in making coffins "given what they are," but the question came up so often, recalls Loren, that "I finally said, 'OK! I'll build one for crying out loud!'"

In his twenty-plus years of woodworking, Loren had never made a coffin. To construct this first one, he trolled the Internet for ideas, studied a book of coffin plans, measured the interiors of standard vaults in which most cemeteries require that coffins be placed. The design he came up with showed an unadorned, rectangular pine box. A single, flat lid lay flush to the coffin case; along both sides and at either end ran a wooden handrail, to be made from birch, since pine wasn't strong enough to support both the weight of the hundred-pound coffin and its occupant. Using some fifty board feet of kiln-dried lumber—roughly a third as much as is used in the construction of a typical, funeral-home casket—and improvising on the hardware (tapping a piano hinge to connect lid to case), Loren built the coffin in about twenty hours. After his wife, Jane, sprayed the exterior with two coats of lacquer, he set it out on a cart by the shop entrance.

And waited for the reaction. Many people had encouraged him to build the casket, but Loren thought the sight of a real one might "freak out" his more squeamish customers. He needn't have worried. "People came in and said, 'Finally, there's an alternative to the high-priced, cookie-cutter metal coffin,'" recounts Loren. Some particularly liked the coffin's simple, basic design, others its handcrafted quality. At $500, the price Loren said he'd probably charge for his novel project—well below the many thousands of dollars anyone would pay for an industry standard metal one—the casket was a bargain to boot. Pleased and surprised by their customers' embrace of the minimal coffin, the Schieuers decided to follow in the tradition of the American woodworker of old and add coffins to their repertoire of handcrafted goods.

For the couple, coffin-making offered an additional, welcome revenue stream in the very tough industry of custom furniture-making, particularly one that took place in the "middle of podunk Iowa," as Loren puts it. And unlike many of the pieces he crafted, the simple coffin, with his streamlined design and mostly straight lines, could be made relatively easily and quickly. The more the Schieuers learned about the funeral trade, the more they also warmed to the idea of offering a handsome, largely handmade coffin at a reasonable price. "We found that the typical funeral director will jack up the price of a casket by three hundred to five hundred percent," says Loren. "That steep markup is just not fair, and made us want to make the caskets even more."

Committed to the new venture, Loren designed a more standard-looking oak model to complement the pine one he'd made; later, he crafted a Mission-style casket from white oak, with ornamental stiles and some curved molding. Unless requested otherwise, the interiors of all three would come upholstered with padded bed, crepe lining on the lid and sides, and outfitted with hinges, latches, and other hardware designed expressly for caskets, which he'd found in a woodworking catalog. He divided the lid into two sections, so, per tradition, only the deceased's upper body would be visible at an open-casket viewing. Jane, who handles the company's finishing work, would stain the exteriors, brush on sealer, and then spray all completed caskets with two coats of lacquer.

The Schieuers priced their caskets in a range they thought reasonable for a piece of handcrafted furniture: pine ($500 initially, without interior accoutrement; today it's $950); oak ($2,000); Mission ($2,500). The cost included finishing, upholstery, and delivery to funeral home or residence within fifty miles of the shop. A down payment was demanded upfront, the rest upon completion. Loren figures their prices are anywhere from fifty to eighty percent lower than what customers would pay for a comparable casket at a funeral home, mostly because families would be buying it directly from the manufacturer—that is, him—and thus bypassing the funeral director and his hefty markup to the wholesale price.

By the fall of 1998, the Schieuers were set to enter the coffin-making business. One final step remained: meeting with the funeral director.

Like all but a handful of states, Iowa permits cabinetmakers and other retailers—such as discount brokers, Internet suppliers, and since 2004 the Costco wholesale club—to sell caskets directly to the public.* Federal law requires that funeral directors accept these "third party" caskets, but the funeral industry does so begrudgingly, since they represent the lost sale of a good that typically comprises the single most expensive item in the long list of funeral goods and services it offers. For a time, directors tried to recoup some of that loss by charging families an extra fee to

* A few states, such as Oklahoma and Virginia, grant funeral directors the exclusive right to sell caskets, on the argument that funeral directors alone have the expertise to determine if a casket is of sound enough quality to protect consumers from fraud and/or injury and to guarantee a sanitary burial. The Funeral Consumers Alliance, among other critics of the restrictions, contends that such laws serve only to protect the funeral industry from competition that would lower the caskets' prices.

handle any casket a family bought elsewhere. In 1994, the Federal Trade Commission, the government entity charged with overseeing the funeral industry, deemed the fee unlawful and banned it.

The Schieuers knew the funeral directors in their area wouldn't welcome what they'd clearly see as an intrusion into a highly profitable corner of the mortuary trade. Nonetheless, Loren and Jane made an appointment with a mortician who handled funerals in the area to explain themselves. "We wanted to lay our cards out on the table so there'd be no surprises," says Loren. "We didn't figure we'd take many sales away from him, since we'd probably only be making a few caskets anyway."

The meeting didn't go well. "He got pretty upset," Loren recalls. At first the director tried to scare the Schieuers off the venture, warning them of the consequences of providing a casket whose handles fell off or whose bottom dropped out in the middle of a funeral service. Loren was too sure of his craftsmanship to worry about that possibility. When he and Jane then declared that they simply wanted to provide families with an affordable alternative to the high-priced casket, the funeral director looked at them and said, "Oh, it won't be cheaper. We'll get their money." Loren knew just how the well-dressed man sitting across the table from him would do it—he'd charge more for some of his other services. The whole exchange surprised and emboldened the Schieuers. By the time they got home, they were more intent than ever on becoming casket-makers.

The Schieuers' first couple of casket sales came through word of mouth: an oak version that a local man dying of cancer wanted decorated with images of roadrunners, another one of oak into which Loren carved shamrocks at the request of an Irishman who'd suffered a stroke. His third casket and, as it would turn out, the first one to make it all the way through the funeral process, was a handsome, walnut make for a customer Loren would have preferred more than anything not to accommodate: his father.

The request had come decades before, when Loren told his dad about the mahogany casket a colleague was making at their shop. "Well, you can make mine when the time comes," Roy had told his son at the time. Standing at his dying father's bedside in a Sioux City hospital more than twenty years later, Loren waited for the right moment to ask if he might make good on an old wish he never forgot. "Yeah, I'd like that," the retired carpenter said with a smile. "Not many men can say their son built them a casket." Roy asked that it be made from walnut—his favorite wood; Loren's mother requested that it have a traditional look, so Loren agreed to pattern it after his standard oak casket instead of the plain pine box he himself preferred.

Back in the shop, Loren cut and glued up the walnut boards but kept putting off actually fashioning them into a casket. "I know it sounds foolish, but I felt that if I made the coffin then Dad might decide to use it right away," Loren says. Six months passed. One morning toward the end of May 1999, Loren's brother called to say he'd better come to the hospital. Hours later Roy Schieuer passed away, surrounded by his family. "The first thing I thought was, 'Oh, Dad, I haven't finished your casket,'" says Loren. There wasn't much time to make it then, either. That was Thursday. The funeral, Loren figured, would be held Monday, the viewing his mother wanted on Sunday, three days away. The coffin, he knew, would take him twenty hours to build.

Loren calculated the few working hours between then and Saturday, when the coffin would need delivering to the Kingsley funeral home, but already he knew what he'd do: "I told Dad I would make his coffin, and I wasn't going to let him down," he says. Learning of his intention, his family expressed its reservations—Loren would be working under both a tight deadline as well as the emotional strain of his father's passing—but gave him its blessing.

Arriving home at nine later that night, Loren told his wife and four children of his plan, and then headed into the shop. With the help of his teenage son, Pete, he spent a couple of hours constructing the casket's main case before turning in. At seven-thirty the next morning, he was back at it. Assisted later by Pete, who'd left school early for the shop, Loren hunkered down to the task, cutting panels to back the crepe lining, sanding exterior wood, grooving out niches to accommodate the handles, hinges, and other hardware, doing more sanding. The pair worked late into the afternoon, when Loren ran out to the funeral home to make final arrangements for the funeral. The director had learned that the family would supply the coffin—a prospect "he was fine with," says Loren—and conferred with Loren to make sure the coffin's dimensions were adequate.

Back at the shop an hour later, Loren was joined by Pete, and for much of the time, Jane, for an all-nighter. At eight o'clock the next morning, the casket was complete. Before heading off to bed Loren and Pete handed it over to Jane, who pulled off hardware, sanded exterior wood, applied sealer, and after wheeling the casket into the finishing room, sprayed it with two coats of lacquer. She was still at it when Loren, too wired to sleep, returned a couple of hours later. After the lacquer dried, Loren then buffed the finished exterior with steel wool and wax, reattached the hardware, and installed the interior panels that their upholsterer had fashioned with crepe lining earlier that morning. Finally, at four that afternoon, the job was done. With Pete's help, Loren loaded his father's coffin into the company van and drove it to the Kingsley funeral home.

Recounting that emotional and physical marathon years later, Loren describes it as a labor of love that proved both satisfying and ultimately therapeutic. "Pete was at my side through the night, and we reminisced about his grandpa while we worked, which helped ease the loss I was feeling," he says. For the family, Loren's coffin helped transform the viewing, funeral, and burial of the man they loved into an even more "touching and personal family affair," he says. The job of building his father's casket proved even more meaningful to Loren himself. Resting at the front of St. Michael's Catholic Church, the wood coffin symbolized both Loren's love of the carpenter it held and of the family tradition of woodworking, which Loren, much to his father's pride, was carrying on. Above all, the work represented a son's parting gift for his father. "The casket was my final tribute to Dad," he tells me in the shop where he built it, "and it was an honor to make it."

In the years since his father's death, the Schieuers have worked with a number of funeral homes in the area. Most have been welcoming. A few give him the cold shoulder, like the mortuary in Sioux City that won't even greet Loren when he pulls up, giving him the impression that he'd best "unload that sucker [coffin] and get out because you're not welcome." Loren suspects it is one of these disgruntled directors who turned him into the state for operating without the "establishment permit" that's required to sell funeral-related products to the public in Iowa. The Schieuers have a business license to sell their woodworks, but neither they nor their attorney knew they needed an additional permit to sell caskets. The first time they learned about the permit was when an official from the state insurance commissioner's office arrived at the shop one afternoon in November 2000 and issued a cease-and-desist order for their casket operation. The Schieuers promptly sent the state the necessary paperwork with a check for $50, and received the establishment permit a couple of weeks later. But the shutdown had hurt. They'd lost almost a month's worth of sales during a boom time in their fledgling business.

Other laws they knew about. Early on the Schieuers had learned that they couldn't build a casket on commission and then store it until the family called for it. The state prohibits the practice in order to protect consumers from ordering caskets that might never get delivered when the time came. To accommodate customers who want to buy a casket in advance—or "preneed" in funeral parlance—Jane has set up an arrangement with the local bank, whereby the customer deposits the full cost of the desired coffin into an interest-bearing CD that's in both his and the Schieuers' names. When the customer, or his family, eventually requests the casket, Loren will either make one or, if time is short, provide them with one he has in stock (or, if none, refund the sale). The family then signs the CD over to the Schieuers.

After building a dozen or so caskets, Loren was able to trim construction time to about twenty hours per oak model, nearly half that for pine. He usually makes two at a time, and tries to keep a couple of finished caskets in stock to accommodate families who call from the hospital and need a casket immediately. "I've pulled four all-nighters to build caskets that were delivered to the funeral home the next day," he says. "After the last one I told Jane no more: they're too draining." Loren will, however, personalize one of the coffins he has in stock—carve a design on the body, set an inlay of a cross into the lid—on short notice. He'll also custom craft caskets to order with enough advance warning. Next to one of his workbenches sits a coffin he built from the walnut boards a family supplied him, both ends of which he's adorning with scenes of farm life.

The demand for the Schieuers' coffins ebbs and flows. Most of their sales are to customers who come into the shop and buy one of the caskets already in stock. The oak model is the most popular. "This area of the Midwest is pretty conservative," Loren says. "People care about what others think, and the oak has a traditional look that's similar to what they see at the mortuary." For that reason, he's had interest in but no actual orders for the eight-sided "shaped" coffins reminiscent of the Old West. Likewise, he's never been asked to build a casket that can serve as a bookcase or coffee table before its final use. One customer says he wants a hickory casket that can convert into a desk, but Loren has yet to receive the order.

*   *   *

Ed McKenna's decision to purchase a handmade coffin from a local woodworker is a return to a once-common arrangement in this country. When death came calling in the Colonial era, a family typically hired the village cabinetmaker or carpenter to produce the coffin, expecting him to turn it out within a day or two of the order, just ahead of its use in the funeral.

Following the traditional English design, the early American coffin resembled a six- or eight-sided chest that roughly approximated the human form, broad at the shoulders and tapering to the feet (a style hence known as a "toe pincher"). The exact wood it was made from reflected the status of the deceased. The coffins of common folk were generally fashioned from pine, an easily worked softwood whose plain, knotty exterior the cabinetmaker might disguise with a paint of gluewater and powdery soot known as lamp black. For more affluent customers, he might use one of the richer-grained hardwoods like walnut, chestnut, sometimes mahogany imported from Cuba, polished to a high sheen.

At first, coffin-making was a side business to the cabinetmaker's regular trade in tables, chairs, bed frames, and other home furnishings. As settlements and villages grew into towns, select craftsmen began to specialize in the funereal chests, and opened "coffin shops" where they stocked ready-made coffins and a range of decorative plates, handles, hinges, and other specialty hardware that could be affixed to them. In the course of producing his burial box, the coffin/cabinetmaker might be asked to coordinate its delivery with the grave-digging sexton, the livery stable owner who supplied the horse and cart to transport the coffin to its final destination, and the minister presiding over the funeral. It wasn't long before the woodworker offered to "undertake" all those arrangements as a regular part of his coffin-making services (for an extra fee), and the undertaker was born.

Stove manufacturers entered the nascent funeral industry in the mid-nineteenth century with a metal coffin they literally pounded out in the very same factories that produced their staple cooking/heating ware. Made at first from iron and eventually from lighter sheet metal, the coffins promised to better protect their occupants from both the elements and the "resurrectionist" grave robbers who supplied medical schools with unearthed cadavers for anatomical study well into the 1920s. To its manufacturer, the metal coffin conferred additional benefits: it could be standardized, made by machine, and thus produced en masse like any other consumer commodity being churned out in the emerging industrial age—and was. For the coffin-making woodworker, the appearance of the mass-produced metal coffin heralded the gradual decline in his trade of single-order, handcrafted funeral boxes and the corner coffin shop where he worked.

A change in name followed the change in material and production techniques. Conforming to the human form, the traditional wedge-shaped coffin reminded families of the dead body it would soon contain, according to one designer. To "obviate" the "disagreeable sensations" such a sight produced, and to win buyers in the process, manufacturers in the late 1800s streamlined the metal coffin's octagonal form, reducing eight sides to four and squaring the remaining corners. The result was the now standard rectangular-shaped box they rechristened a "casket." At the time, the word *casket* referred to a jewelry box or small chest for valuables. Now affixed to the straight-sided coffin, the new appellation served not only to further divert consumers' attention from the death the burial case was needed for, but to likewise suggest that the earthly remains within were, like jewelry itself, precious and thus worthy of the increasing attention the growing funeral trade would lavish on them.

Today, some three-quarters of the nearly two million caskets sold every year are metal, the vast majority of them mass produced by three corporations. Industry figures put the average price of a casket at $2,200, but it easily goes much higher.

On an early Saturday morning near the end of October 2004, some two years after Ed arrived home with his coffin, Evelyn complained of a splitting headache while making breakfast and lay down on the couch. On the advice of his daughter Joan, a nurse, Ed took her to the hospital in Sioux City. Doctors there told Ed that Evelyn had suffered a "head bleed," a break in a blood vessel feeding the brain, and they'd need to operate.

The surgery later that day was successful. But when Evelyn suffered another episode the following night, the doctor said Evelyn's long-term prospects looked grim. The vessels were brittle, the physician informed Ed, and the slightest pressure would continue to rupture them. Further surgery would do little good, so the doctor moved Evelyn into respite care, expecting her to die by morning.

To his surprise, she recovered and after a couple of days stabilized enough to be discharged. Back at home, Evelyn slowly regained some of her strength and occasionally got out of the house, taking daily walks to the park with Ed, attending Mass, shopping with her daughters. Ed counted each day with his wife a blessing but harbored no illusions. Years ago, he'd sat down with a funeral director in a nearby town to make arrangements for his own funeral. In early November, Ed met with the same funeral director to plan for Evelyn's. The McKennas had often talked about the kind of funerals each of them wanted, so Ed was clear about his wife's final wishes: a private funeral Mass at St. Joseph's, burial in the church cemetery, and, as the couple had agreed, use of the pine casket Ed had bought. There'd be no public viewing—Evelyn "didn't want her friends looking at her," says Ed—or memorial service.

Most of the family lived nearby, so the service and burial would be held the day following her death. Embalming, therefore, wouldn't be necessary. Ed would, however, want the director to pick up his deceased wife and "clean her up" and dress her before bringing Evelyn to the church the next day in the casket Ed would supply, and after the service, deliver her to the cemetery. Having years ago volunteered to help rehabilitate St. Joseph's neglected cemetery, Ed knew burial there required the use of a vault, the buried casement into which the coffin is lowered, and asked the funeral director to provide a basic concrete one. The director noted Ed's instructions as he laid them out. If he was upset at not being able to sell Ed one of his caskets, the embalming, or any of his other standard services, he never showed it, says Ed. For the goods and services he would provide, the director charged Ed $3,934.60—the bulk of it for his nondeclinable assistance fee ($1,282) and for the vault ($775).

After finishing with the funeral director, Ed contacted the church sexton, who agreed to excavate the grave on short notice when the time came.

That April, five months after returning home, Evelyn suffered another bleed returning from the bathroom, collapsed in the utility room, and broke her hip. Again, the doctors in Sioux City said there was nothing they could do to stop the cranial bleeding, but pinned Evelyn's hip so the family could take her home to die.

Evelyn needed constant care now. The family called in hospice, and the McKennas' daughters—all six of them—set up a daily rotation so that one of them was always at their mother's side. Evelyn, though unable to communicate, was alert during this time, and in no obvious pain. On the morning of May 1, a Sunday, she slipped into a coma and her breathing, says Joan, grew irregular, coming in rapid gasps followed by slow, shallow breaths. Ed ran out to an early Mass, and asked the priest to come by to administer last rights.

As it turned out, the family had planned a brunch that morning at the house to celebrate Ed and Evelyn's sixty-third wedding anniversary a day before the actual date, and had assembled by the time Ed got home from church. When the priest, Father Slaven, arrived shortly afterward, he joined Ed and nine of the McKennas' ten children in Evelyn's bedroom, where they had just finished praying the Rosary. Stepping to the head of the bed, the priest prayed over Evelyn and anointed her with oil, once on her hands, chest, and forehead. Evelyn's breathing continued to come in hard, halting gasps but with longer pauses between breaths, and then, just minutes after Father Slaven had finished the final sacrament, it stopped for good.

"It was real peaceful," says Ed of that last moment. "She didn't suffer at all." Everyone knew Evelyn had passed, but Joan handed a stethoscope to her sister Jane, also a nurse, who listened for but found no pulse. Joan then told the assembled family that her mother had, indeed, passed. For a few moments, no one moved. "You know the end is coming, but when Mom died we all just looked at one another, not saying anything," says Joan. Jane then broke away to call the hospice nurse; Ed called the funeral director. The brothers trickled out of the room and, after a time, headed up to the attic to retrieve the pine coffin that would be needed now. The daughters, meanwhile, prepared their mother for the funeral director, washing her hair and folding her hands on top of her chest, because, says Joan, "it just made us feel good." A few of them collected the clothing Evelyn had told them she wanted to be buried in: a purple dress she'd last worn at her oldest son's wedding, plus the earrings, necklace, and other jewelry she'd worn that day, according to a wedding picture they consulted. Ed conferred with the priest, who agreed to preside over a private Mass at eight the following morning. Ed asked that no homily be given, and said no family members would speak. Ed then called the sexton to ask that the grave be dug in time for a nine-thirty burial.

Within the hour the hospice nurse came and officially declared Evelyn's death. The funeral director arrived shortly afterward. Using the bedsheet she'd died on, he and an assistant lifted Evelyn into the open bag on top of their gurney and then wheeled her out to the black hearse parked at the curb, her body zipped into the bag. Her sons had maneuvered the coffin down the tight staircase, having removed all but the pair of quilts Evelyn had asked to be buried in. With the coffin resting in the living room, the girls arranged the interior of the box the way they wanted it for their mother: spreading a quilt over a bunch of throw pillows they'd placed in the bottom and positioning a wedge-shaped pillow at the head; the other quilt they'd later tell the funeral director to drape around their mother like a wrap. They finished, and the boys closed the coffin and carried it out to a brother's truck. The girls had already assembled Evelyn's effects by then—the dress and jewelry, as well as her makeup and eyeglasses. When the funeral director then pulled out for the thirty-minute drive back to the funeral home, Evelyn's family trailed him, Ed and his sons in the truck carrying the coffin, the oldest girls in a car with their mother's clothing.

Early the next morning, the family of Evelyn McKenna gathered at St. Joseph's Catholic Church in downtown Salix to bury the woman Ed had married exactly sixty-three years ago to the day.

Evelyn had requested a private funeral, but between her children, grandchildren, and a few of her great-grandchildren, a large clan of McKennas—more than forty in all—had gathered to mark her passing. Most of them waited inside the church, the group filling nearly a quarter of the pews there, a dozen others remaining outside on the sidewalk, awaiting the hearse. When it pulled up at seven forty-five and the funeral director opened the rear door to the bed where Evelyn lay in the coffin that until yesterday had stored her quilts, six of Evelyn's children—three sons, three daughters—stepped forward to carry it into the church. "I had tripped over that coffin so many times going up into the attic that the sight of it wasn't shocking anymore," says Joan. "It was very sobering, though, knowing my mother was in it now."

Grasping the birch rail, Evelyn's pallbearers carried the coffin up the steps and, reaching the vestibule, set it down on top of the dolly where Father Slaven stood. The priest blessed the coffin, which the oldest daughter then draped with a plain white pall. At the foot of the coffin, one of them laid a small bunch of pink roses, Evelyn's favorite color.

Following the priest, the funeral director wheeled the closed coffin into the church, bringing it to rest in front of the altar. It was a bright May morning, and the light filtering through the stained-glass windows illuminated this high-ceilinged space, bringing out the interior's mostly pink hues, plus those in the banners that happened to be hanging that season—a sight that would have pleased her mother, Joan thought.

The Mass was the simple, family service Evelyn had wanted. Two of her grandsons served as altar boys. Jane did the readings.

Following the final blessing, Father Slaven processed out, the funeral director wheeling the coffin behind him. When the director reached the last row of pews, he stopped and turned the coffin to face the aisle. The pall came off the coffin, the flowers were resettled on the bottom half of the now bare lid.

Loren Schieuer says his plain coffin makes an impression not many mourners forget. Stationed near the entrance of this handsomely appointed church, with its stained-glass windows, carved Stations of the Cross, mural of Christ's ascension adorning the high arch behind the altar, the unvarnished, knot-mottled pine casket Loren built in his Pierson woodshop indeed stood out. In this setting, the plain, wood coffin struck a simple, yet elegant note that in both form and function served to remind those here of the most basic fact of all: that we live and, no matter what our station in life, we die. And as will happen to the humble pine boards enclosing Evelyn McKenna, we all return to dust.

The McKenna family exited their pews and began to walk up the aisle. The priest had come to stand behind the coffin, at the head, and as he did, the funeral director opened the lid of the coffin and stepped away. Evelyn was visible now, her head resting on the white pillow it lay on in her final weeks of life, the quilt draped around her shoulders. She was wearing her glasses, the diamond earrings, her purple dress. And looked at peace.

As they came up the aisle, Evelyn's family took one last look at this mother, grandmother, great-grandmother, and, for Ed, who headed this funeral procession, wife. And whatever tears were held back during the Mass came now. Looking at his wife, Ed had one clear thought: "She should have been the one standing there looking down at me, not the other way around."

When the last of the mourners left, the funeral director closed the coffin, latched it, and wheeled the coffin into the vestibule. Here, the pallbearers again grasped the birch bar running the length of each side, and hoisted the coffin off the bier. With Ed now taking a handle at the coffin's head and the funeral director grabbing the foot, they slowly descended the steps leading down to the street and carried the coffin to the waiting hearse.

The cemetery lies half a mile from the church. More than three-quarters of a century ago, Ed had followed the horse-drawn cart carrying his grandmother to that very place. With the rest of his family, he now trailed the gray hearse that held his wife's remains. When they reached the grave site, the pallbearers took up their mother's casket for the last time and laid it on the bier stretched across the cavity the sexton dug just yesterday afternoon.

The burial service was as simple as the Mass. Fanning out around the casket, Ed and three of his daughters seated, the family watched the priest as he anointed the casket, recited his prayers, and, finally, committed the spirit of Evelyn McKenna into God's hands.

In August, three months after his wife's burial, Ed called Schieuer Woodworks for the second time. He'd like to buy a plain pine casket, he told Loren, and wondered if there were any in stock. Ed said he'd bought one before, and when he told Loren who he was, Loren had Jane pull the invoice of that first sale. "I've got a pine casket already made up," Loren informed his former customer. "Looking at your old invoice I can tell the casket's the exact same kind you bought last time: pine, no varnish, no liner. Just a plain box." Loren had been planning on taking it into the finishing room, but told Ed he'd hold off if he was interested in buying it. "Good," Ed replied. "I'll be there this afternoon to get it. I didn't want to come up without hauling a load back."

As promised, Ed showed up a few hours later, accompanied by Joan. He told Loren of Evelyn's passing and how she'd been buried in Loren's first coffin, the one he'd planned for his own burial. He'd come back to get another exactly like it, for just himself this time. "You could tell he was hurting," Loren says, recalling that visit. "I felt sorry for him, poor guy."

The price of lumber had gone up since that 2002 sale. The pine casket cost $800 now, which Ed paid with a check. Loren again loaded the plain pine box, this time into the back of Joan's pickup, and, after wishing Ed well, watched them drive off.

Not long after Evelyn's death, Ed sold his home to his youngest daughter and moved in with Joan to await an opening in one of the senior apartments in town that Evelyn had been instrumental in getting built. Not wanting to take up additional space in Joan's house, Ed had asked one of his sons in town to store the casket at his place until it was needed. It's in the son's basement now. "The coffin's up on a couple of sawhorses and covered over with a tarp," Ed tells me. "And there it sits, just waiting to be filled."

Resource Guide: *A Plain Pine Box*

What:
A simple coffin made from pine or other inexpensive, common material.

The Laws:
No federal or state law requires that you purchase a coffin from a funeral director. You can make a coffin yourself or buy one from a "third-party provider"—be it a coffin-maker, mail-order discount broker, or even the Costco department store—and the funeral home you deliver it to is legally compelled to accept it, and without charging you an extra fee to handle it.

A handful of states—Virginia, Louisiana, and Oklahoma, among them—allow only funeral directors to sell caskets. If you live in one of these states, you may still purchase a so-called third-party casket from an out-of-state provider and have it delivered to the funeral home. Or follow the advice of Lisa Carlson, author of *Caring for the Dead* (1998, Upper Access Books): call the casket you purchase in state from your local woodworker a "hope chest." No law she's aware of prohibits families from buying hope chests and then burying their dead in them.

How and Where:
Your local woodworker/cabinetmaker may be willing to make a basic coffin for you (under "carpenters," "wood turning," and/or "woodworking" in the Yellow Pages). Some of them actively produce coffins on the side, others solely. The Funeral Consumers Alliance maintains a good though somewhat dated online list of some five dozen coffin-builders by state (www.funerals.org, click on "Frequently Asked Questions," follow link to "Burial, Cemeteries, Etc.," click on "Caskets"). For a basic pine casket, you can generally expect to pay anywhere in the $400 to $900 range, more if you add interior lining, bedding, or any personalizing. If you want a casket that serves both the living and the dead, ask the carpenter if he/she can outfit the coffin with shelves so it can double as a bookcase until its final use, or construct the coffin to function as a coffee table.

Loren Schieuer, the woodworker profiled in this chapter, offers three kinds of wood caskets: pine ($1,200, more with upholstery, etc.), oak ($2,100, including upholstery), and Mission ($2,500). For more information, contact Schieuer Woodworks, 211 Main Street, Pierson, Iowa 51048; 712-375-5316; www.schiwoodworks.com.

You can also build the casket yourself. For a basic design, measurements, and instructions, see Ernest Morgan's *Dealing Creatively with Death* (2001, Upper Access Books).

What You Need to Know:
Most cemeteries require that caskets be placed inside a vault, a buried concrete, metal, or plastic "box" that's designed to prevent the ground from collapsing around a decaying casket. The vault thus prevents the casket from ever touching the ground and the body from fully rejoining the elements. Before purchasing cemetery space, ask if any ground on site is open to nonvaulted burial or, if in place of a vault, you may use a concrete grave liner, which is open at the bottom. If you're burying in Vermont or New York, you may, per state law, refuse use of a vault for unspecified religious reasons.

Alternative Coffins:
A few manufacturers offer wood coffins made from "green" wood. Kent Casket Industries (888-534-7239; www.kentcasket.com) manufactures rectangular-shaped coffins from solid pine that's culled from forests certified as sustainable by the Forest Stewardship Council ($420, plus shipping). The Eco Casket ($2,795, shipping included) is made from oak grown in sustainably managed forests (800-914-9145, www.environmentalcaskets.com).

Nonwood caskets are another option. Cremation Products (800-837-0701) sells a basic corrugated cardboard container strong enough to support 450 pounds ($20, plus shipping, which runs in the $70 range, about half that within California). The cardboard coffins manufactured by Eternity International (408-777-0308; www.eeternity.com) are painted with a faux cherry, pine, or "plain" finish that gives them a woodlike appearance ($295, includes shipping). Your local crematory and/or funeral home may be willing to sell you one of its cardboard "cremation" containers for a modest price.

The Natural Burial Company (503-493-9258; www.naturalburial company.com) and Colorful Coffins (650-726-5255; www.colorful coffins.com) are among a number of companies selling caskets made from willow, bamboo, hemp, paper, and other natural materials.

It doesn't take me two minutes to walk down from the house to the little private cemetery where Sharyn is buried. I know her body is inert matter; it's not her. But her memory is there, my memory for her is there, and that is the last place we saw each other. For me, it's a comfort to have her close by.

Robert "Smiggy" Smith,
husband of Sharyn Nicholson

⚬⚭⚬

CHAPTER EIGHT:

Backyard Burial

Whenever Robert Smith feels the pull to visit his wife's grave—to remember their ten years together, maybe say a prayer—he walks down the gravel lane that slopes from the rustic cabin he and Sharyn shared in the forested foothills of the Virginia Blue Ridge. At the bottom, he crosses a narrow dirt road that snakes up from the flatlands of Sperryville and, after stepping through an opening in the thicket, enters a small clearing.

The ground's level here and ringed with towering yellow poplars mostly, smaller sassafras, the odd locust. On a mid-afternoon in early November, their brown-and-gold leaves litter this secluded glade, all but covering the rectangle of stones in the center, the flat grave marker at the near end engraved with the name of Sharyn Nicholson. Opposite the marker, rising before a fan of rosebushes, stands a statue of a winged angel, its head bowed to the spot where the forty-nine-year-old wife and mother was buried in nothing but a winding bedsheet almost seven years ago to the day.

"Sharyn loved the beauty and peace of these woods," says Robert, a bearded, Scotland-born carpenter and musician known to his friends as Smiggy, as he stands at the foot of his wife's grave on a break from felling the last of the apple trees previous homesteaders once cultivated in this hollow. "When her cancer came back, she knew it just had to run its course. We'd been up here awhile by then, and she said she wanted to die at home and be buried on the property. She even picked out the grave site."

Like many rural regions across the country, Virginia's Rappahannock County allows residents to legally bury family members on their land. And many families here have done so, going back for generations. Of the burials the Rappahannock historical society has documented from the Revolutionary War on, almost ten thousand have occurred in private cemeteries scattered throughout the county. For Smiggy, who moved into this mountain community with Sharyn not long before her breast cancer returned in the late 1990s, the tradition makes a lot of sense. "This allows you to return a body directly to the earth we all came from, without a casket, right in the woods," he says. The home burial also means he and other families don't have to use (and pay for) the burial vaults most cemeteries require or abide by their rules, which typically dictate the kind of marker a family must install, the flowers and decorations that can be placed around the grave. For Smiggy, the biggest benefit of having a family graveyard is even more basic. "Sharyn's little graveyard is just down the hill from the house," he says, "so I can walk down and visit with her anytime I feel like it."

The kind of small, family graveyard where Sharyn Nicholson now rests was a common feature of the early American landscape. Colonial-era farmers often buried their dead on their own homesteads, typically near shade trees that grew along the margins of their fields. The first wave of pioneers established similar cemeteries on land they inhabited for brief periods during their trek west, some of them creating more permanent domestic burial grounds on their settled claims.

The family graveyard took strong root in the rural South. Faithful Southerners generally lived at a greater distance from the town church and its neighboring graveyard than their Northern counterparts did; travel was difficult and the parish large, sometimes served by a single church and few clergy. Geographically and emotionally removed from church and community, the rural Southern family practiced self-sufficiency by necessity, and as with other matters of daily existence, took the care of the dead into its own hands—and burial onto its own land.

In siting the graveyard on its home turf, the Southern family had a model to work from: the plantation cemetery. Notably at Mount Vernon and Monticello, plantation families buried their own dead—and, at times, beloved hired hands—on the grounds of their estates. Though more humble than Washington's burial vault or Jefferson's enclosed grave site cum marble obelisk, the backyard cemeteries of more common folk were nonetheless lovingly tended, their gravestones maintained and the ground sometimes planted with crepe myrtles, mimosas, red cedars, or other native trees that would come to be associated with the Southern burial ground.

The home burial eventually fell from favor in the decades following the Civil War, as isolated farms and communities grew into towns, and public, as well as an increasing number of parochial, cemeteries cropped up within their boundaries. Still, in some agricultural regions, the practice continued—and continues—to take place. Sharyn Nicholson's rural burial is one of up to a dozen that occur every year in this county, according to one official; farmers throughout the South and elsewhere often bury family members in private graveyards on their grounds. And while plantation burial largely ended with the decline of plantation life, estate burials still take place. The most famous examples are those of popular entertainers. When Elvis Presley died of a heart attack in 1977, his family eventually convinced the county board of adjustment to grant a zoning variance to allow the King to be buried at Graceland, which sits within the Memphis, Tennessee, city limits.

More recently, Bill Cosby legally established a private cemetery on his family estate in Shelburne, Massachusetts, a semirural hamlet of just over two thousand residents. There, on a bitter cold afternoon at the end of January 1997, the Cosby family and a few friends buried the actor's only son, Ennis, who had been killed in a robbery attempt off the Los Angeles freeway. Walking down a snowy slope from the ground's barn, they carried Ennis's coffin to a grave freshly dug into an herb garden and, joining hands, conducted a brief service in which Cosby asked the assembled mourners to praise God for allowing them to know Ennis. Beside the grave the family later planted a pine tree, which, Cosby said, they would string with lights on his son's birthday.

*   *   *

Sharyn picked out her grave site on a mid-summer afternoon almost three months before she died. Rebounding from a round of chemotherapy, she'd taken a walk through the nearby hillside with her two dogs. At some point, she looked up and found herself standing in a level clearing of land encircled by half a dozen big poplars. "I've found the spot," she told her neighbor Jane Mullan in a phone call describing the locale when she got home. "Can you come over and take a look?"

Jane was a longtime friend who had first rented out and later sold to Sharyn and Smiggy the cabin and land where they now lived. Sharyn had called her that afternoon partly because the site she'd picked out for her grave, though just across the driveway from Sharyn's house, actually lay on land that Jane and her husband, Kevin, owned. Sharyn knew her friends were amenable to the idea of establishing a cemetery somewhere on their sixty acres. The couple had long talked about setting aside a private burial ground for their own pair of graves and those of any family and friends who wished it; after Sharyn's cancer had returned, they'd offered her the chance to start it. On a couple of occasions when Sharyn felt up to it, she and Jane had taken short hikes together through the grounds, searching for potential sites. Considering her family's needs and the general lay of the land, Jane had pointed out swaths of ground she thought suitable for a cemetery. Its exact locale she left for Sharyn to decide.

Even in decline, Sharyn brought a clear-thinking practicality to the selection of her final resting place. The grounds she had to work with would guarantee that any place she eventually picked out would be beautiful. What she wanted, though, was more than something lovely to look at: her burial site had to work for the living after she was gone.

The ground she settled on more than met her needs. For one, it offered a rare patch of level ground on this steep-climbing terrain, and with room enough to accommodate the backhoe that would be needed for the grave digging. It also lay right off the lone road that led past Sharyn's home, so, unlike other private cemeteries that are scattered throughout these hills, visitors wouldn't have to trek into the woods to reach it. Such easy access would matter particularly to Sharyn's almost seventy-year-old mother, who, Sharyn thought, might regularly visit her grave site.

Best of all to Sharyn was the glade's proximity to her beloved cabin, nestled into the forested hillside, with the huge flower and vegetable garden she tended out front. Smiggy would be able walk the hundred yards down their lane anytime he wanted; her friends and family would have easy going, as well, on the one day they'd carry her body on its final journey from house to grave.

Jane had seen the spot Sharyn described over the phone, and knew it was an ideal site for a cemetery. Walking it with Sharyn after that call, she and Kevin saw the benefits Sharyn had enumerated and then some. For their purposes, the clearing sits on a section of property they had no intention of later building on or selling out of the family. The land itself falls away on two sides, but it could be expanded along the western edge to accommodate additional graves, for the two of them and a handful of other friends. Potential contamination of water supplies wasn't an issue, either. The stream that flows at the base of the mountain lies more than a hundred yards down, and the site itself doesn't rest directly above it. Standing in the clearing with Sharyn, Jane and Kevin told her she could use it for her burial.

"She was relieved to have that taken care of," Jane says. Afterward, when she drove Sharyn back from chemotherapy treatments in Charlottesville, Jane would sometimes stop the car at the opening of the now claimed cemetery ground. Sharyn was often too weak to get out of the car and walk into the glade itself, so the women would look over at it from their seats. "I really like it here," Sharyn would say on occasion, according to Jane. "I'm glad this is where I'm going to be buried."

Sharyn gained strength over the rest of that summer, and by September felt well enough to take a vacation in Hawaii with her teenage daughter, Summer. Back in Sperryville, Jane researched laws regarding the home cemetery her friend wanted to be buried in. She knew other people who had established private burial grounds on their land, but wanted to know exactly what was required. The first thing she did was consult Lisa Carlson's *Caring for the Dead*. The state-by-state compendium of funeral laws mentioned no explicit roadblocks against burial on one's private property in Virginia.

The family lawyer she then called and visited confirmed Carlson's reading of the Virginia Code. The state law, she said, expressly permits family cemeteries, as long as they're two hundred fifty yards from the nearest residence (or closer with the home owner's permission) and three hundred yards from wells that supply drinking water to the public. Individual counties, municipalities, and towns may impose their own additional restrictions. But Rappahannock County, the largely rural county in which Jane's acreage sat, offered few. The county code permits families to establish "family graveyards" on their property in all but commercial districts and mobile home parks. Jane's land, which rests within a large agricultural zone and is far from any drinking water (Smiggy, whose home was less than two hundred fifty yards from the planned site, would, of course, give his approval), may thus legally hold her planned cemetery. She didn't even have to notify the county of her intention or gain a permit to start it.*

Virginia's not unusual in allowing private cemeteries. "Many states allow you to bury a body on your own property if you live in a rural area outside the city or village limits," says Lisa Carlson, author of the book Jane consulted. Several of those states spell out a couple of specific requirements, mostly having to do with how deep the grave must be dug and how far away from water supplies it has to be. In New Mexico, for example, home burials can't take place within fifty yards of any body of water; to comply with New Jersey law, families have to cover any adult-size casket with at least four feet of earth.

Just because a state allows—or doesn't expressly disallow—a domestic cemetery doesn't mean families may necessarily establish one. County and municipal zoning and/or health boards often weigh in with their own set of laws addressing the siting of home cemeteries within their boundaries. Generally, those laws ban private graveyards outright unless they're out in the country. "If you're in an urban or suburban area, the town isn't likely to take too kindly if you bury Aunt Minnie twenty-five feet from your neighbor's badminton net," as Carlson puts it.

In areas where backyard burials are allowed, local authorities may require families to meet a number of requirements to gain a cemetery permit, such as getting the land surveyed and declared a cemetery, recording the cemetery with the deed to the land, setting up a trust fund to pay for the ground's upkeep in perpetuity, enclosing the site with a fence. Some governments may leave final approval up to the zoning/planning boards and/or boards of health.

---

* There may be some argument as to the legality of Jane's claim. County code does not define what exactly constitutes a "family graveyard," but one county official contends it means only family members may be buried there. Jane's lawyer, who says plenty of non-family members have been buried in family graveyards with no issue, disagrees. If Jane wanted, she could seek to have her graveyard reclassified as a non-church-related cemetery where both family and friends may be buried, which is allowed by special permit in the agricultural zone in which her property sits.

Jane was in the middle of researching those legalities in the state and local codes when she got a call from Smiggy. Sharyn had collapsed in her hotel in Hawaii, he told her, and she'd been taken to the hospital. Doctors there found that her cancer had spread to the brain, liver, kidneys, and intestines. Immediate treatment would shrink the tumors enough so Sharyn could endure a flight home, but no medical intervention would stop the spread. Jane flew out to nurse Sharyn through the treatments and bring her home to die.

When Sharyn returned a month later Smiggy had just about finished building a sunroom, where his wife could lie on a hospital bed Jane had brought over and take in the views of their hollow. Sharyn called hospice, so she'd be able to easily get medication for the pain. But Jane, who had attended other deaths in the area through her work as a healing arts practitioner, set up a daily rotation of nurses who were longtime friends of Sharyn's to handle her day-to-day care—tending to Sharyn, cleaning the house, making the meals. The doctors in Hawaii didn't expect Sharyn to last more than a couple of weeks, but back at home she battled on for two months. Looking back, Smiggy's grateful for the time he had with his wife there in their house and for the community of women who made it possible. "It was so much better to have her here than in some hospital or nursing home, where she'd have strangers looking after her," he says. "I don't know how I would have managed without these angels of mercy."

Sharyn Nicholson took her last breath on a rainy evening in November. She had been in and out of consciousness and had gone without food or water for days. That afternoon her breathing had come slower and slower. Around sundown, with no sign of a struggle, it stopped for good.

Smiggy, Jane, and one of the nurses were at Sharyn's bedside when she died. "We all knew she was near death, but you're never really ready for it to happen," Smiggy tells me at his kitchen table one bright October afternoon, looking into the sunroom where his wife passed away. When the end, indeed, came, Smiggy was so distraught that he staggered into the yard howling in grief and, with the rain pouring down, took refuge for the night in one of the cars parked on the grounds. "It was too much to be in the house," he says. "I just had to get out."

Like most states, Virginia allows families to handle the after-death care of their own. Jane had "midwifed" a number of home deaths in the area, and so called Sharyn's caretakers to ask for their help in laying out the body. It was dark by the time they all assembled a few hours later. Summer, Sharyn's teenage daughter from a previous marriage who'd just learned of her mother's death herself after returning home, joined them.

The lights had been on in the house, but before the work began someone turned them off and placed lit candles around the sunroom, illuminating this place of final death—and Sharyn herself—in a soft glow. Circling their friend's body, the women removed the pajamas Sharyn had died in and, dipping hand cloths into a basin of soapy water, washed and then dried her; the hospital bed they made over with fresh sheets. Sharyn had asked to be buried in a long, white nightgown a friend had made her. Working together, the women fit the nightgown onto her still-limp frame and rubbed lotion onto Sharyn's face and hands. The arms they then crossed at the chest, covering the lower half of her body with a sheet. Thinking of Sharyn's mother, Susan Levick, an oncology nurse who'd known Sharyn for more than twenty years, took a moment to tie a bandanna around her friend's head and jaw, so Sharyn's mouth would be closed when her mother first saw her.

The laying out, which Susan describes as a "beautiful experience," took less than an hour. When it was done, Jane began a round of calls to Sharyn's mother and a few close friends, informing them of the death and funeral arrangements. During her decline, Sharyn had given specific instructions for her funeral and burial. "She wanted to keep it all very simple," says Jane, who had taken to writing down Sharyn's wishes whenever her friend relayed them. "There'd be no embalming, no coffin, no public viewing. Just her wrapped in a sheet and buried in the ground." All of which was permitted by law. Burial in a coffin is the usual requirement of an individual cemetery, not of federal, state, or local legislation; in a private burial ground, a body could be buried without any kind of container at all.

Sharyn liked the idea of being interred with only a sheet wound around her. An uncoffined burial was the most direct way she could think of to rejoin the cycles of nature so evident in the woods surrounding them, she told Smiggy, of returning her body to the dust it was drawn from, unhindered. In choosing such a burial, Sharyn was also reviving an ancient tradition that others before her had practiced for similar reasons, including the Hebrews and some early Romans, and that orthodox Israeli Jews and some Muslims around the world continue to practice to this day. As late as the seventeenth century, the majority of English families routinely laid their dead to rest sans coffin, wrapping them in linen sheets knotted at the foot and head or, later, in robelike shrouds, and lowering the bundled remains directly into the grave. The coffin, with its ability to protect the body for its literal resurrection on Judgment Day, eventually displaced the sheet and shroud as the primary covering for the dead. The burial cloth itself, however, wasn't entirely lost, reappearing in the "grave clothes" in which we outfit the dead for their coffined burial today.

Sharyn could have been laid out indefinitely. States almost never require that a body be embalmed. Unlike many of them, Virginia sets no limit on the amount of time an unembalmed body can be held before it's buried, without at least cooling it via refrigeration or dry ice. Still, since Sharyn didn't want a viewing, the women saw no reason to delay the burial, and scheduled it for eleven the next morning. In a final call, Jane asked her husband, Kevin, to contact the backhoe operator and ask him to dig the grave in the early morning.

Susan then got on the phone to the hospice social worker who'd been assigned to Sharyn and told her of the death. Susan had once worked with this same hospice unit and said she'd handle the after-death-care matters, saving the social worker a trip up the mountain. Before hanging up, Susan asked about gaining and filing a death certificate. Smiggy could legally handle the form himself, filling out the top part, getting Sharyn's primary physician in nearby Culpeper to complete the medical section, and then filing the finished form at the local health department. It requires a lot of running around, so the social worker recommended that the family use a local funeral director to handle those multiple transactions. In the deaths she'd attended over the years, Jane had sometimes worked with Found and Sons Funeral Homes in Culpeper. That night she talked to Scott Found, who agreed to take care of the death certificate and file obituaries with local newspapers. For his services, he charged Jane $100.

With the paperwork handled, the women settled into the kitchen and made plans for tomorrow's burial and a larger memorial service to take place the day after. Soon after Sharyn's death, her cousin Michael had come to the house and offered to sit for the vigil. "Sharyn and I were very close," says Michael, who lives in a cabin just down the mountain road from Sharyn and Smiggy's home. "I knew her spirit would still be near her body and I wanted to be there with her." The women left around eleven, and Michael settled into a chair next to his cousin, now dressed for her burial. "I told her how much I was going to miss her, but that I was glad her suffering was over. I was also reassuring her that I'd look after Smiggy and Summer. 'Don't worry, honey,' I told her. 'We'll take care of everything here. You've got nothing to worry about now. You just go on.'"

Susan returns to the house early the next morning. It's a beautiful start to an autumn day, clear and crisp, and Susan had come to clean up the flower beds outside the sunroom so they'd look nice for the morning's burial and for the memorial service the following day. Susan will remember many of the details of these three days, but the strongest memory she'll take away happens now. Weeding the garden, she looks into the sunroom and sees Sharyn laid out on her raised hospital bed. "The sun was pouring through the window right down on her, and shining through the stained-glass panel that hung above her head," Susan recalls. "She looked really gorgeous, like in a painting."

While Susan tends the garden, her husband, Phil, works in a neighbor's woodshop, crafting a board on which to carry Sharyn down to the grave site. When he brings it to the house a little before ten o'clock, a small group has already collected in the sunroom, mostly the same women who'd prepared Sharyn's body, plus Smiggy, Michael, and Sharyn's mother, who'd been able to spend some time alone with her daughter earlier that morning.

Sharyn had told Jane she wanted to be wrapped in a blue sheet and buried with objects that held special meaning for her. Now, as the sheet is spread out beneath her body, the women in turn place those objects on top of Sharyn: small stones, crystals, favorite pieces of jewelry, feathers, pictures of people she loved, notes from friends. With each winding of the sheet, more objects are laid on, until, finally, Sharyn is completely bound up and covered in the last of the cloth.

With its rounded edges and sanded top, the plank Phil had crafted resembles a surfboard. After the wrapping's done, he, Michael, and Smiggy lift Sharyn off the bed and slip the board beneath her, squarely positioning the body on top. At this point it occurs to the group that they'll need to somehow secure the body to the board so it won't slide off during the procession to the grave. Using regular rope seemed too vulgar, somehow. To some gentle laughter, someone suggests enlisting Smiggy's neckties for the task. A bunch are then produced from Smiggy's closet and knotted together to form two straps. One of them is then stretched across Sharyn's chest, each end tied to the hand grips Phil cut into both sides of the plank; the other strap reaches over her legs.

Sharyn hadn't asked anyone in particular to serve as her pallbearers, but four of the men automatically step forward, Smiggy and Michael, plus Phil and Kevin. After her body's secured to the board, each man grasps a handle and raises the board off the bed on which Sharyn had died and been laid out. They walk the board through the sliding glass doors into the yard, where they're met by a dozen or so close friends, neighbors, and their children, who fall in with the others.

Smiggy, grasping a front corner of the board, leads the procession down the hill. No one speaks. "It was fall, leaves were all over the ground," says Jane. "So all you heard was the sound of our feet crunching the leaves as we walked."

The excavator Kevin called had come and gone early that morning. Entering the clearing, the silent funeral train sees the rectangular, six-foot hole the backhoe had scooped out of the earth, a mound of dirt piled off to the side with a bunch of long-handled shovels lying beside it. At the foot of the grave, someone had placed a cardboard box filled with the scores of get-well cards Sharyn wanted buried with her.

Careful of their footing in the leaf litter, the men walk into the glade. At a spot near the grave they set Sharyn down and begin to loop a pair of ropes through the handles of the board, one each supporting the head and feet. As they do, the group fans out around the hole. Jane uses this unscripted moment to strew into the darkened cavity handfuls of dried rose petals she'd carried down in a large bowl. Sharyn loved roses, Jane tells me later, and the two of them had plucked and dried petals from the flowers she'd received for just this purpose.

The bare earth at the bottom of the grave is covered in a red blanket of petals by the time the men pull the ropes secured to the board and raise Sharyn off the ground. Working in tandem the two teams of men shuffle to positions that leave them standing on opposite sides of the grave, Sharyn suspended over the cavity between them. This is the last time anyone will be able to touch Sharyn, and Susan takes the opportunity to reach over and quickly slip her hand beneath her friend's shoulder blade, a spot "that always hurt her and I would sometimes rub at night to ease the pain," she says.

And then the men lower Sharyn into the grave. She descends slowly as the ropes slip through each man's grip, and then gently touches bottom. After the men drop the rope ends into the grave, Jane invites some of the children to sprinkle the last of the rose petals down on top of their friend and neighbor. Other adults now step forward and toss in their own flowers and, because they knew of Sharyn's last wishes, handfuls of the get-well cards and letters from that box.

When the last of the cards is delivered to the grave Jane asks the assembled group to join hands and recite the Lord's Prayer. "Anyone's welcome to share a few words about Sharyn if they'd like," Jane says following the prayer. One by one most everyone offers a blessing, thanks, some expression of love. Referring to Sharyn's strong will, Michael remarks that "Sharyn didn't just touch your life, she punched it!" which gets a laugh. Another close friend of Sharyn and Jane's then begins to sing "Swing Low, Sweet Chariot" and all join in. Some people are crying now; many are looking into the inhabited grave. Without planning it, Sharyn's daughter, Summer, and Smiggy simultaneously reach for shovels and laden them with dirt. Standing on opposite sides of the grave, they pitch their earthen load into the cavity, on top of the mother and wife lying at the bottom, wound in a blue sheet and covered over with rose petals and cards. "You know the sound dirt makes when it hits something," says Susan recalling that poignant moment. "With all those cards on top of Sharyn, the dirt made a really different sound when it hit. Like a rustling or tinkling, that was soft and beautiful."

His part of this ages-old ritual done, Smiggy hands his shovel to Sharyn's mother, who pitches another spadeful of dirt into the grave before passing the shovel on to her neighbor. Most everyone takes a turn with the shovel; a few grab dirt with their bare hands and drop it into the hole. When the round is done, the women and children head back to the house. The half dozen men left behind—Smiggy and the other pallbearers, a few others—grab the remaining shovels and begin filling in the grave. In twenty minutes, the last of the dirt mound is gone. The men then smooth the top of the grave with their shovels and walk back up the lane to the house, just as silently as they'd come.

Two days following Sharyn's burial, Smiggy returns to her grave for the first time. "I walked down to say my final farewells in peace and quiet," he says. "Just the two of us together."

A memorial service had been held the day before in his yard. Nearly two hundred people had shown up. The hillside couldn't accommodate their cars, so the guests parked at the base of the mountain and either hiked up or hopped one of the carpools that shuttled them to the house. Like the day of the burial, this one was clear, a bit warmer, the woods in peak color. Standing in front of a makeshift altar, Jane led the group in prayers and hymns. Children at the local school where Sharyn sometimes taught read poems and sang songs for their former teacher; a woman played the harp. Family and friends then walked to the altar or stood up from the seats filling the yard to offer their own words in favor of Sharyn. Susan, who sat with Sharyn's inconsolable mother, remembers one little girl mustering the courage to stand up before the large crowd to say, "I want you to know that Sharyn was my friend. I am going to miss her. I know we all are."

There was potluck lunch afterward, the dishes set out on tables outside. Over the next couple of hours, guests mingled in the yard and walked down to Sharyn's grave site in small groups, some planting the bulbs Jane had laid out there—tulips, lilies, daffodils that would adorn the now barren mound in the coming spring. Others added their own personal touches.

When Smiggy comes down that next morning alone, the grave site shows their handiwork. A statue of a winged angel stands at the head of the grave. Flowers cover the mounded earth. Wind chimes, crystal amulets, and webbed dreamcatchers hang from the tree branches. The grave itself has been lined with blocks of blue quartz that half a dozen local children had found on the mountain and laid down here; the rose-shaped candles they'd fashioned from melted wax are stuck in the dirt near the angel.

Standing at his wife's grave, decorated by the community that loved her, Smiggy feels a mix of emotions. "I was devastated by her death. She was my happiness in life," he says. "But she had been so tormented by pain and aches that I was glad she was at peace." Smiggy found some solace, too, in knowing he'd been by her side, in their own home, during much of her decline and, with the help of her friends, had handled her sickness and burial just as she wanted.

And at least Sharyn is nearby. "I feel she's still around," he says, motioning toward the poplars ringing this little cemetery. "Somehow her spirit, her vibration is out here, whether it's lingering in the woods or among the trees." Smiggy often comes here to connect with that spirit; one day, he'll join what remains of the body. "I've made it clear to my friends that when my time comes, I want them to cart me down the hill and plant me back in Mother Earth, right next to Sharyn."

Resource Guide: *Backyard Burial*

What:

Burying the body of a family member on one's own, usually rural, property.

The Laws:

A few states—including California, Indiana, and Washington—require their residents to bury their dead in established cemeteries (unless, in the case of Washington, they're interring someone on their own island). Other states, however, allow families to create domestic burial grounds on their own land. Some of these states place certain restrictions on the placement of the graveyard (requiring a certain distance from water bodies, neighboring residences, utility poles, and the like) and the amount of soil that must cover the casket (anywhere from eighteen inches to four feet), among others.

Even if your state permits, or doesn't expressly ban, private graveyards, you'll still need to meet county and municipal/town regulations to do it legally. (Contact your county/town clerk for the exact requirements.) Laws vary from place to place, but in general they tend to prohibit home cemeteries in urban and suburban locales.

You're likely to have better luck if you live out in the country, in land falling within rural or agricultural zones. Even then you'll probably have to follow some guidelines in siting the graveyard. In addition to the kinds of requirements demanded by the state and county, local regulations may ask that you survey the land, record the plot, and register the cemetery with the county clerk; set up a fund to maintain the grounds well after your death; and perhaps even use a grave liner. In some cases, you'll have to gain the approval of the zoning board and/or board of health.

If you live in a rural area where no specific laws regulate home burial, you'll reduce your risk of potential conflicts with authorities now or later by considering the lay of the land. "The *E. coli* that's naturally in a body will disappear through natural decomposition, but when choosing a spot for a family burial ground it's good practice to locate it one hundred fifty feet or more from a water supply," says Lisa Carlson, author of *Caring for the Dead*. The site should also be a good distance from overhead power lines (which could be replaced with buried cable some day, possibly intruding on the home burial site and, in some cases, requiring the body's removal), and the bottom of the casket should rest six feet below the surface of the earth.

What You Should Know:
No state law requires that a body be buried in a casket or other container. Regular cemeteries generally insist that a casket be used and that the casket be placed in a vault. In your own graveyard, however, you may bury a family member in nothing but a cloth or shroud. If you do, it's a good idea to bury remains many feet below the ground to keep animals at bay.

Establishing a family burial ground on your own land offers plenty of benefits—the freedom to visit when you wish, plant your own flowers, erect markers of your own choosing or skip them altogether. But there are risks as well, says Carlson. Property that boasts a backyard graveyard may be harder to sell, and if it is sold, there's nothing to compel future owners to treat the space with reverence. In many states, the cemetery becomes a permanent easement on the land, which ensures the graves can never be moved. Some states, however, may allow future owners to declare a private graveyard on their property "abandoned" after so many years of disuse and have the bodies moved to an established cemetery elsewhere.

Some states require the owners of land on which a private cemetery sits to allow family members of the deceased the right to visit the grave. You'll help secure your progeny's visitation rights by recording the burial plot with the deed to the land.

No law prevents you from burying the cremated remains of your loved ones on your private property, rural or urban.

Chris was very much in touch with nature. The [woodland grave] where he's buried at Ramsey Creek is the kind of place I could see him camping out in for the weekend, just sitting there by the stream, listening to the water and the birds, watching everything emerge from its winter slumber, like it is now. And I'm sure he's pushing it all along.

Rebecca Cochran,
cousin of Chris Nichols

CHAPTER NINE:

The Natural Cemetery

More than a hundred grave sites lie scattered across the burial ground of Ramsey Creek Preserve, an ecological cemetery that sits in the shadow of the Blue Ridge Mountains, just outside Westminster, South Carolina. But if you hike the two-mile network of rough trail that winds through these thirty acres of heavily forested wood, you might never know bodies were buried here. You'll come across no upright headstone or monument to the dead, no burial plot marked off with stone edging or linked chain. Nowhere will you find vases of perfect plastic flowers, live plants blooming in cellophane-wrapped pottery.

What greets you when you join the trail at a gap in the trees that serves as an entrance to Ramsey Creek is an eastern woodland timbered with mostly yellow and short-leaf pine, half a dozen varieties of oak, American beech. In the understory, white-and-pink flowering dogwood rise from the matted forest floor, with chalk maples and a broad-leafed rhododendron the locals call deer tongue laurel. Altogether some two hundred twenty-five different plant species cover this landscape, a few of them rare and endangered—like the crested coral root, a tiny, leafless orchid never before seen in this county.

White-tailed deer regularly pass through here on their way to the big wilds of Sumter National Forest, three miles west. Wild turkey has been spotted in the brush, the occasional black bear. The Ramsey Creek itself, a narrow, curving stream that fixes the property's eastern border, teems with redeye bass, chubbs, and yellow-fin shiners. The creek rushes the granite shoals forcefully at one stretch, producing a din loud enough to be heard nearly anywhere you stand in the preserve.

Walking through Ramsey Creek is to experience Carolina country as it must have looked when Cherokee still roamed these hillsides, before cotton farmers settled the piedmont in the early 1800s and began clearing land. With one important difference: scores of flat fieldstones that lie at irregular intervals along the trail's edge. Half buried in the dirt and covered over with vegetation and decaying pine nettles, the stones are often inconspicuous enough that you wouldn't be the first hiker to walk right by them. But stumble onto one, brush it clean, and you'll see that its face is engraved with a name, range of dates, and, often, an epitaph. These native fieldstones, you then realize, are more than the mere product of local geology; they're grave markers, and below each one a body or its ashes lies buried.

Ramsey Creek is a cemetery, but its grounds are so natural, so free of the usual funereal structures that you could wander into it by chance on an afternoon hike through these hills and never even know you've strayed into a graveyard. "Visitors are surprised when they first see Ramsey Creek because they expect it to look like a regular cemetery with a little bit of nature around it," says Billy Campbell, a fifty-something Westminster family physician who founded Ramsey Creek and serves as president of Memorial Ecosystems, the cemetery's parent company. "We're a woodland burial ground, an actual forest where burials also take place."

Since the fall of 1998, when a stillborn infant named Hope was laid to rest in a small grave Billy dug with two rafting buddies, well over a hundred burials have been conducted in these woods. In keeping with its leafy environs, each has followed a natural course. "We take a dust-to-dust approach to burial," Billy tells me one bright afternoon, taking a break from hauling construction debris from an abandoned country church he'd recently moved into a clearing at the burial wood's edge, for future use as an all-faith chapel. Remains are returned directly to the earth, in either plain cloth shrouds or simple coffins manufactured from nontoxic, easily biodegradable materials, like cardboard or pine. Vaults are banned, embalmed remains prohibited. "Our idea is to allow physical bodies to degrade naturally and be incorporated into other living things, the trees and flowers," explains Billy. "We want them to be caught up in life's continuing cycles of growth and death, decomposition and rebirth."

In Billy's green scheme—his resurrection of an ages-old, traditional burial he dubs "people plantings"—the dead literally nourish and sustain a living forest. When Billy gets around to punching out a floor-to-ceiling window in a part of the chapel that backs onto his cemetery, visitors will be able to sit in pews and take in the native piedmont their beloved departed are perpetuating for future generations. No stately monument or grand headstone will disturb the picturesque scene before them. Ramsey Creek allows only small, flat fieldstones collected on site or taken from a similar geological stratum to serve as grave markers; within a hundred years, even they will weather into the landscape. Eventually, the only sign that bodies were ever buried here will be the wood itself. For Billy, that's the whole idea. A fitting monument to a life well lived isn't an inert headstone devoted to one's memory, he asserts: it's more good earth. "What finer legacy could you leave behind than acres of beautiful woods, your final act in death contributing to the preservation of wild life?"

If such a place had existed in 1985, Billy would have buried his father there. But when George Campbell died of respiratory failure at the age of fifty-four, his family, like the rest of us, was left with the less than green services proffered by the local funeral home. The director, who happened to be a friend, presented the family with the gold standard of American burial: a top-of-the-line metal casket that cost almost as much as a new car and a lined concrete vault guaranteed to remain leak-free for a hundred years. The Campbells chose a cheaper oak casket (the same model the actor who played *Bonanza*'s Hoss Cartwright was buried in). But when Billy suggested a vault was unnecessary—because it didn't matter if it leaked and, even if it did, who would ever know?—the director was aghast.

Without a vault, a wooden casket would quickly disintegrate, the director told Billy, and the family would have to "deal with the fact that dirt and water would go in on the loved one." The argument held little sway with Billy—the body would decay with or without the vault, he contended—but the rest of the family was cool to Billy's attempts to green up his father's burial. In the end, the Campbells, to Billy's dismay, plunked down $4,000 for the standard send-off. "My father's body was pumped full of toxic [embalming] chemicals, placed in a casket, which was placed in a vault, buried in an overmanicured graveyard, and covered with pea gravel," he says. At the open casket viewing in the local funeral home, Billy's father, preserved to appear as if he had just slipped off to sleep and outfitted in his best suit, "looked like he was going to a great sales meeting in the sky."

Billy and his family buried George Campbell at the Hopewell Cemetery on a cold, windy day in mid-March. Billy, who would rather have "laid my father's body to rest in a wild setting, full of the peace and quiet of nature," found the whole funeral experience more distressing than soothing. It also inspired him to consider what that ideal, working cemetery in a "wild setting" might look like and how he might actually bury the dead there.

One model he'd already read about: the *ples masalai,* or sacred forests, of New Guinea. The native Fore buried their dead just outside these wooded areas, Billy learned, and because they believed the spirits of their dead took up residence there, held these woods as sacred and thus off-limits to most human activity. As a consequence, New Guinea was filled with pockets of unspoiled wilderness, stands of original forest in the midst of densely populated settlements and farmlands.

Another Fore burial practice proved equally intriguing: the burying of the dead in vegetable gardens. At some point the Fore had recognized that plants grew better in places were bodies were buried, and began planting crops there. The burials reminded Billy of the film strips he'd watched in grade school that showed American Indians using fish to fertilize corn crops. For a people considered primitive, the Fore, like Native Americans, had been amazingly astute, Billy thought; they'd made the connection between death and fertility.

These ideas were churning inside Billy's head around the time his father died. A couple of months later they came together: "I was thinking about the Fore when I was working out how to create a cemetery I'd want my father to be buried in, and this little light went off," says Billy. "I thought: Why not combine the Fore's insights into death and fertility with their ideas about the sacred forest?"

The latter, as Billy originally conceived it, would translate into a kind of nature preserve whose cemetery designation would place it off-limits to a popular manifestation of "human activity" in the industrialized Western world: development. The "memorial forest," as Billy would eventually call it, would thus serve a dual purpose. It would offer families a truly natural environment to be buried in, and, in doing so, also serve to actually preserve land threatened by the bulldozer. The natural cemetery scheme even provided a means to fund the land's purchase and maintenance: the burial fees themselves. Taking the idea a step further, Billy envisioned combining burial with ecological restoration of the land. Working with biologists, he'd craft a science-based plan to return the cemetery ground to its more natural state, using bodies to renew depleted soil, planting native species at grave sites, regreening areas prone to erosion.

As for a piece of rural land that could serve as a testing ground for his ecological cemetery, Billy knew just the place: the forty acres he owned along the banks of Ramsey Creek. A former cotton farm a few miles down the road from where *Deliverance* was filmed, the land boasted a broad meadow and a large parcel of second-growth forest that bordered the fast-running Ramsey Creek.

Billy couldn't have picked a more ideal state in which to site a cemetery preserve. At the time, South Carolina lacked the restrictive funeral laws that govern many states, which limit the size and placement of cemeteries and require a host of conditions for approval (such as the posting of expensive bonds, the creation of paved access roads to graves). State oversight, in fact, seemed completely lacking. When Billy's wife, Kimberley, called the state capitol to inquire about requirements for establishing a cemetery, she was told the cemetery board had disbanded and that the "power of authority" in such matters had disappeared with it. In early 1998, the state's Department of Natural Resources came up to survey the property, mostly out of curiosity, says Billy. Later that year, he and Kimberley incorporated Memorial Ecosystems and officially opened Ramsey Creek Preserve to burials in the fall of 1998.

Sharon Perry can't say for sure just how her son Chris Nichols learned about Ramsey Creek, but isn't surprised he had. An ecological cemetery in the middle of the woods is just the kind of place her "gentle New Age hippie" would have heard about in the circle of environmentalists in which he traveled. It was also, she knew, an idea sure to appeal to a twenty-eight-year-old stonemason who lived on a ten-acre farm in the rural, northwest corner of South Carolina and supplied vegetarian restaurants in nearby Greenville with his own organic produce.

Sharon first heard of Ramsey Creek herself in the fall of 2003, just weeks after she'd taken Chris to the emergency room when he'd called to tell her he'd gone to the bathroom and found a large pool of blood in the toilet bowl. At the Greenville hospital a team of doctors started Chris through a protracted battery of procedures—CAT scans, MRIs, a colonoscopy. In mid-October, they announced their diagnosis: Chris had aggressive colon cancer. Surgery to remove the cancerous tumor would dangerously compromise Chris's immune system, they said, and scheduled him instead for radical chemotherapy.

In the following months Sharon and Chris shuttled back and forth to Greenville for the treatments and, with the rest of the family, worked to remain upbeat. Early on, sometime after his mother had shorn his beloved dreadlocks—a moment Sharon, who'd always hated her son's hair, calls "bittersweet"—Chris broached the possibility of his death. "Mom, I'm not ready to die. I don't want to die," he told her. "But if that's what happens, I want you to look at this place in Westminster that does green burial." Sharon had never heard of the concept and didn't want to pursue it, still hopeful of a cure and, by her own admission, "not ready to talk about death." By New Year's, however, even she had to admit there seemed little reason for optimism. Despite all the chemo treatments, cancer had spread into Chris's liver, lungs, and pancreas, progressing, as she says, "like a fast-moving monster."

All this time, Chris's medical team had offered little on his prognosis, sensing perhaps the family's reluctance to accept the fact of Chris's decline. At the end of January, the family finally sat down with Chris's primary physician to ask the hard questions. In so many words the doctor told them the truth of what they were facing: Chris was dying, and the end was just a matter of time.

The family moved Chris into a comfortable lake house that friends had offered them—one that Chris's dad, James, a home builder, had constructed and lived two doors down from—and in mid-February called in hospice. Sharon and her sister, Debbie, a nurse, attended to Chris around the clock. In the mornings and evenings they prayed with him, every night they gave him sponge baths; the two read him stories aloud and sat quietly with him. Visitors came and went. At the beginning of May, Chris took a marked turn for the worse, and the family decided the time had come to talk with him about funeral arrangements. Jim,

Sharon's oldest son, offered to raise the subject. On a quiet afternoon when his brother was alert, he went into Chris's room, sat down next to his bed, and, admitting later that "it was all I could do to get it out," asked his brother if he'd thought about what kind of burial and funeral he'd like. Tilting his head, Chris considered a moment before telling Jim that he wanted a "green burial" at an eco cemetery over in Westminster, so he could join "all the other living organisms in the ground." As for the funeral, he said, growing more animated, he wanted everyone to wear tie-dyed T-shirts. For Jim, his brother's wish to be buried at Ramsey Creek was remarkable on many levels, including the cemetery's proximity to their home. "At the time, Ramsey Creek was only one of two places in the country where you could do the kind of green burial Chris wanted," says Jim, "and it just happens to be no more than twenty minutes from here."

Ramsey Creek is the first—and until recently, the only—modern woodland burial ground in the United States. But the idea of a green burial in nature is hardly novel, says Billy. "For most of human history, it used to be the default."

In the early years of civilization and probably well before, the bodies of commoners were sometimes buried in simple pits dug into the ground, with corpses covered in little more than the clothing already on their backs. As with the aboriginal Fore who first inspired Billy's own woodland cemetery, many rural villages in old India buried the remains of their dead in "sacred groves," forested preserves that were thought to shelter mighty spirits and deities and were thus placed off-limits to timbering, fruit harvesting, and most other human activities.

For thousands of years, orthodox Jews have honored the Old Testament admonition to return "dust to dust" by interring unembalmed remains wrapped in nothing but shrouds or in plain, wood coffins into whose bottoms holes have sometimes been bored to invite the elements.

The garden has been a particularly popular natural burial site. In the 1600s, British Quakers often chose to be buried in their gardens, sans grave markers, preferring a simple return there than to the crowded churchyard, with its landscape of headstones. A century-plus later, Jean-Jacques Rousseau followed a similar course. In keeping with his belief in the superiority of the natural state of things, the French philosopher was laid to rest on an island of poplar boughs within the estate garden of a friend at Ermenonville.

The very first settlers to the New World took a natural approach to burial, mostly by necessity. Early colonists sometimes buried their dead in whatever outdoor environment they happened to expire in, laid to rest in rude graves marked with fieldstones or simple wooden crosses. Pioneers trundling across the American frontier reserved sections of prairie for their domestic burying grounds. Spared from the plow, some of these pioneer graveyards today serve as rare exemplars of native, tall grass prairieland; dozens throughout the Midwest boast such troves of native species that they've been designated nature preserves. Naturalist Aldo Leopold noted a similar botanical phenomenon farther north, calling one aged, country grave site near his sand farm a "yard-square relic of original Wisconsin."

Ramsey Creek's truest forebear, however, may be the rural cemetery movement of the early to late 1800s. Up to that time the popular city cemetery had grown so overcrowded with rotting corpses that some produced fetid odors that wafted into nearby neighborhoods and, according to prominent physicians of the day, spread disease-causing "miasmas." The miasma theory never proved itself out, but it nonetheless spurred city officials and groups of private citizens to explore a healthier means of burial.

Taking inspiration from Rousseau's garden burial and a then-widespread romantic idealization of nature, they crafted what came to be known as "garden cemeteries." First at Père-Lachaise (1804) in Paris and, in this country, at Mount Auburn (1831) outside Boston, the new graveyard took root in spacious, pastoral landscapes of bosky glens and grassy meadows, ponds teeming with fish and bird life, babbling brooks, and, typically, promontories that afforded dramatic views of the nearby city. Undulating networks of foot and cart paths, well shaded by tall, native timbers, wound throughout.

Families adorned the woodsy precincts with prominent, often stylized grave markers, including statues of petal-strewing maidens, towering white marble obelisks, massive chamber tombs built in the classical style. But the Arcadian, naturalist quality of the burial ground prevailed, and attracted harried urbanites from the crowded urban cores. By the thousands they came, delighting in the fresh air, quiet, shaded strolling paths, the safe and increasingly rare communion with the natural world. Mount Auburn and its followers—Laurel Hill in Philadelphia, Brooklyn's Green-Wood, among them—proved such popular pleasure grounds that they inspired the creation of the first public parks in North

America, which were essentially rural cemeteries devoid of graves and overt reminders of mortality.

To its designers, the rural cemetery served a moral as well as recreational purpose. Contact with the bucolic burial ground was thought to provide frenetic, stressed city dwellers with what Romantic poet William Wordsworth called the "soothing influences of nature . . . [the] renovation and decay which the fields and woods offer to the notice of the serious and contemplative mind."

The rural cemetery gradually faded from the funereal landscape by century's end, replaced by the parklike "forest lawns" that are still popular today. The new ground maintained some of the pastoral character that marked its predecessor, but the natural features assumed a well-pruned, orderly look that could be replicated on any property, anywhere—and was. Expansive mowed greens replaced the rural cemetery's leafy glens; ornamental headstones were leveled into flat, nondescript grave markers, a benefit mostly to efficient lawn mowing.

For Billy, the forest lawn represents a "bastardization" of the rural model, a banning of real nature from a funereal Eden. Ramsey Creek is his effort to regreen the deathscape. "We're reviving the idea of those 1830s rural cemeteries. We have a place for people, the babbling brook, and woodlands, examples that produce the Wordsworthian stimulation to the 'contemplative mind,'" he says. "At the same time, we're taking the rural model forward, adding to it conservation science—the land-saving and restoration components."

In both spirit and intent, the best fit to Billy's model lies four thousand miles across the Atlantic in parts of Great Britain. Home to the natural death movement that has since sprung up on these shores, Great Britain produced the first modern woodland burial grounds in the early 1990s. Today, more than two hundred twenty exist. Like Ramsey Creek, the British grounds offer green burial (no embalming, no vaults, etc.) in a green setting. What sets his project apart from the British model, says Billy, who learned of that country's natural cemeteries after conceiving his own, is its strong ecological focus. Before opening Ramsey Creek for burial Billy drafted a plan to return the former cotton farm to ecological health, which included siting graves in areas where burials would benefit the land and crafting a list of native plants that could be introduced onto each grave. "Our goal is to restore the land," says Billy, "and we're using burials to do it."

*   *   *

Some time before noon in the middle of May, Jim and his parents arrived at Ramsey Creek to pick out Chris's grave site. Their guide that morning was Kimberley Campbell, Billy's wife and Memorial Ecosystems's vice president of sales. After learning of Chris's wishes, Sharon had called over to Ramsey Creek and talked to Kimberley, who had explained the green burial concept and the requirements for interment in Ramsey Creek: no embalmed remains, only biodegradable caskets allowed, headstones permitted if cut from flat fieldstone. The cost for burial, she told Sharon, was $1,950. Ramsey Creek lacked facilities to hold remains until the service, so Sharon would have to either keep Chris at home or call a funeral home that offered refrigeration. Before hanging up, the women planned to meet at Ramsey Creek later that morning.

Sharon then called the local funeral director, who agreed to hold Chris in their refrigeration unit and deliver his casketed remains to Ramsey Creek. For his services, the director quoted Sharon a charge of $1,500.

A few hours later, Sharon, James, and Jim followed Kimberley into the woodland cemetery of Ramsey Creek. A gentle breeze swept the pines, sunlight filtered through the tall canopy overhead. From the head of the trail they could hear Ramsey Creek running the shoals below and see lizards darting through the underbrush, dragonflies flitting in and out of vision. Having known only the institutional, somber cemeteries of their hometowns, the family was struck by the vitality of this one. "It was this thriving, little ecosystem, a place full of life, not death," Sharon says of that first introduction to Ramsey Creek. "We knew right off it was the perfect place for Chris."

From the wood's edge, the group took the western bluff trail, a half-mile-long footpath that winds down to the creek. Kimberley led the way, noting some of the graves that had been installed—the site of a buried child, the corner overlooking the creek where a colleague of Billy's at the hospital had been buried. All graves were located just off trail, in spots the Campbells had deemed that grave digging would have the least impact on the environment—and where remains might actually best work to push up new plants, enrich depleted soil, renew natural life. Locating graves along the trail's edge also prevented visitors from tramping deeper into the forest, harming vegetation. Kimberley told the family it could choose a more remote site, but Memorial Ecosystems would restrict the number of guests that could visit it at any one time. When she mentioned that the families of some of those buried here had made the coffins themselves, James announced that he would build Chris's.

The four hikers trekked through the preserve for nearly an hour before turning back to collect their thoughts. At a place some hundred yards from the top of the trail, Jim stopped in his tracks. In front of him lay a small clearing, bathed in sunlight. "The light was shining through the canopy onto the top of this little ridge," he recalls. "The land fell away on both sides, and you could hear birds chirping and the running of the creek." Addressing his parents he said, "I think this is the spot." As it happened, the place was the very one James and Sharon had each fixed on when they'd first seen it on the way in. For Kimberley, the plot was an ideal grave site for other reasons as well. It lay within a swath of land Billy had reserved for burials, and was free of big rocks, trees, and other objects that might hinder the grave digging.

The party exited the woods and hiked the dirt path back to the parking lot, a mowed clearing fringed by black-eyed Susans. Standing by the cars, Kimberley wished her new clients well in the trying days ahead and said she'd keep them in her prayers. She produced no contract, demanded no down payment. "I tell you what, dears," Kimberley told the family before everyone departed, hugging each one of them. "You just give me a call when you need me."

Back at the lake house, Sharon went into Chris's bedroom and told her son about the woodland cemetery he'd never see and the site they'd selected for his grave. Chris was heavily medicated against pain by this time and in and out of consciousness, though alert enough to follow his mother. When Sharon finished describing the morning's venture, he looked at her and in a quiet voice said, "Cool, Mom. It's all good," before nodding off to sleep.

In the late-night hours of May 18 the sound of Chris struggling for breath woke Sharon and Debbie, who'd taken to sleeping in Chris's room. Sharon went over to her son's bed and laid her hand on his chest. "Hey, Chris," she whispered. "It's Mom." Chris drew another breath and, then, the room grew silent. "Chris just slipped away," says Sharon years later, "and it was as peaceful as it could be." Sharon and Debbie sat in the silence of the death, embracing each other and, then, saying a quiet prayer over Chris. After a few minutes, Debbie went out to call hospice and Sharon headed into the bedroom where Jim lay sleeping on a cot, to tell him of his brother's passing. She then called James, who walked up to the house and joined the others in Chris's room. For a time, father, mother, brother, and aunt touched, held, kissed, and caressed their suddenly lifeless loved one, taking in the loss of the passionate idealist, the stonemason and organic farmer, who after high school had taken to the road in a Winnebago with two friends, traveling the West and working on farms before returning home. Sharon says it isn't her family's style to join hands and pray together; sitting beside Chris she privately thanked God for the gift of her son and for the twenty-eight years she had with him.

Within half an hour of Debbie's call, the hospice nurse arrived at the house and, checking Chris's vital signs, pronounced his death. She called the funeral home and left. Sharon and Debbie had given Chris a sponge bath before he'd gone to sleep that night, so Jim and his father proceeded to dress him for his funeral in the outfit they thought he'd have liked: a pair of his favorite corduroy pants, the size-thirteen skateboarder shoes he often wore, and an Army green T-shirt that, as much as anything, says Jim, literally spelled out his brother's free-spirited philosophy of life: "Listen to Bob Marley." Over his head, they pulled the baseball cap he'd been wearing to cover the peach fuzz that had replaced his dreadlocks.

Jim and his father had finished dressing Chris by the time the funeral director and his assistant, both dressed in dark suits, pulled up to the house in a black hearse and wheeled the gurney into Chris's bedroom. When they reappeared, Chris was lying on the gurney, a sheet pulled over his body. "That was the way he left the house," says Sharon, recalling the last time she would ever see her son. "It was just like you see on TV, and it was terrible."

Later that morning Jim called Kimberley with the news of Chris's passing, and they scheduled the funeral for noon that Friday, two days away. And then the family dispersed. Accompanied by her brother-in-law Sharon went down to the funeral home to pay its $1,500 charge for handling Chris. In the director's office, the brother-in-law questioned the high price, given the little work involved, and the director agreed to accept $300 instead. Jim, meanwhile, crashed at his house, emotionally and physically drained. James went home to await the funeral director, who said he'd return to retrieve the coffin James had finished in his basement workshop the day before. Working without plans, the home builder had cobbled together a rectangular box from plain pine boards, with a detachable lid. To both sides of the coffin base he'd attached a trio of loop handles, fashioning them from the same thick rope he strings between the posts of the lakefront boardwalks he builds. Inside the coffin he and Sharon had later placed two quilts they wanted Chris to be wrapped in, one made by his grandmother, the other by Sharon's.

The day after Chris's death, Billy began digging his grave. Billy, with help, hand-dug many of the graves at Ramsey Creek. His efforts resemble an excavation more than a simple grave-digging. "We create a pretty big hole in the ground when we bury a body," he says, "so we're careful to limit our impact on the ecosystem."

Having dug dozens of graves, Billy had by then honed his method: trenching out the few plants by their rootballs and setting them aside, and then, literally, digging in. State law requires that caskets be at least ten inches below the surface of the earth. The requirement suffices for urban cemeteries, for which it was clearly written, but not for burial grounds out in the wild. "Animals live in these woods—we've got bears, foxes, bobcats—and they could dig up a dead body if it's in a grave that shallow," says Billy. "To keep them out, we go down three and a half feet."

The actual digging Billy approaches in stages. He starts by setting out a couple of tarps beside the site. With a pointed shovel, he turfs off the top layer of forest floor and sets it on one of the tarps, then digs up the topsoil and deposits that onto another tarp. At around two feet, sometimes less, he reaches the subsoil, and puts that onto a third tarp. After a body—and casket, if used—has been laid into the cavity, Billy covers it with the excavated soil, returning each pile of dirt in the same order in which it was dug out. The last step is to replant whatever greenery had been removed earlier and, depending on the time of year, introducing native plants to the site, if appropriate.

The strategy returns the grave site to a close approximation of its original state. The addition of a body to the site does, of course, raise an earthen mound, but the mound's temporary, Billy says; it will fall as the casket and corpse below it decay. The burial mound's not even that unnatural, he contends. Though man-made, that mound neatly replicates the pit-mound that's formed when storm winds knock a tree to the ground. "When a tree topples over, its root ball pitches up, creating a pit below it," he says. "As the dirt settles and the roots decay, a mound forms next to the pit." Research in forests of the eastern United States and Canada shows that a pit-mound's freshly aerated soil provides a hospitable bed for seeds that otherwise struggle to sink roots into the more compact soil of the forest floor; the mound's soil also attracts ant colonies, which both take refuge there and carry seeds to its newly fertile home ground, wildflowers in particular. Recent studies have suggested that ants are, in fact, major players in forests, says Billy, distributing as much as sixty percent of all wildflower seeds that are produced there.

You won't see many natural pit-mounds at Ramsey Creek. For the better part of the twentieth century, much of this well-forested wood was cropland, plowed to level grade by farmers and trod upon by grazing cattle. The forest that arose when farming ceased here fifty years ago is still young in ecological terms, boasting sprightly pines not yet easily felled in big storms. The way Billy sees it, his burial mounds stand in for the pit mounds that would have been formed were the land never farmed. "If it's done right—if we locate the grave in the best place, for instance—each burial plays a role in restoring the land to the way it used to be," says Billy.

The buried corpse only aids that restoration. As it decays, the body releases into the surrounding soil its cache of organic nutrients. The microbes, insects, and other organisms that attend a decaying corpse further nourish the ground with their leavings and remains; they also aerate the dirt, loosening compacted earth and thereby creating fertile ground for vegetation.

The body itself harbors its own cache of bacteria, including the E. coli, staph, and strep microbes that naturally reside in the intestines, as well as traces of whatever viruses, pathogens, and disease that killed the deceased. The vast majority of these bacteria perish in the grave, but not all. Trace amounts of still-vibrant contaminants may leach from a corpse, carried by trickling body fluids or percolating rainwater into the surrounding soil and groundwaters. British researchers recently discovered as much when they tested groundwaters around a number of the country's inland cemeteries. Water samples there showed traces of staph, fecal strep, and coliform bacteria, pathogens they tracked back to the population of decaying corpses at crowded cemeteries nearby.

Billy isn't worried about corpses tainting his ground or surface waters. Burials take place well above the water table, some twenty feet above Ramsey Creek; they're banned entirely from the preserve's low-lying wetlands. From the burial site, any living pathogen that leached from a cadaver would have to percolate through multitiered layers of earth, including loam, clay, rock, and finally sand, before hitting groundwater. "Those layers make up a deep natural filter," says Billy. "It would work to trap bacteria before they reached the water."

The low density of burial plots at Ramsey Creek further minimizes the risk of ground and surface water contamination. Most cemeteries typically accommodate some thousand graves per acre; in some metropolitan areas the number can approach two thousand. Such high density of bodies to land may overwhelm the soil's ability to absorb all the bacteria, pathogens, and body fluids leaching from corpses, particularly in older cemeteries sited on shallow soils. Not at Ramsey Creek. "Right now we're burying only three to five percent as many people per acre as a contemporary cemetery does," about twenty-five corpses an acre, says Billy; the most bodies he'd allow on any one acre is one hundred. "So the risk of any problem to the water is small and transient." If water tests ever turned up positive for bacteria, Billy says he would consider adding to grave sites certain soil amendments, like activated charcoal, to absorb and neutralize them. The bigger threat to water purity from cemeteries, Billy contends, is less pathogens than chemicals that are entirely absent from his property: the formaldehyde that leaches from embalmed bodies.

It was late evening when Billy and his crew stopped digging Chris Nichols's grave, four hours after they'd started. It usually takes them three hours to dig to the standard three-and-a-half-foot depth, but they'd needed longer because Billy, who was on call at the hospital, had had to run out to answer a page. (Later Billy would return to increase the size of the grave, after learning that Chris's homemade coffin was longer than average.) Across the open grave the crew now laid three wooden slats and, on top of them, a piece of plywood, to keep out any animals or rainfall, and covered the piles of dirt with tarps. On the morning of Chris's burial, Billy would return to prepare the grave for the service, removing the plywood cover, laying a set of casket-lowering straps into and out of the cavity, and setting aside shovels for any mourner who would want to help close the grave.

Shortly after eleven o'clock on Friday morning, the funeral directors who have been holding Chris pull their hearse up to the unfinished chapel at the edge of Ramsey Creek's woodland cemetery. In front of the steps stands a long, folding table covered with a blue cloth. Pulling Chris's coffin out of the hearse, the men carry it across the lawn and place it on top of the table. Their part in the funeral is over, but after parking the hearse back at the cemetery entrance the directors return to witness the singular, woodland burial; later, one of them will tell Sharon he'd never seen a service that felt so "pure and personal."

Gradually family and friends, dressed in khaki pants or blue jeans, many of them wearing dark glasses against the bright sun, begin to gather around the chapel. Most of the hundred or so who eventually collect here take up the colored markers Sharon has set out on the coffin, and on the unvarnished, wood lid write their parting messages to Chris. At a spot near the framed photograph of her son that she had placed in the middle of the coffin top, Sharon writes about "looking out, not down," in reference to Chris's admonition that she not mourn during his illness. Other notes express love and appreciation, the best wishes for a good journey into the afterlife. In black marker, James simply writes: Chris, You are the love of my life.

The day after Chris's death, Jim had asked half a dozen of his brother's friends to serve as pallbearers. Jim now asks them to gather around the coffin and grasp the rope handles. As they do, Jim and his parents position themselves behind the coffin, the others falling in line behind them, and the pallbearers hoist the coffin off the table and process into the woods.

Like the morning four days ago when the family had entered the preserve for the first time, this one's bright and balmy. A gentle breeze sounds wind chimes hanging in some of the pines, birds are chirping. The party wends its way through the woodland, just springing into bloom. About halfway down the trail, Jim relieves one of the pallbearers who struggles under the coffin's weight, now helping to carry his brother the rest of the way to the grave.

When they come to the site, Billy Campbell is already there, standing beside the rectangular-shaped hole in the earth, piles of dirt mounded off to the side with a couple of shovels lying beside them. Earlier that morning Kimberley had strewn pine needles into and around the grave, and over them sprinkled red and white rose petals, which now catch the sun, brightening this final resting place. At the head of the grave, a brilliant magnolia blossom sits in a blanket of needles, a bouquet of roses and wildflowers spilling from a basket behind it.

Three wooden slats stretch across the mouth of the grave. Under Billy's direction, the pallbearers place the casket on the ground at the near end of the grave, and then advance the casket to the first slat and then to the second and third. As they do, the crowd fans out around the grave site, finding a place to stand or sit among the trees and saplings and ferns and other greenery rising from the forest floor. One person climbs a tree to gain a better view.

Accompanied by Jim, Sharon steps to the head of the grave. In a voice so clear and unwavering it amazes those gathered here, she offers a prayer of thanks for Chris and asks for the strength to endure his loss. Chris had kept a journal in the months before his death. Sharon now recites one of his poems, which she found particularly fitting given the woodland burial he wanted: "One beautiful flower my life seems to be, then my petals fall off and I burst into seed. . . . [And] after all is said and done, the seed becomes life."

When Sharon finishes, Jim steps forward. Recalling his younger sibling, Jim describes the surprise he felt in later years to realize that Chris had become the hipper one and that just being Chris's older brother earned him a certain cachet of "cool." Coming to the end of the remarks he'd jotted down, Jim now looks out to the group assembled around him and, remembering his brother's wishes, says, "I know that Chris is up there looking down on us, and this will definitely get a smile on his face." With that, Jim pulls off his khaki shirt to reveal a tie-dyed T-shirt underneath it, and, to much laughter, reaches into his backpack. Inside are stashed half a dozen other tie-dyed T-shirts, which he tosses into the crowd.

As those few don the colorful shirts, two of Chris's close friends speak, one reading a poem honoring Chris's "warrior spirit," the other recounting funny stories about Chris. Afterward, Sharon's mother prays in a quavering voice for her grandson, and then Jim thanks everyone for coming and invites them back to his father's house for a cookout in celebration of Chris's life.

The coffin had remained closed before and during the service, because Chris "didn't like the idea of people looking at him," says Sharon. She was worried that the lid might come off as it was lowered in the grave, so James takes a minute now to screw the lid of his son's coffin to its base. Billy asks the pallbearers to come forward. On his cue, each of them grabs an end of one of three belts that run beneath the coffin. Pulling the belts taut they raise the coffin off the slats, which Billy pulls out, and then slowly lower the coffin—and the twenty-eight-year-old son, brother, friend, and stonemason, who is wrapped in the quilts of his great-grandmothers—into the grave.

With no prompting, Jim grabs a shovel from the mound of dirt, scoops out a spadeful of earth, and dumps it onto the casket lid. The thud of dirt resounds in the grave, a sound that Kimberley says "puts your life into perspective like no other in the world." Jim returns the shovel to the mound and embraces his family, most of them, like others here, now crying. Sharon breaks away to grab a shovel herself and tosses in her own spadeful of dirt, an act she describes as "almost cathartic." And then the others join in, grabbing the remaining shovels, each one unloading a bit of dirt into the grave, and passing the shovel on. A few people begin to leave, but most remain to watch the closing to the end. A few of Chris's friends undertake the bulk of the spadework at this point, returning dirt into the grave in the order in which Billy and his crew had removed it. Half an hour later red earth mounds over the grave site, and the burial is done. Thinking that no one would leave until she did, Sharon heads back up the trail, arm and arm with Debbie, their mother coming up behind them.

A week after Chris's burial, James asked Sharon to come over and look at a stone in his yard. A flat fieldstone about the size of a large open book, the stone was one Chris had returned to his dad after being unable to fit it into the stone profile of a house he was working on. "I can't use this rock right now, but keep it," he told his father. "I know a time will come when this rock will be useful." Walking his property after Chris's death, James had come across that discarded rock. Looking at it he recalled his son's advice and then remembered the quote he'd seen on one of Chris's business cards: The stone that the mason refuses will be his headstone. The best place for the stone, he now told Sharon, was on their son's grave, and Sharon agreed.

James loaded the stone into the back of his pickup and brought it to a local monument engraver. A couple of months later, he and Sharon gathered the family again at Ramsey Creek to install the finished headstone on the grave. After Chris's burial Kimberley had placed a fieldstone on top of his grave to serve as a temporary marker. Sharon and the family now moved it off and gently pushed aside the plants that grew there, wild ginger, some ferns. James, Jim, and a couple of other family members then hoisted the new stone off the golfcart they'd driven it down on and lugged it to the grave, laying it at the foot. In the middle of the stone was carved Love Your Mother Earth. On one side an angel with dreadlocks was engraved; a dragonfly, which had presented itself to the family when it first walked into these grounds and has since become its symbol of everlasting life, on the other. At the base Chris's name was inscribed, with his birth and death dates. "And then we just reveled in the beauty of the place," says Sharon, "and had another great visit with Chris."

Sharon's mom lives on the way to Ramsey Creek, so after visiting her Sharon will drive on to the cemetery, usually with Chris's dog, Briar. While Briar wanders the woods, Sharon sits next to Chris's grave. "I look at the plants and the sky, and have a conversation with Chris," she says. "It's not sad to visit, but sometimes I cry. It's just the raw emotion of being in a place that's so lush and green and living and beautiful, and that's all so representative of Chris."

Resource Guide: *The Natural Cemetery*

What:
Form of burial whose purpose is to return the body to the natural environment as directly as possible, usually within rustic, often wooded settings. To speed the body's dissolution and incorporation into the elements, vaults and metal coffins are prohibited. Embalmed remains, which may leach formaldehyde into soil and groundwaters, are likewise banned. Only simple grave markers are permitted, typically fieldstones or vegetation (trees/shrubs) that are native to the area. Bodies may be interred in shrouds or coffins made from common softwoods or cardboard, sometimes available from the woodland group. Scattering or interring ashes is also possible.

Some woodland schemes use burial fees and the grave sites themselves in an effort to restore the grounds to ecological health.

To help families understand how their natural cemetery of choice works, the Green Burial Council (www.greenburialcouncil.org) divides eco burial grounds into three types. The greenest is the *conservation burial ground,* which offers green burial (vaultless, embalming-free, etc.) and uses it to restore the land. These grounds thus follow science-based restoration plans that are overseen and documented by independent conservation partners. A *natural burial ground* offers a green burial that may or may not involve ecological restoration of the land. Finally, a *hybrid burial ground* is a conventional cemetery that accommodates green burial, by offering vaultless burial or reserving sections within the grounds specifically for green burial, among other strategies. The cemeteries below are grouped according to the council's standards. An asterisk below identifies cemeteries that have earned the council's certification.

How:

Staff at the woodland ground can help you make arrangements in advance or at time of need, including arranging transport of a body to the cemetery, obtaining a suitable casket, planning ceremonies.

Where:

The cemeteries below accept bodies for burial, as well as ashes for burial or scattering. Many more are in the exploratory and/or planning stages, including those in California (Humboldt County), Colorado (Denver area), Connecticut (northwest), Georgia (Macon, Milton), Hawaii (Maui), Illinois (downstate), Indiana (Bloomington, Indianapolis), Iowa (Cedar Rapids), Michigan (southeastern part of state), the greater Midwest (group based in Wisconsin), Missouri (Columbia), New York (Tarrytown, Hudson Valley area), Pennsylvania (Philadelphia area, Pittsburgh), Texas (Houston, Austin, Big Bend), Virginia (Roanoke, Culpeper), and in Canada (Victoria, BC; Paisley, ON; Nova Scotia).

Conservation Burial Grounds

Ramsey Creek*
Memorial Ecosystems
111 West Main Street
Westminster, SC 29693
864-647-4491
E-mail: Kimberley@memorialecosystems.com
www.memorialecosystems.com

> *Place:* A seventy-acre largely wooded preserve in the shadow of South Carolina's Blue Ridge Mountains. Burial of bodies and ashes are sited within the second-growth forest that runs down to the Ramsey Creek; scatterings take place in a meadow of wildflowers. The ground's parent company is in the process of securing an additional twenty acres of neighboring land.
>
> *Cost:* Burial of body ($2,000 to $3,000, depending on location). Burial of cremated remains ($500 to $1,000). Scatter-

ing of cremated remains ($250). Opening/closing grave ($250 to $500). Grave marker ($50).

Honey Creek Woodlands
2625 Highway 212 SW
Conyers, GA 30094
770-483-7535
E-mail: info@honeycreekwoodlands.com
www.honeycreekwoodlands.com

Place: A conservation burial ground for people of all faiths on the grounds of a 2,100-acre monastery half an hour's drive southeast of Atlanta. The cemetery lies within an 8,000-acre greenway of nature preserves and state parkland.

Cost: Burial of body (from $2,500 to $4,500, depending on location, plus $400 for opening and closing the grave). Burial of cremated remains (from $750 to $1,250, depending on location; opening and closing included in cost). Family and group discounts are available.

Galisteo Basin Preserve★
117 Guadalupe, Suite C
Santa Fe, NM 87501
505-982-0071
E-mail: Info@commonwealconservancy.org
www.commonwealconservancy.org

Place: A natural burial ground within a 13,000-acre, permanently protected conservation area outside Santa Fe.

Cost: Burial plot for whole bodies ($4,000 donation to the Commonweal Conservancy). Opening and closing of grave ($650). Cremation burial plots ($1,500 donation). Opening and closing of cremation grave ($100). Half the cost of burial plots is tax-deductible. Cremation scattering ($500).

Foxfield Preserve*
9877 Alabama Avenue SW
Wilmot, OH 44689
330-763-1331
E-mail: jennifer@wildernesscenter.org
www.foxfieldpreserve.org

Place: Former farmland on 43 acres in northeast Ohio that's being restored to original prairie and forest. Owned and operated by a nonprofit nature center and land trust.

Cost: Burial plot ($3,200). Opening and closing of grave ($1,000). Burial of cremated remains ($3,200 for plot, which may accommodate two urns of created remains, plus $500 for each opening and closing of grave). Scattering of cremated remains ($250).

Natural Burial Grounds

Glendale Memorial Nature Preserve
297 Railroad Avenue
DeFuniak Springs, FL 32433
850-859-2141
E-mail: info@glendalenaturepreserve.org
www.glendalenaturepreserve.org

Place: A seventy-acre burial ground within a larger expanse of creeks, ponds, and woods on the Florida panhandle.

Cost: Burial plot (free). Opening/closing grave ($1,800). Scattering ashes from historic Fire Tower or outdoor chapel ($100). Burial of cremated remains with survey marker and map ($225), without survey marker and map ($150).

Cedar Brook Burial Ground
175 Boothby Road
Limington, ME 04049

207-637-2085
E-mail: a.green.cemetery@gmail.com
Web: greencemetery.blogspot.com

Place: A two-acre wood of mostly pine and hemlock some thirty miles due west of Portland. Within its borders sits the rock wall–enclosed Joshua Small Cemetery, a tiny historic graveyard whose dozen burials date back to the early 1800s.

Cost: Single plot ($800; $600 for military veterans, $300 for cremated remains). Double plot ($1,400). Pet burials free.

Rainbow's End
52 Mill Creek Road
Orrington, ME 04474
207-825-3843
E-mail: joanhoward@att.net
www.rainbowsendcemetery.com

Place: Fourteen acres of meadow and pine forest that overlook the lower run of the Penobscot River just south of Bangor, Maine.

Cost: "Burial rights" for whole body or for up to four cremated remains ($750). Opening and closing of grave ($350 approximately, more during winter months). Scattering (donation requested).

Steelmantown Cemetery★
Located on Steelmantown Road
Mailing address:
327 Marshallville Road
Tuckahoe, NJ 08270
E-mail: bixby17@msn.com
609-628-2297

Place: An active cemetery dating back to the 1700s, where green burial has been practiced by default. Its one-acre grounds are overspread with oak, cedar, and pine and border the Belle Plain State Forest.

Cost: Plot, for two whole bodies ($2,000), for cremated remains ($100). Scattering of cremated remains ($100). Opening and closing of grave ($1,500).

Greensprings Natural Cemetery Preserve*
293 Irish Hill Road
Newfield, NY 14867
607-564-7577
E-mail: info@naturalburial.org
www.naturalburial.org

Place: A hundred acres of rolling hilltop meadows south of Cayuga Lake in the Finger Lakes region of New York, bounded by two forests. The preserve includes two main burial grounds: one eight-acre site and another two-acre area reserved for Jewish burials.

Cost: Single plot ($750). Opening and closing of grave ($600).

Ethician Family Cemetery
1401 19th Street
Huntsville, TX 77340
Contact: George Russell (936-891-5245)
E-mail: info@ethicianfamilycemetery.org
www.ethicianfamilycemetery.org

Place: Over eighty acres of mostly pine woods ninety minutes north of Houston, on the shores of Lake Livingston.

Cost: Single plot ($500). "Family" plot, large enough for twelve burials ($5,000).

White Eagle Memorial Preserve★
401 Ekone Road
Goldendale, WA 98620
206-350-7353
E-mail: whiteeagle@naturalburialground.com
www.naturalburialground.org

Place: A twenty-acre cemetery within 1,300 acres of permanently protected oak and ponderosa forest, meadow, and steppe on the edge of Rock Creek Canyon near the Columbia River Gorge National Scenic Area.

Cost: Burial plot ($2,000). Opening and closing of grave ($600). Burial of cremated remains ($500), scattering of cremated remains ($250). Additional $200 for deposit into state-mandated endowment fund.

Hybrid Burial Grounds

Forever Fernwood
301 Tennessee Valley Road
Mill Valley, CA 94941
415-383-7100
www.foreverfernwood.com

Sebastopol Memorial Lawn
7951 Bodega Avenue
Sebastopol, CA 95472
707-823-7473

Eternal Rest Memories Park
2966 Belcher Road
Dunedin, FL 34698
727-733-2300
www.eternalrest.com

Valley Memorial Park★
3929 SE Tualatin Valley Hwy
Hillsboro, OR 97123
503-648-5444

Central Texas, Mt. Zion, Garden of Memories
8101 Old U.S. 81
Temple, TX 76501
254-742-0441

Forest Home Cemetery
2405 West Forest Home Avenue
Milwaukee, WI 53215
414-645-2632
www.foresthomecemetery.com

Natural Cemeteries for Cremated Remains Only

EcoEternity Forests
P.O. Box 105
White Stone, VA 22578
804-435-1869
www.ecoeternity.com

Place: Wooded, natural cemeteries where only cremated remains may be buried. Ashes, either free or in biodegradable urns, are buried along the drip line of selected mature trees. Trees may be marked with small memorial tags. EcoEternity Forests, which originated and are popular in Germany, have been sited in eastern south-central Pennsylvania and in north- and southeast Virginia. The company plans to open a cemetery in North Carolina.

Cost: Familes may "lease" a single tree ($4,500, for up to fifteen urns) or claim one of some dozen burial plots beneath a "community tree" ($500). Opening and closing of site ($250, with a ceremony; $175 without).

Afterword

When I emerged from the woodland cemetery at Ramsey Creek for the first time that summer of 2004, I knew I'd just witnessed the biggest change in American funeral traditions since battlefield surgeons began embalming Union casualties during the Civil War.

On this thirty-two-acre pine forest in the foothills of South Carolina, the dead were lowered into vaultless graves dug by hand and marked with small, rough fieldstones collected on-site and laid flush to the ground. Bodies returned to the earth unembalmed and, when not buried in cloth shrouds, were laid into simple caskets of pine or cardboard. As I hiked the dirt footpath that cut through the memorial preserve the afternoon of my visit, I felt I was communing not with the dead but with the living—the trees, the flowers, and other wildlife that abounded in this thriving southern ecosystem.

Ramsey Creek was like no cemetery I'd ever seen: it was lush and vibrant and, for a graveyard, oddly welcoming. When my guide, Kimberley Campbell—the wife and business partner of Billy Campbell, the family doctor who'd first conceived the idea of a woodland cemetery—drove me back to town, I dropped all pretense of journalistic impartiality. "Ramsey Creek will define a new American Way of Death," I enthused to Kimberley before climbing out of her car. "And I think it's going to happen soon."

That was four years ago. Today, a dozen other green cemeteries have cropped up across the country since Billy dug that first tiny grave at Ramsey Creek for a stillborn infant in the fall of 1998. And more cemeteries like it are on the way. As I write this, the Campbells have recently opened Honey Creek Woodlands, a conservation burial ground that takes root in a Trappist monastery outside Atlanta. On its heels followed Rainbow's End, a fourteen-acre meadow and pineland cemetery that hugs the lower run of Maine's Penobscot River, and a memorial preserve on a onetime cattle ranch south of Santa Fe.

Within the year, additional natural cemeteries will appear in Michigan, Virginia, and parts of Texas. Scores of others will soon join them. I've heard from individuals, families, community groups, and government entities from almost every state in the Union—from Hawaii to New Jersey—all of which are working to grow green graveyards in rural backyards, on family farms and historic estates, within state parks, and even the gated environs of existing cemeteries close to home. Joe Sehee, the director of the Green Burial Council, who is working to get a number of these projects off—and in—the ground, believes we'll see as many as two hundred natural cemeteries open to burial within the next five years.

Once niched as an eco-phenomenon that spoke solely to off-gridders and back-to-landers, green burial has broken into the great mainstream. Big media—CNN, the *Chicago Tribune, Time,* and, yes, the Weather Channel—are tracking the trend. In the summer of 2007, eco-interment became almost chic, the subject of a four-page spread in *People* magazine, sandwiched between profiles of Paris Hilton and Matthew McConaughey.

Clearly, green burial is an idea whose time has come.

The reason? Americans are starting to accept, if not embrace, this fundamental fact of biology: that the natural end of all life is decomposition and decay. Instead of fighting it at almost all cost as we have for the better part of the last century—with toxic chemicals, bulletproof metal caskets, and the concrete bunker that is the burial vault, all of which will only delay, not halt, the inevitable—we're finally seeing the wisdom of allowing Mother Nature to run her natural course. As I see it, more of us are coming to believe that a lasting legacy to a life well lived may be as basic as good earth. Our best last act may, in fact, be the simple act of using what remains of our physical existence to fertilize depleted soil, push up a tree, preserve a bit of wild from development, and, in the process, perpetuate the natural cycle of life that turns to support those we leave behind. All the better that such basic, earth-friendly send-offs are sparing of resources, driven by families, and easy on the pocketbook.

And that's just burial. Deathcare is going green on all fronts—and finding converts. The strategies I write about in this book, from cremation and home funerals to memorial reefs and the use of biodegradable coffins, continue to gain traction. The cremation rate, for one, ticks ever upward. Currently some thirty-three percent of Americans are cremated; by the year 2025, that percentage will nearly double. More of the resulting "ashes" are finding final rest in artificial reefs. Since I last reported on Eternal Reefs, the Atlanta-based company has helped families add cremated remains to some seven hundred reef structures off mostly southern shores. In the coming year, the company will wade into new waters in Chesapeake Bay and on the opposite coast in the Pacific Northwest.

Taking inspiration—and training—from pioneers Beth Knox and Jerrigrace Lyons, a growing community of "deathcare midwives" is teaching families how to lay out and wake their deceased in their own homes, without the assistance of a funeral director. They're members of a burgeoning network of so-called "alternative funeral providers." These pro-earth and consumer advocates are being called on to handle the raft of postdeath matters that families face in their time of loss, from writing personalized eulogies and filing death certificates to arranging with local funeral homes for viewings of loved ones who haven't been embalmed. They'll even acquire the appropriate eco-coffin, perhaps a plain pine box from the local carpenter or a cardboard container via the crematory operator. In the coming year, these alt.providers—and family members themselves—can peruse funerary goods at old-fashioned coffin shops that stock caskets crafted from an earth-friendly biomass of materials, such as bamboo, wicker, papier mâché, cardboard, formaldehyde-free plywood, and sustainably harvested timbers.

Once the sole province of a modern funeral industry, deathcare is increasingly passing to independent caretakers and families who work quite literally outside of the box.

That said, I would not—nor would I want to—count the mainstream mortician out of green burial. One of the more encouraging developments I've witnessed in the last year is the willingness of main-street funeral homes to at least consider and, in some cases, actually venture into planet-friendly burial. Since this book's publication, many funeral directors have told me that they actually welcome send-offs that are easier on families, the earth, and, not coincidentally, their own health. In fact, some have resolutely cheered the opportunity green burial affords them to step out of the embalming room, with its toxic chemicals and gruesome procedures. A few, like the funeral director I met in Bloomington, Indiana, are sold enough on the idea that they've already added eco-friendly goods and services to their general price lists, offering refrigeration in lieu of embalming (minus the hassle) and a handsome wood casket for just over $400. A licensed funeral director I chatted with in Maine said he'd be happy to come to families' homes and help them lay out and wake their deceased there. By the time this paperback appears, the Green Burial Council will have recognized some fifty funeral directors and the like around the country who have proved particularly helpful to families that chose natural returns.

Not every funeral director is thrilled by this green turn of events, of course. With its simpler, sparer partings, ecological burial represents a hit to the bottom line of an industry whose profits accrue from sales of high-end merchandise ($10,000 caskets of brush bronze) and a multiplicity of services (from $800 embalmings to $100 "flower cars"). Even members that look kindly on the alternative strategies in *Grave Matters* struggle to find ways to make them profitable (and thus worth doing) in their hometown parlors. Or as one funeral director put it to me recently, "Simplified funerals will make sense to more and more people. Still, I need to get three children through college and eventually fund some sort of retirement."

Making the economics work will challenge an industry accustomed to bigger profit margins. As it matures, the green burial movement will face challenges of its own. For one, it will need to define itself. Already some advocates (including this one) have questioned the authenticity of woodland burials that use recycled paper or bamboo coffins that boast high sticker prices and are imported many thousands of carbon-spewing miles from their final destinations. Embalming may prove a sticking point. The practice is anathema to the movement, but should it still be so if the fluids involved are "natural" and "biodegradable"? The biggest questions will be reserved for cemeteries. Nearly anyone can open ground for burial, label it "green"—and then, say, allow the burial of bodies embalmed with toxic chemicals or mark graves with non-native trees that would eventually shoulder aside indigenous vegetation. (The Green Burial Council is working to address this issue. The Santa Fe–based nonprofit has established science-based standards that cemeteries must meet in order to earn the council's seal of approval, making it possible for families to identify the true green from the merely greenwashed.)

Like all movements, natural burial will experience its own growing pains. But as the greening deathscape in this country suggests, grow it will nonetheless—to the benefit of the planet, the memory of our deceased, and the families who lay them to rest.

It's too strong an idea not to. After their ninety-eight-year-old mother recently passed away, two sisters who'd learned about green burial arranged with the Wisconsin funeral home for a cremation but no embalming. "[My sister] and I dressed Mother's body," one of the women wrote to me. "Though somewhat awkward, the process took away the distance I felt. It was an intimate experience, indeed. I appreciate what [green burial is doing] to help survivors cope with our losses."

Acknowledgments

Every book is in some way a communal act, and this one has benefited from the involvement of a particularly rich community. Numerous families granted lengthy and repeated interviews in which they recounted the decline, passing, and memorialization of their loved ones, and then sent along a wealth of materials—from photographs and funeral programs to eulogies and death certificates—that made the writing of this book possible. I'm indebted, in particular, to the following for their willingness to share the story of perhaps the most profound event in their lives: Sandy Booth, Cheryl Hedman, Joan Hopkins, Janet King, Ed McKenna, Dan Mullen, Jim Nichols, Sharon Perry, Carrie Slowe, and Smiggy Smith. I hope to have done their trust justice in these pages.

Bill Sucharski welcomed me into his Philadelphia crematory with an openness I frankly found astonishing, and allowed me to witness much of the cremation process. My warmest thanks to him and to staffers Andrew Meredith and Jay McGee. Paul Rahill at Matthews Cremation Division explained in detail the operation of the company's cremation units, and Jack Springer of the Cremation Association of North America provided valuable insights on a number of issues relating to cremation. The Mercury Policy Project's Michael Bender offered background on the mercury emissions of crematoria.

Ken and Anya Shortridge arranged to have me witness a sea burial with the King family only to later deal with the stress of my late arrival into San Diego. Many thanks to them for their forbearance and willingness to help out in numerous ways with this project. On board the *Bay Watch,* Bill Whalen and Jerry Heath patiently answered my many queries as they went about their duties. Ellis Kjer of the California Cemetery and Funeral Bureau and Patricia Pechko at the EPA were particularly helpful in explaining regulations regarding burial at sea, as was Tim Nicholson at the U.S. Naval Mortuary Affairs about requirements for military sea burial.

For the chapter on memorial reefs, George Frankel went out of his way to connect me with Carrie Slowe, and he and Don Brawley invited me to observe the casting process in Sarasota and later deployment of finished memorial reefs off Ocean City. Larry Little of Reef Innovations helped make sense of what I was seeing. Todd Barber of the Reef Ball Foundation told the story of Eternal Reefs's genesis. Bill Figley reviewed for me the history of and purpose behind the reef building program he launched in New Jersey. Little of my interviews with Dave O'Ferrall and Mary Simpson made it into the final chapter, but I'm grateful to them for sharing their thoughts at the Sarasota casting.

Donna Belk took my cold call looking for leads to families in the Austin, Texas-area, who had conducted home funerals, directed me to "Sally Barnsley," and offered her insights into home funerals and the role she played in Sally's mother-in-law's. A kind thank-you to "Regina," who told me about the evening she spent at her deceased aunt's bedside, and to Robert Cisneros for his history of Old Jones Cemetery. Susan Rodriguez filled me in on Texas law as it relates to home funerals. Beth Knox relived, yet again, the events surrounding her daughter's death and home wake, and invited me to attend one of her workshops on home funerals. I'm indebted to Beth for her many contributions to this book.

Jane and Loren Schieuer agreed to ask a number of their customers to indulge me with an interview, and Loren freed up an afternoon to show me around his Iowa woodworking shop. Many other woodworkers around the country talked to me about their forays into coffin-building, among them Horace Bailey, James Casey, Craig Convissor, Bud Davis, Dienna Genther, Davis Griffith, Mark Hansen, Rand Herzberg, Paul Kester, Paul Meehan, Eric Tamm, and Byron Worley. A special thanks to Carolyn Jensen and Willy von Bracht for sending leads to their clients.

I met Jane Mullan at Beth Knox's home funeral workshop in Virginia, where she told me about the private cemetery where she helped bury her good friend. As much as anyone, Jane has had to tolerate my multiple interviews, and did so with much grace. Michael Soule and Susan Levick helped me to picture Sharyn's burial. For information on backyard cemeteries, I'm grateful to Isabel Berney, Greg Jeane, Gregory Stoner, and Donna Fisher.

This book started as an idea that formed as I walked through the woodland burial ground at Ramsey Creek in South Carolina one summer afternoon a few years ago with Kimberley Campbell, and then afterward as I interviewed Billy Campbell over many cups of tea in the warm company of Kimberley and her parents. Billy and Kimberley have generously shared their many experiences and insights into the green burial movement they've launched and nurtured in this country. This book would have been a much poorer venture without their on-going assistance.

Of the many funeral directors I interviewed, Dan Rohling, author of *Funeral Information,* was the most forthcoming and helpful, spending many hours spelling out the details of and rationale behind embalming and the modern funeral, with a candor that bespeaks an honest and caring professional. Thanks also to Joe Weigel at Batesville Casket and to George Lemke, of the Casket & Funeral Supply Association of America, for fielding my queries on issues related to casket production.

At the EPA, Karen Johnson and Mark Nelson educated me on septic systems and embalming waste. Regarding funeral home effluent and sewer treatment plants, pretreatment coordinators Tom Uva, Andy Rudzinski, and David Houston were most helpful.

I cannot thank Lisa Carlson (of the Funeral Ethics Organization) and Josh Slocum (of the Funeral Consumers Alliance) enough. They graciously shared their vast wealth of knowledge from the beginning of this project, fed me countless leads, willingly and quickly reviewed and corrected selections I beamed up to them. An early conversation with Josh redirected the focus of the coffin chapter. Lisa and Josh are a family's best advocates in all things related to death care in this country, and their efforts on behalf of this book proved why.

Mary Woodsen could have written this book herself. I'm indebted to her for her encouragement, assistance, and invitation into the green burial movement she has been instrumental in getting off the ground.

I didn't connect with Joe Sehee, executive director of the Green Burial Council, until I'd finished most of the manuscript for the hardcover. Since then, Joe has been a constant source of information and insight into the movement he's growing, while keeping true to its best principles. My many thanks to him for his continued, wise council and friendship.

Among the many researchers, proconsumer funeral advocates, and assorted experts who offered leads and information, I'd particularly like to thank Bill Bass, Gary Laderman, Karen Leonard, Jerrigrace Lyons, Julian Trick, Julie Weatherington-Rice, and John Wilkerson. My work occasioned numerous discussions about death and burial, many of them drawn from personal experience. For those I thank Adelaide and Leonard Ortwein, Don Midway, Gayle Justice, and Michele Mullen. A special thanks to Bob Brill, Rik Scarce, and Tom and Mary Dougal for pursuing leads in the funeral industry. I'm grateful, as well, to the families whose stories I was not able to use but which added to my understanding of natural burial: Elmer Blackburn, Luann Dunkerley, Teri Hackler, Lauri Werth, Patrick Ginnaty, Christina Haskin, Craig Gidding, and Bonnie Ramey, among them.

At Moravian College, the AfterWords Cafe in Reeves Library provided a welcoming work environment when the walls of my home office closed in. Reeves's reference librarians—Bonnie Falla, Dorothy Glew, and Linda Lapointe, in particular—helped me tap the wealth of resource material at the library's command, and Debbi Gaspar and Nancy Strobel retrieved a raft of research materials I consulted in the course of my research. Many thanks to them, and to Moravian's environmental readers group, which critiqued an early draft of the natural cemetery chapter.

The friends in my mostly monthly writers' group—Ruth Setton, Paul Acampora, Virginia Wiles, and Joyce Hinnefeld—followed this project from proposal to finished manuscript, and gave constructive advice and, for me, the first sense that natural burial had merit as a book topic. I owe a special debt to Joyce, who encouraged my foray into book writing and believed in this idea. For Jim Hauser, a heartfelt thanks for, among many other things, the reality checks, the push I needed to finally submit this proposal, and a way to present the concept.

Russ Galen saw potential in a book on natural burial well before Nate's green burial in *Six Feet Under,* and landed the proposal with an editor who couldn't have been more enthusiastic and supportive. Beth Wareham is the editor writers dream of but few are fortunate enough to encounter. Thank you, Beth. At Scribner, Jill Vogel and Katie Rizzo shepherded the manuscript through the editorial and production process with great aplomb. Jane Herman sharpened the copy, and Marcell Rosenblatt's keen eye caught many an error. It has been my good fortune (and great pleasure) to work with Kate Bittman, fellow runner, good soul, and publicist extraordinaire. My thanks to her, and to Whitney Frick and Heidi Richter for their work on the paperback.

My father, Don Harris, spent many summers of his youth on the grounds crew of White Haven Memorial Park in Pittsford, New York, which was cofounded by my great-grandfather, George Harris. Dad fielded my many questions about grave digging and general cemetery matters. Thanks to Dad and Mom for their support of this book and of this writer.

My young daughters endured their father's obsession with death and burial with good humor, and dealt with his absence, both physically and, at times, emotionally, with remarkable maturity. My wife, Tesia, has long endured what should be the private anxieties of the independent journalist, and the writing of this book occasioned only more of the same, and with greater intensity. She read and listened to every word of my many drafts multiple times and in numerous iterations, offering the usual insightful comment, suggestion for improvement, and unflagging encouragement. She has made this project possible in so many ways, and made it worthwhile.

I consulted a great many published sources in the course of my research. My brief review of the modern funeral draws heavily on Gary Laderman's fine companion histories of the dismal trade, *The Sacred Remains* and *Rest in Peace*. Robert Habenstein and William Lamers's *The History of American Funeral Directing* also proved helpful. The emphasis I've placed on the role that the cult of gentility and sensibility plays in the rise of the modern funeral comes from Brent Tharp's unpublished dissertation, *Preserving Their Forms and Features*.

David Charles Sloane's *The Last Great Necessity* informs my review of the rural cemetery movement and the memorial parks it gave way to. On numerous occasions I turned to Stephen Prothero's *Purified by Fire,* Paul Irion's *Cremation,* and Fred Rosen's *Cremation in America* for background information on cremation.

In addition to my interviews with funeral directors, I consulted a number of resources to gain a deeper understanding of embalming. Among those I found most useful were standard textbooks—Robert Mayer's *Embalming: History, Theory & Practice* and *The Principles and Practice of Embalming* (various editions) by Clarence Strub and Lawrence Frederick—as well as back issues of trade magazines, including *The Dodge Magazine, The Director,* and *The American Funeral Director.* I also viewed two videos that show the procedure: *Unlocking the Mysteries of Embalming* (William Ellenberg) and *Embalming Techniques* (Gary Sokoll).

The epigraphs that open this book I turned up in Johnny Slowe's article, "Toxic Burials." I'm grateful to Jack Loeffler for permission to quote from *Headed Upstream,* the source of Edward Abbey's remark.

Lisa Carlson's *Caring for the Dead,* which I mention throughout this book, was an invaluable resource, as was Kenneth Iserson's voluminous *Death to Dust* and Jessica Mitford's *The American Way of Death.*

Index

coffins for, 106, 109, 113, 115–16
cremation after, 107, 113–15, 117–18
history of, 104–5
legal requirements for, 107–8, 118
memorial service in, 115–17
preparation of body for, 108–11, 118, 119, 188
preservation of body for, 107–12, 118, 119
resources for, 119–24
Homer, 54
Honey Creek Woodlands, 179, 185
Hospice care, 29, 136–37, 149, 164, 169, 170
home funerals and, 104, 110, 111, 113
Hospitals, deaths in, 29, 46, 103, 151
home funerals after, 105–7, 118
Hybrid burial grounds, 177, 183–84
Hydrogen chloride, 62

Illinois, natural cemeteries in, 178
India
cremation in, 53, 55, 74–76
sacred groves in, 165
Indiana
home funerals in, 118
natural cemeteries in, 178
traditional burials in, 156, 165
Industrialization, 42, 43
Interment, 31–33
Internet, 128
ordering caskets on, 13, 129
Iowa,
natural cemeteries in, 178
plain wood coffins made in, 125–41
Iserson, Kenneth, 56
Islam, 46n, 108, 150

Japan, cremation in, 55
Jefferson, Thomas, 145
Jewish funerals and burials, *see* Judaism
Johnson, Karen, 34
Joplin, Janis, 75

Judaism, 9, 46n, 108, 126, 182
ancient burial customs of, 55, 150, 165

Kennedy, Caroline, 75
Kennedy, Edward M., 75
Kennedy, John F., 101
Kennedy, John F., Jr., 75–76
Kent Casket Industries, 142
King family, 69–71, 76–83
Kjer, Ellis, 70–71, 73, 85
Knox, Beth, 105–10, 116, 118–19, 187
death of daughter of, 103, 105–6, 119
Konefes, John, 39

Laderman, Gary, 44
Land preservation, 56
see also Natural cemeteries
Last rights, administration of, 137
Last Things, 120
Laurel Hill Cemetery (Philadelphia), 166
Laying out, 3, 45, 46, 126
for backyard burial, 149–50, 152
for home funeral, 103, 106, 107, 109–13, 118
Lennon, John, 116
Leo XIII, Pope, 55
Leopold, Aldo, vii, 166
Levick, Susan, 150–52, 155
Limousines, 10
Lincoln, Abraham, 45, 46
Louisiana
casket sale regulations in, 141
home funerals in, 118
Lyons, Jerrigrace, 119, 187

Maine
discharge of funeral home effluent in, 33
home funerals in, 120–21
natural cemeteries in, 180–81, 185–86
Marine Protection, Research and Sanctuary Act (1972), 83

201

Index

About the Author

Mark Harris is a former environmental columnist with the Los Angeles Times Syndicate. His articles and essays have appeared in the *Chicago Tribune, Reader's Digest, E/The Environmental Magazine,* and *Hope,* among others. He lives with his family in Pennsylvania.

Portland Community College